MW00650764

Monsoon Marketplace

Monsoon Marketplace

Capitalism, Media, and Modernity in Manila and Singapore

Elmo Gonzaga

FORDHAM UNIVERSITY PRESS
NEW YORK 2024

Copyright © 2024 Fordham University Press

All rights reserved. No part of this publication may be reproduced, stored in a retrieval system, or transmitted in any form
or by any means—electronic, mechanical, photocopy, recording,
or any other—except for brief quotations in printed reviews,
without the prior permission of the publisher.

Fordham University Press has no responsibility for the persistence or accuracy of URLs for external or third-party Internet
websites referred to in this publication and does not guarantee
that any content on such websites is, or will remain, accurate or
appropriate.

Fordham University Press also publishes its books in a variety
of electronic formats.

Some content that appears in print may not be available in
electronic books.

Visit us online at www.fordhampress.com.
Library of Congress Cataloging-in-Publication Data available
online at https://catalog.loc.gov.

Printed in the United States of America
26 25 24 5 4 3 2 1
First edition

CONTENTS

Monsoon Marketplace was written, reviewed, and revised over a span of twelve years. This book almost never came to be published.

Through the long, tireless process of bringing its narratives and arguments to life, I was married and my daughter was born. I divided my time between Berkeley and Manila. I taught in Singapore, then in Hong Kong. As my manuscript gestated, all this unfolded, although not necessarily in the order I describe.

Doing archival work for this manuscript, I spent a significant amount of my time in libraries. I benefited from two University of California grants that enabled me to conduct preliminary research in Manila and Singapore in the incipient stages of this study. I was fortunate to be able to visit the Library of Congress in Washington, D.C., and the National Archives in Kew, London, where I learned about the disparities in how marginalized colonial materials are preserved and loaned. Institutional and financial support from the Chinese University of Hong Kong's Faculty of Arts, Department of Cultural and Religious Studies, and the Master of Arts in Intercultural Studies Programme funded respites from my teaching duties that allowed me to complete my monograph.

My experience of libraries inspired the book's methods. I remember straining my eyes for hours in the darkness of the microfilm section of the Lee Kong Chian Reference Library in Singapore. I thought a lot about comparison and juxtaposition through the physical act of browsing its Southeast Asian Studies collection, which allowed me to see affinities among the seemingly unrelated volumes on its shelves. In Metro Manila, doing archival work was less straightforward and efficient, as I needed to travel to various libraries scattered across the traffic-choked megalopolis to be able to access issues from the same periodicals. Delving into the Rizal Library's American Historical Collection and Filipiniana Section, I carefully flipped through brittle, yellowing pages of long discontinued newspapers and magazines, cognizant of the fragility of memory. I consumed a wide range of materials produced and circulated during the periods I was studying, beguiled by the ultimately futile goal of immersing myself in their now disparate, alien cultures.

I am indebted to scholars whose influence permeates this work. Trinh T. Minh-ha's indefatigable advocacy of underrepresented perspectives and experiences has informed *Monsoon Marketplace*'s sensibility. Despite its unconventional structure, Jeff Wasserstrom's publication of an earlier extract in the *Journal of Asian Studies* helped nurture its ideas. The late Jeff Hadler's ebullient passion for Southeast Asian Studies will always be an inspiration, even in his absence. In ways I had been unaware of, they highlighted the ethics and politics behind our choices as scholars about the objects and methods we grapple with in our analyses.

My deep gratitude goes to my editor, Fred Nachbaur, without whose support and commitment this book would not have been published. I am enormously appreciative of his effort to shepherd my manuscript through the precarious process of peer evaluation and editorial approval. Thank you to my two anonymous referees, who were equally encouraging and critical. One expert incisively read different versions of my manuscript with a meticulous eye for structure, argumentation, and evidence. The other referee's unconditional enthusiasm for my book project gave it a final, crucial push over the goal line. Their comments and questions stressed upon me the importance of negotiating the tension between theory and history, which I am still striving to resolve.

Having taught in three different cities and countries, I am lucky to have been enriched by the insight and encouragement of diverse and erudite coworkers, collaborators, and friends who have shaped my thoughts. Ruanni Tupas was an early proponent with his shared interest in decolonizing critical frameworks. Bearing the same engagement with the history and culture of our city, Vince Serrano's poetry about Manila forms the creative counterpoint to this monograph. I am extremely thankful for present and former colleagues at the Chinese University of Hong Kong's Department of Cultural and Religious Studies, including Laikwan Pang, Song Lim, Kaming Wu, Katrien Jacobs, Janet Pang, Benny Lim, Jia Tan, Peichi Chung, Yongwoo Lee, Tiecheng Li, Virginia Lo, Grace Ng, Elaine Chow, Nocus Yung, Yu Cheung, and Chris Patterson, whose conviviality and generosity have furnished a dynamic intellectual space for this project. Nicolo Ludovice helped verify historical facts and claims. Cindy Wu assisted in contacting libraries and searching databases for images I could use in my book. I would also be remiss if I failed to mention my postgraduate students, whose passion for their work has motivated me to be passionate about my own projects, despite the difficulties that I often encounter realizing them.

Close friends back in Manila, who will probably never read this book, are a godsend for keeping me grounded with their constant care and humor. To the Gonzaga and Limsico families, I could barely even begin to repay their unwavering compassion and encouragement beyond the bounds of necessity. Having the courage and diligence to raise me on her own, my mother gave me the freedom and confidence to explore my own interests and projects.

This book is dedicated to two people in particular: Taryn is a boundless ball of energy and affection who suspects me of being the hardest-working teacher for typing furiously on my MacBook each waking day. Tiffany, my harshest critic, constantly urges me never to settle for the mundane or overdone. As she always reminds me, living in the world means loving and striving intensely.

Beyond the discrete traces of their influence, this book is inescapably indebted to the divergent interpretations and expectations of readers about how its pages should have been written or what its ideas might imply.

Monsoon Marketplace

Introduction: Methods of Archipelagic Capitalism

In the shadow of the Asian century, the center of the globe is said to have shifted away from the Western hemisphere. Concentrated in the so-called emerging or developing metropolitan areas and city clusters, this economic passage from West to East, however, has continued to marginalize other parts of the world, such as the highly diverse archipelagic subregion of Southeast Asia, which encompasses over 660 million people, 350 ethnicities, and 1,000 languages. Separated by decades across the span of a century, three important moments in the understudied urban microhistories of its two capitals, Singapore and Manila, during the 1930s, 1960s, and 2000s could be seen to disclose the changing spaces and practices of capitalist modernity, mass consumption, and media spectatorship.

Completed in 1932, the Crystal Arcade was a stylish Art Deco building with striking horizontal lines, circular edges, and geometrical patterns that stood midway on Calle Escolta, the main commercial street of Manila, capital of the Philippine Islands, before the Pacific War. After four decades of occupation under U.S. imperialism, which transformed the landscape of the archipelago after Spain's stagnant three-century rule, the Philippines was granted a definite path to independence as a commonwealth. As an important hub for transpacific shipping and trading routes, especially the galleon trade of silk and silver between Amoy and Acapulco, Manila was the first city in Southeast Asia to have air-conditioning installed in its buildings and theaters. Featuring department stores and retail boutiques with glass window displays selling imported luxury and electronic goods, the Escolta epitomized the convergence of social prestige and material progress. Despite discourses about their innate barbarism, filth, and sentimentality, the Crystal Arcade illustrated the potential of Filipino entrepreneurs and artists to mimic how foreign governments and businesses harnessed seemingly unmanageable modern forces.

Proliferating across Singapore's central island in the first half of the 1960s, seemingly primitive *pasar malams*, or night markets, served as provisional sources for basic supplies in the early stage of *merdeka*, or postcolonial independence, from the British Empire and Malaysian Federation. Denouncing youthful students, politicians, and professionals protesting on the streets for their alleged infiltration by the Communist Party of China, the ruling People's Action Party built new public housing estates that reconfigured social relations away from civil unrest toward industrial discipline. Far from the commercial streets, department stores, and movie theaters of one of the world's most congested city centers at the time, their Hokkien, Teochew, Cantonese, Malay, Javanese, and Tamil residents would gather in crowds at the makeshift stalls of itinerant markets, whose mobility and informality refused the official health and legal codes of the state. Popular multiracial fantasy movies produced by Cathay-Keris Studios and Malay Film Productions, the local subsidiaries of the Cathay and Shaw Organizations in the subregion's film production hub, visualized the restless movement and dynamism characteristic of a moment of transition.

Occupying the end of this genealogy, newly constructed or refurbished shopping malls Ion Orchard and SM Megamall were inaugurated in Singapore in 2009 and in Manila in 2014, exemplifying their utopian aspirations to become world cities of investment, tourism, and innovation. Whereas Singapore followed a linear master plan of development under the impassiveness of its ruling party to rise to the top of rankings of per-capita income and quality of life, Manila struggled in the period after the 1986 People Power Revolution to realize the gains of neoliberal democracy with a congested, overwhelmed metropolis beset by corrupt, incompetent governance. If one-third of the Singapore workforce comprised foreign migrants, one-fifth of the Philippine population resided overseas for work. Singapore competed against London, New York, and Hong Kong to become the leading financial hub as the Philippines overtook India as the center of the Business Processing Outsourcing industry. Emulating the logic of global capitalism toward continual accumulation and addition, the malls on Singapore's Orchard Road and Manila's EDSA incorporated consumer spaces that were previously separate under bright, air-conditioned enclosures free from the crime, heat, and congestion of the tropical metropolis. Featuring luxury brands and video screens, the deconstructivist Ion Orchard and brutalist SM Megamall incarnated the normalcy and buzz of neoliberal cosmopolitanism by reproducing its prevailing disparities between affluence and scarcity.

Monsoon Marketplace aims to trace the entangled genealogies of capitalist modernity, mass consumption, and media spectatorship in two understudied cities across three historical periods in the twentieth and twenty-first centuries. Instead of dwelling on neoliberal conditions of atomization and apathy, this book applies them as frames of reference to uncover the multiplicity of changing vernacular configurations and experiences. News magazines and political analysts have heralded the coming of the Asian century by emphasizing the East and South Asian economies of China, South Korea, and India and their financial capitals, Shanghai, Shenzhen, Hong Kong, Seoul, Mumbai, Chennai, and Bangalore. Reexamining the dominant worldview of Southeast Asia in modernization theory as occupying a subordinate stage of progress not only to Western Europe and North America but also to Australia and East Asia, the book explores how the print, audiovisual, and spatial cultures of its cities and populations might offer divergent ways of comprehending the contingencies of colonialism, nationalism, development, and neoliberalism.

Looking at the commercial and leisure spaces that have captivated the collective imaginaries of their cities and populations, *Monsoon Marketplace* studies the changing perceptions and understandings not only of movie theaters, supermarkets, and shopping malls, but also of bazaars, coffee shops, and amusement parks. If many critical theories and cultural studies of capitalist modernity and mass consumption see the department store and shopping mall as the height of the linear trajectory of progress, *Monsoon Marketplace* dialogues with the scholarship of the Global South metropolis, which explores their coexistence and interaction with similar consumer spaces commonly perceived to be more traditional and primitive. While designed for commercial profit, these consumer spaces have unfolded as vernacular sites of interaction and tension among colonial, local, national, regional, and transnational flows of discourses, narratives, practices, and images, where multicultural workers, migrants, and activists encountered and negotiated new, ambivalent ideas and lifestyles. Interdisciplinary and comparative, this book analyzes print and audiovisual media representations of commercial, administrative, technological, and infrastructural innovations, which such spaces introduced to enhance their sanitary modernity, social order, and spectatorial experience.

Marking shifts in the regimes of political sovereignty, economic production, and mass entertainment, the emergence of each of these spatial innovations could be situated within an important moment of change and uncertainty in Asian cities—namely, colonial occupation in the 1930s, national development in the 1960s, and neoliberal globalization in the 2000s, when the established order was threatened with upheaval or collapse. While local consumers in Calle Escolta, Avenida Rizal, Battery Road, and Raffles Place in Manila and Singapore awkwardly experimented with modern products and lifestyles in the 1930s, the colonial regimes of the United Kingdom and United States sweepingly introduced their visions of sanitation and civilization to tropical environments, whose diversity and complexity they struggled to completely grasp and subdue. The ambitious visions and programs of postcolonial authoritarian governments under Lee Kuan Yew and Ferdinand Edralin Marcos to transform congested metropolises for the sake of rapid industrial production and material prosperity during the 1960s were challenged by youthful activists who demanded their democratic right to more humane living and working conditions. As competing world cities after the turn of the millennium that depended on their incorporation of transnational flows according to the economic instrumentality of market capitalism, their worsening wealth inequalities intensified between super-rich investors and migrant professionals.

Dichotomies of Development

The book's geographic focal points are Southeast Asian cities, which first emerged in the world market as trading ports but have long had a peripheral relation to the more prosperous urban centers of North America, Western Europe, and Northeast Asia. Its title, *Monsoon Marketplace*, alludes to these commercial origins, when trade in the South China Sea, in the "lands below the winds," would be reliant on the monsoon season. The history of the subregion shows that Southeast Asia has served as a crossroads between East and West, with its multiracial, multireligious, and multilinguistic communities shaped by merchants from South Asia and Northeast Asia and colonizers from Western Europe and North America. Impacted by the encounter with Hinduism and Islam, the populations of its port cities have long engaged with Chinese, Indian, and Arab cultures because of their strategic location in the South China Sea, which has contributed to the subregion's syncretic, cosmopolitan character. These early influences have commingled with colonial occupation from the United States, United Kingdom, Spain, Netherlands, France, and Japan from the sixteenth to twentieth centuries, which introduced bureaucratic and autocratic mechanisms of governance as well as rigid racial and sexual categories to their fluid, pluralistic societies.

Today, the subregion is an increasingly vital component of the global economy, especially with the further integration of the nation-states that constitute it into the Association for Southeast Asian Nations, or ASEAN,[1] which is projected to be the world's fourth-largest economy by 2030. As the world system of capitalist production, distribution, and exchange has been reorganized, Asian cities have become key engines with the development of their industrial, financial, and service sectors.[2] Before the COVID-19 pandemic, the world was shaped by planetary urbanization, with tens of thousands of people around the world moving to burgeoning metropolitan areas and city clusters, which have needed to manage transnational and intraregional flows of goods, ideas, technologies, bodies, and images according to their given social, economic, and cultural conditions. In Southeast Asia, the transnational class of consumers will supposedly have doubled over two decades to 163 million households by 2030.[3] Because of their rich history at the junction between different cultures, religions, and worldviews as pluralistic, multiracial trading ports, Southeast Asian cities are important examples for grasping the emergence of complex economic and social changes transpiring in the world because of capitalism, media, and modernity.

Monsoon Marketplace seeks to excavate and map entangled genealogies of capitalist modernity, mass consumption, and media spectatorship in Southeast Asia by uncovering affinities, variances, and disparities in the circumstances of Manila and Singapore, which are said to offer two contrasting paradigms of the Asian metropolis. In a world with rapidly urbanizing consumer societies, these two urban environments are frequently cited by international news magazines and policy reports as prototypical cities of the twenty-first century.

Manila is the teeming capital of an emerging economy with a high demographic of poverty, but it has three of the fifteen largest shopping malls in the world, a paradox indicative of the Philippine archipelago's long-standing class disparities. The political struggle for autonomy from the United States in the early twentieth century was succeeded by the failed efforts of nationalist politicians to govern the repercussions of import substitution and internal migration in the decades after the Pacific War. Pervasive corruption under the Martial Law dictatorship of Ferdinand Marcos in the 1970s and 1980s resulted in the collapse of the national economy. The Philippines was relatively successful at braving the global financial crisis of 2008 with the earnings of call center agents and overseas migrant workers fueling domestic consumption through the aspirational lifestyles of its expanding middle class.

With shopping described as its national pastime, Singapore, a small city-state that sits atop global city indexes with the highest per-capita income and standard of living in the world, is characterized by the prevalence of malls. Under the laissez-faire governance of the British Empire in the early twentieth century, the multicultural entrepôt of Singapore gained international notoriety as an abyss of vice and sin. Prompted by independence from the Federation of Malaya in 1965, Lee Kuan Yew and his People's Action Party refashioned the urban environment and eliminated political dissent to boost economic growth and industrial productivity. By the 2010s, inequality and congestion had intensified once more with relaxed restrictions on external flows of foreign professionals and workers, which the government declared to be essential for maintaining the prosperity of its local citizens in a competitive world market.

Both Manila and Singapore flourished in the colonial era as international ports, which facilitated the dynamic circulation and exchange of goods, bodies, and ideas. Both populations suffered under Japanese occupation during the Pacific War; in particular, Manila's landscape was devastated by Allied bombing during Liberation. Whereas Singaporeans have been governed by the same political party for more than half a century, Manila was the site of two popular revolutions that ousted corrupt administrations by drawing millions of ordinary Filipinos into the streets. Shaped by postcolonial national sovereignty and transnational business investment, their spatial environments experienced distinct forms of urban renewal with new buildings, infrastructures, and malls that have transformed their city centers with various degrees of success and failure. Today, the two metropolises occupy contrasting poles of political sovereignty, urban infrastructure, economic prosperity, and social order, a sphere of variance that would enable patterns to be discerned in the multiple articulations of capitalism, modernity, consumerism, and spectatorship across the Southeast Asian archipelago. Looking at changes to images, discourses, narratives, practices, and spaces, this book interrogates the prevailing hierarchy between progress in world-class cities and underdevelopment in Third World megacities that is apparent in news reports, policy documents, and even cultural exhibitions and arthouse films.[4]

Urban Histories of Consumerism

As an interdisciplinary work, *Monsoon Marketplace* is in conversation with existing studies of capitalism and consumerism from different fields and subfields. Scholarship about the history of capitalism and consumerism tends to dwell on the business history of objects and spaces. This book explores how capitalism and consumerism could be understood to involve changing arrays of spaces, discourses, and images, which urban residents negotiate cognitively and collectively as they aspire for transcendence from the necessity of their given economic, social, and environmental conditions.

Studies about the world history of capitalism have focused on the production, distribution, and consumption of commodities essential to everyday life such as sugar, cotton, and tea. Many of such works—namely, Mintz's seminal

Sweetness and Power and more recently Trocki's *Opium, Empire, and the Global Political Economy*, Beckert's *Empire of Cotton*, and Liu's *Tea War*, uncover the entanglement of industrial capitalism and colonial occupation in expanding transnational supply chains over several centuries.[5] They shift the locus of discussion to seemingly more peripheral locations, which, commonly understood to be lacking in economic development and infrastructural innovation, are revealed to have been essential in supplying cheap manufacturing and slave labor that have guaranteed the prosperity and freedom of the United Kingdom and United States. Instead of comprehending the local experiences of colonies in reference to industrial processes in the metropole, *Monsoon Marketplace* uncovers their entanglement with vernacular discourses and images of prestige and progress in the commercial and leisure spaces of burgeoning metropolises amid the cultural history of colonial occupation and national development in Southeast Asia.

Tracing the cultural history of commercial and leisure spaces, *Monsoon Marketplace* builds on Rachel Bowlby's *Carried Away* and Sharon Zukin's *Points of Purchase*, which discuss department stores, retail boutiques, and supermarkets in London, Paris, and New York across the nineteenth and twentieth centuries.[6] Looking at innovations to their spatial configurations, distribution systems, and consumer practices, these seminal works examine how sites of capitalist exchange and mass consumption are important public spaces where residents have encountered and negotiated modern flows in the form of consumer products, fashion styles, and media spectacles in diverse ways. Presenting a picture of the linear trajectory of economic and material growth in the cities of North America and Western Europe, they highlight how sanitary and air-conditioned commercial spaces such as department stores emerged that segregated gender, race, and class to prevent moral contagion and degeneration. As these cities became reconfigured with internal migration to the suburbs, postwar supermarkets and brands marketed themselves to a more inclusive range of consumers amid an economic boom by espousing democracy as the personal freedom of mass consumption.

Instead of treating these examples from North America and Western Europe as universalized models of the rise of capitalism and consumerism, *Monsoon Marketplace* juxtaposes two postcolonial Asian metropolises, Manila and Singapore, to uncover the vernacular entanglements of capitalism and consumerism with colonial occupation, national development, and neoliberal globalization. While consumerism managed the energies and mobilities of urban residents in Southeast Asia through the sanitary, air-conditioned spaces of supermarkets, department stores, and shopping malls, it often meant immersion in the congestion, diversity, and profusion of tropical urban environments. Instead of being emptied by the flight of their populations to the suburbs, the city centers of Southeast Asia have flourished as bustling, neon-lit environments.

Critical studies about the commercial spaces of Southeast Asian metropolises have often looked at shopping malls in the 1990s to examine the vernacular practices of popular culture at the onset of neoliberal globalization. Prescient critic and activist Rolando Tolentino's *Sa Loob at Labas ng Mall kong Sawi, Kaliluhay Siyang Nangyayaring Hari* elaborates on the processes of neoliberal globalization and labor contractualization that shape parameters of agency and collectivity in SM Megamall.[7] Discussing the prosperous consumer society of Singapore, pioneering sociologist Chua Beng Huat's *Life Is Not Complete Without Shopping* examines sites of entertainment and shopping on Orchard Road that undergo mediation and localization.[8] Using the framework of postmodernism to analyze the shopping mall, however, Tolentino and Chua tend to assume that capitalist modernity is an overarching, transnational system that homogeneously instills alienation, docility, and atomization among urban residents as their national governments aspire to deliver progress to them. Uncovering their interconnections with shopping malls, *Monsoon Marketplace* maps the multiplicity of configurations and experiences of capitalism and consumerism in amusement parks, coffee shops, and night markets as vibrant public spaces for intellectual exchange and political community.

Looking at different sites for capitalist exchange and mass consumption such as department stores and shopping malls in a Southeast Asian metropolis, anthropologist Ara Wilson's *The Intimate Economies of Bangkok* studies the changing spatial and social forms of neoliberal globalization over a period of national development.[9] Focusing on Chinese migrants and same-sex intimacies in Bangkok's commercial and leisure spaces, Wilson uncovers how the personal freedoms and social relations of modern consumers in a Southeast Asian metropolis are shaped by race, gender, and tradition. Highlighting the transformative potential of capitalism and consumerism, Wilson examines how shoppers, entrepreneurs, and merchants negotiate market relations according to their own vernacular terms of distinction and transcendence.

While defining capitalism as a market-oriented system that "uses money to measure value, pay people for work or debts, and conduct exchange,"[10] Wilson uncovers how the users of public and private spaces grapple and experiment with the norms of discourses and practices borne by diverse colonial, local, national, regional, and global flows of capital and media according to their own aspirations and fantasies. If cultural studies about mass consumption in commercial and leisure spaces understand it to entail self-fashioning and performance, I see capitalism as a regime of variable spatial configurations, social practices, and media ecologies for producing, circulating, exchanging, and consuming goods and services across disparate, changing contexts. Although oriented toward market rationality and economic profit, their varying discourses, narratives, and images affect, reshape, and impel agency, identity, and collectivity in unforeseen, contingent, and multitudinous ways.

Media Histories of Spectatorship

In addition to cultural studies of capitalism and consumerism, *Monsoon Marketplace* draws on histories of media and modernity that have centered on Asian global cities such as Tokyo, Shanghai, Beijing, Delhi, and Hong Kong. Shifting away from a focus on the cognitive absorption of the cinematographic gaze by examining the coexistence and interaction of different media forms, this book explores how spectatorship is a popular activity of mass consumption that involves the vernacular experience of sensorial immersion in bustling, multicultural metropolises.

Such scholarship is typically limited to a single city or period in the world history of capitalism when the emergence of urban modern forces was most prominent, such as nineteenth-century Paris (Clark's *The Painting of Modern Life* [1984] and Schwartz's *Spectacular Realities* [1999]), early twentieth-century Shanghai (Lee's *Shanghai Modern* [1999] and Zhang's *An Amorous History of the Silver Screen* [2005]), late twentieth-century Hong Kong (Abbas's *Hong Kong: The Culture and Politics of Disappearance* [1997]), late twentieth-century Delhi (Sundaram's *Pirate Modernity* [2009]), and early twenty-first-century Beijing (Braester's *Painting the City Red* [2010] and Neves's *Underglobalization* [2020]).[11] *Monsoon Marketplace* aims to contribute to this extensive body of scholarship by examining the entangled spaces and practices of capitalist modernity and media spectatorship in two understudied cities, Manila and Singapore, during the 1930s, 1960s, and 2000s. While such works typically define modernity as a transformation or transition marked by a "flowering" or "disappearance," the genealogical scope of my book aims to situate this transition within two urban microhistories that unfold in diverging, meandering, or opposing trajectories.

Writing about media spectatorship in the metropolis, both Miriam Hansen and Zhang Zhen highlight the limitations of dominant critical theories of capitalist modernity and mass consumption, which presume that the cognitive absorption of spectators automatically renders them docile, alienated, and homogeneous. Critiquing such theories for their "discursive construction" of spectatorship, Hansen argues that they perceive the act of film viewing to be abstracted from the collective, sensorial experience of urban spaces where audiovisual media representations are encountered and consumed. Hansen highlights how spectatorship must be "contextualized" within its public sphere, which she defines as comprising a "particular" site and mode of exhibition addressed to a contingent audience. In addition to studying similar audiovisual media representations that circulate within the same urban environment, Hansen uncovers the impact on spectatorial experience of the "horizon" of historical and cultural conditions of gender, race, and class.[12]

Zhang echoes Hansen when she argues for the "grounding" or "historicization" of cinema amid the "phenomenology" of the "metropolis" and "modernity."[13] Expanding Hansen's scope, she examines how spectatorial experience is shaped by collective, sensorial practices of consumerism and spectatorship in the diverse commercial and leisure spaces of the Asian metropolis in a distinct historical period. Departing from the conventional focus on the cosmopolitan modernity of print literature, which, for her, tends to overlook the importance of cinema, Zhang uncovers the vernacular modernity of mass entertainment in 1930s Shanghai amid the dominance of industrial capitalism. Looking at the stylish commercial and leisure spaces of 1930s Shanghai, which strove to incorporate and exhibit elements of progress and prestige, Zhang remarks how the articulation and experience of their modernity were more heightened and intense than that of New York and Paris. Whereas both Hansen and Zhang presume capitalism in the early twentieth-century metropolis to be dehumanizing, atomizing, and alienating, I explore how its profusion and intensity amid the bustle and diversity of the developing postcolonial city in Southeast Asia could be seen to produce a multiplicity of vernacular configurations of agency, transcendence, and collectivity.

Moving away from a focus on the cognitive absorption of the solitary voyeur and flaneur, Zhang analyzes how the interaction or "permeability" of cinema with other forms of print, audiovisual, and spatial culture in the metropolis, including theater performances, newspaper advertisements, and amusement centers, constituted this modernity.[14] Zhang understands spectatorial experience to encompass not only the consumption of print and audiovisual media but also the occupation of a mediatized spatial environment. Working with Zhang's more expansive conception of spectatorial experience, I look at different innovative commercial and media infrastructures such as glass windows, carnival rides, neon signs, and advertising billboards. I would suggest that permeability could be taken to refer not only to the coexistence and interaction between different forms of commercial exhibition and media spectacle, but also the transition and transformation between dominant regimes of mass entertainment and visual perception.

Defining "permeability" as the "mixing" of different forms of print and audiovisual culture including blueprints, CDs, cassettes, posters, and flyers, Ravi Sundaram, a faculty member at the Centre for the Study of Developing Societies in Delhi, explores the "media urbanism" of postcolonial cities such as Delhi amid the rise of transnational capitalism and failure of the welfare state during the 1980s and 1990s. Describing this coexistence and proliferation together with a multiplicity of media technologies, urban plans, and commercial infrastructures as a "hyperstimulus," Sundaram understands spectatorial experience less as visual apprehension than as sensorial immersion amid the contradictions and anxieties of the slippage between authoritarianism, neoliberalism, and development.

Looking at the entanglement of ideologies and fantasies of urban renewal and technological progress, Sundaram highlights how governments and businesses have deployed them to create and facilitate opportunities for investment and industrialization, which have been characterized by varying degrees of failure and breakdown. Amid the intensified profusion of capitalist flows, which eluded and resisted government control, overarching blueprints of sanitary modernity in late twentieth-century Delhi interacted and conflicted with subversive, everyday practices of bazaar informality, whose pirated media provided access to new technologies, representations, and lifestyles. In the emergent tropical metropolis, which is characterized by low-cost, pirated technologies and their constant, improvised repair, Sundaram highlights the blurring of the distinctions among producers, consumers, distributers, and proliferators that have shaped their ambivalent agency.

Both Zhang and Sundaram conceive of the permeability or mixing of different consumer and media products coexisting in a bustling metropolis where colonial, local, nationalist, regional, and cosmopolitan images, narratives, and discourses interact and overlap. Diverging from Zhang, however, I share Sundaram's understanding of how media does not simply domesticate the shocks of capitalist modernity but bears a transformative potential that is part of the collective, sensorial immersion in the postcolonial developmental city. In *Monsoon Marketplace*, I similarly explore how commercial, administrative, infrastructural, and technological innovations have enabled urban residents to navigate the limits of given conditions by appropriating and experimenting with available resources of public space, cultural imagination, and political community in night markets, amusement parks, movie theaters, coffee shops, and shopping malls. In these examples, consumerism is not simply characterized by the move toward the solitary freedom it instills but also the collective agency it encourages in a dynamic urban environment.

Beyond Postcolonialism and Area

Juxtaposing Singapore and Manila across different historical periods, this book is informed by comparative cultural studies about Singapore and the Philippines. The method of comparativism in these existing works tends to focus on Singapore or the Philippines' relationship with nations commonly regarded as economically and geopolitically dominant, which has translated to their prevalence in global imaginaries. Shifting its critical attention toward interconnections within the marginalized subregion of Southeast Asia,

Monsoon Marketplace examines the public cultures of these two cities through an Inter-Asian approach.

Chua Beng Huat has been a pioneer not only in uncovering the complex changes to Singapore's spatial and social landscapes but also in exploring comparative approaches to Asian urban and media cultures. On the one hand, Chua's singular work has offered a seminal critique of the neoliberal pragmatism in the People's Action Party's ideology of communitarian democracy and policy of mass housing in a public sphere bereft of dissent.[15] On the other, as one of the main proponents of Inter-Asia Cultural Studies, Chua situates Singapore within East Asia alongside Tokyo, Shanghai, and Seoul. For Chua, these cities are more analogous in pop culture because they share equivalent levels of economic prosperity and technological advancement in contrast to other Southeast Asian cities, which he assumes to be afflicted by political and social turmoil.[16] Throughout his extensive body of work, Chua has emphasized Singapore's exceptionalism as a model of capitalist development, urban renewal, and mass consumption in relation to other postcolonial cities, which has made visible its operations of governmentality over its population and its hegemony in the region.[17]

Much comparative scholarship about the Philippines is interested in its relationship with its former colonizer the United States. Such works presume that social, economic, and cultural conditions in the Philippines have profoundly and inescapably been impacted by its occupation under the United States, whose hegemonic rise as a global superpower in the twentieth and twenty-first centuries was prefaced by its first colonial experiment. Among the groundbreaking writings of Postcolonial Studies in the Philippines, essays collected in the anthology of University of the Philippines professors Cristina Pantoja Hidalgo and Priscelina Patoja-Legasto look at how norms of white beauty and English grammar have maintained the consciousness of Filipinos in a subordinate position based on the notion they promote visual and linguistic practices that originate from elsewhere.[18] E. San Juan Jr. is more critical of how Postcolonial Studies overlooks uneven capitalist development in the world. In two of his noteworthy works, *Beyond Postcolonial Theory* (1998) and *After Postcolonialism* (2000), San Juan uncovers how its reproduction of the United States' dominant discourses of neoliberal democracy and multiculturalism obscures the racism and violence of U.S. imperialism and militarism.[19] Emphasizing how the Philippines and the

United States exist in a dialectical relationship, he argues that the knowledge production of Philippine Studies emphasizes the subordinated history of the Philippines to the United States.

The other leading proponent of Inter-Asia Cultural Studies, National Chiao Tung University professor Chen Kuan-hsing, calls for the multiplication of alternate frames of reference other than North America, Western Europe, and even East Asia.[20] To decenter the focus on the United States as a universal model, *Monsoon Marketplace* juxtaposes its economic, geopolitical, and cultural hegemony with that of the United Kingdom in Singapore, which has been less of a concern in Singapore Studies. This book looks at the intertwined microhistories of capitalism, modernity, consumerism, and spectatorship in two Southeast Asian cities, where colonial occupation forms one stage together with national development and neoliberal globalization.

Challenging overarching claims of uneven, hierarchical development, which can be limited to a single historical period, *Monsoon Marketplace* explores how capitalist modernity translates to the diverging, meandering, and opposing trajectories of economic growth and technological advancement in Singapore and the Philippines across the twentieth and twenty-first centuries. The book attempts to uncover the entangled genealogies of development and consumerism in postcolonial Southeast Asian metropolises by foregrounding how Manila under U.S. occupation was perceived to be one of the paragons of capitalist modernity in the Asian region in the 1930s and 1960s, before the rise of poverty and violence under the despotism and corruption of Ferdinand Marcos's Martial Law dictatorship in the early 1970s. Occupying a converse trajectory, Singapore was internationally notorious for its congestion, unrest, and crime until the 1960s before commencing its exemplary rapid growth, under Lee Kuan Yew and the People's Action Party, into a leading world-class city. Instead of adhering to a linear, evolutionary teleology of progress, the cultural histories of capitalist modernity, mass consumption, and media spectatorship in more marginal, understudied locations reveal how they assume discrepant, oscillatory temporalities of abundance, decline, abundance, and decline.

Instead of emphasizing a linear, evolutionary trajectory of capitalist development in which each new period is presented as an advancement over the previous one driven by the historical inevitability of progress, this book is interested in the contingencies, tensions, and possibilities of historical shifts and transitions. Writing about the emergence of modernity, Reinhart Koselleck sees historical or epochal shifts as a "period of transition" between disparate structures of knowledge and experience.[21] Perceiving them to be distinct, existing means of representation and language, according to Koselleck, may not succeed in comprehending the changing conditions that have transpired. *Monsoon Marketplace* focuses on historical shifts or transitions that trace the passage between different regimes of political sovereignty, economic production, and visual perception. It looks at how such transitions unfold as fissures and adjustments among prominent and popular infrastructures and practices of capitalist exchange, mass consumption, and media spectatorship in which dominant norms are unsettled without necessarily resulting in the constitution of a new established order. In the historical moments that this book examines, the shift in the dominant forms of mass entertainment and media representation from theater to cinema is facilitated by the emergence of glass window displays in the main commercial street that shaped the prevailing modes of visual perception and social prestige among urban residents. The book uncovers how the changing spatial configurations of commercial exhibition and public life in bazaars, department stores, supermarkets, and shopping malls redefine the possibilities of personal transcendence, national self-determination, and revolutionary upheaval.

Archipelagic as Comparativism

To comparatively study capitalism, media, and modernity in Southeast Asia, *Monsoon Marketplace* aims to uncover their entangled genealogies in the spatial environments and media ecologies of two cities, Manila and Singapore, during the 1930s, 1960s, and 2000s. Foucault defines genealogy as a diachronic method for tracing the changing configurations of knowledge and practice by identifying affinities, variances, and disparities across different historical periods.[22] For Foucault, genealogy is rooted in archeology, which, synchronic in orientation, excavates the multiple trajectories and temporalities that often remain invisible because they are deemed illegitimate or inconsequential according to the established norms of sociological inquiry or scientific objectivity. Archeology maps interconnections and arrangements among seemingly unrelated images, discourses, narratives, objects, practices, and spaces. Applying archeology to a wider period, genealogy exposes the coherent linearity of history as a shifting network whose vernacular configurations and experiences are liable to change based on the circumstances of the milieu.

As an archeology of capitalist modernity in Southeast Asia during the 1930s, Su Lin Lewis's *Cities in Motion* (2016) diverges from the typical focus on national development in Southeast Asian history to uncover the affinities and interconnections among the public cultures of colonial port cities Bangkok, Penang, and Rangoon.[23] Lewis adopts what I would call a panoramic approach, which flattens planetary space to map the interaction and convergence among global flows across different locations. Looking at how cosmopolitanism is produced in the commercial and leisure spaces of the burgeoning middle class such as amusement parks and social clubs, she excavates their transformative potential for refashioning established norms of identity and collectivity.

Tracing capitalist modernity in postcolonial Asian Tiger Economies Singapore, Seoul, and Taipei through a genealogical approach, Jini Kim Watson's *The New Asian City* (2011) analyzes the interactions and conflicts among different ideologies and imaginaries of space in fiction and poetry about urban development and neoliberal capitalism.[24] For Watson, literary and visual representations inscribe the complex, uneven interactions among individuals, infrastructures, and markets. Like Watson, I am interested in mapping affinities, variances, and disparities across the different scales of colonial, local, national, regional, and global flows. Whereas Watson looks at alienation in Tiger Economies, whose trajectories of material growth appear to be linear and evolutionary, I explore the limits of postcolonial analysis by examining Southeast Asian cities whose forms of political sovereignty, social order, and financial prosperity have diverged, meandered, and contrasted under shifting conditions of colonial occupation, postcolonial development, and neoliberal globalization.

Dipesh Chakrabarty argues that a comparative approach, which juxtaposes analogous realities from disparate milieus, enables scholars and critics to engage closely with theories without having to treat them as universalized abstractions.[25] Being comparative means opening up a critical epistemological space where concepts and categories such as capitalism, modernity, consumerism, and spectatorship could be seen to undergo variation and transformation across different locations and periods outside the limits of a linear historical framework.

The analytical work of comparison typically rests on a common ground or similarity, which would provide the thematic or conceptual basis for examining different objects of inquiry. For instance, while Watson focuses on postcolonial development in the urban spaces of East Asian Tiger Economies, Lewis elaborates on cosmopolitan modernity in the public cultures of Southeast Asian port cities. One of the dangers of comparison when studying different geographic and historical milieus is that the pervading logic of modernization theory might cause these milieus to become arranged under a linear hierarchy of economic and material growth. For instance, engaging with Philippine and Indonesian literature to trace the historical emergence of a national consciousness, Benedict Anderson's method of comparison as an "inverted telescope" examines one location using the frame of reference of a different, more marginal location such that the less discernible affinities and interconnections between the two are made visible.[26] While the "inverted telescope" enables the contradictions of the West to be uncovered and comprehended from the lens of Southeast Asia, this comparative method has been criticized by Partha Chatterjee and Harry Harootunian for failing to overcome the cultural dominance of North America and Western Europe through their continued use as frames of reference.[27]

Critiquing the typical reliance on North America and Western Europe as main frames of reference, Kuan-Hsing Chen seeks to decolonize and diversify knowledge production through his conception of "Asia as Method," which entails the juxtaposition of different locations within greater Asia by applying frameworks and perspectives developed in the same contexts.[28] Chen criticizes the tendency of established scholarship to study Asia by taking East Asia or South Asia as a proxy for the entire region while disregarding its plurality and complexity. Chen's comparative approach consists of "interreferencing," which maps the "base-entities" in a location by multiplying its points of reference while treating each location as coeval with one another such that each location is reciprocally apprehended by seeing affinities and resonances in the "base-entities" of other locations. Chen chooses the term "base-entity" to examine how the complex conditions in a singular spatial environment are shaped by their distinct agglomeration of "social practices" and "historical experiences."

Instead of merely engaging in *comparison*, *Monsoon Marketplace* is interested in *juxtaposition*. Informed by Chen's method of interreferencing the complex conditions of different locations in Asia, the book juxtaposes the urban environments and media ecologies of two Southeast Asian cities. Whereas *comparison* assumes the rational completeness and precision of a closed system of conditions based on scientific and sociological categories, *juxtaposition* explores possible affinities and interconnections among ambiguous or discontinuous realities, whose correspondence or relationship with each other may not be immediately evident.

By mapping affinities and interconnections among seemingly disparate objects of inquiry, the method of juxtaposition enables me to uncover, within a particular geographical and historical milieu, what Raymond Williams calls the "structure of feeling," a pattern of "meanings and values as they are actively lived and felt."[29] Described as constituting a "practical consciousness," such imaginaries and significations are implicit in the public culture but without congealing into the coherent formality or precise validity of scientific and sociological knowledge. According to this method of juxtaposition, fragmentary objects in the public print, audiovisual, and spatial cultures could be analyzed to disclose the prevailing tendencies from the milieu in which they were produced, disseminated, or consumed. For example, Leo Ou-Fan Lee examines the vernacular entanglement of capitalist modernity and mass consumption in everyday spaces, discourses, objects, and practices that were experienced as modern in cosmopolitan Shanghai before the Pacific War. Lee's goal is to uncover its *cultural imaginary*, which he defines as "a contour of collective sensibilities and significations resulting from cultural production."[30] Looking at the prevalent forms of urban infrastructure, transportation, and leisure in prominent commercial districts like Foochow Road and The Bund,[31] he identifies what for him are salient spatial and cultural realities characteristic of his geographic and historical milieu of 1930s Shanghai such as concrete, electricity, automobiles, trams, fashion, and cinema.[32] In this book, I aim for a similar interdisciplinary and multimodal scope by covering a range of print and audiovisual media that resonated in the collective imaginaries of different milieus. However, unlike Lee's *Shanghai Modern* or Harootunian's *Overcome by Modernity*,[33] I devote less attention to the reflexive writings of intellectuals and artists about capitalist modernity or mass consumption than its implicit articulation in the public culture of their time.

For each period, I identified a span of approximately five years, based on which I perused a wide range of materials from the print, audiovisual, and spatial cultures of the time to gain a sense of the prevailing trajectories and tendencies in its everyday life. Some of the recurrent words and images I gleaned include those of sanitation and femininity in the 1930s, nationalism and youthfulness in the 1960s, and globalization and competition in the 2000s.

I delved into the archive using newspapers, advertisements, maps, blueprints, speeches, brochures, novels, photographs, postcards, and films. In these multiple archival print and audiovisual media representations, I aimed to excavate and trace changes to the configurations, uses, and significations of images, discourses, narratives, practices, and spaces commonly associated with capitalist modernity, public life, mass consumption, leisure time, and media spectatorship across different locations and periods.

Monsoon Marketplace's method of juxtaposition builds on Édouard Glissant's conception of the *archipelagic* as an analytical framework for excavating, connecting, and mapping seemingly disparate, unrelated objects. Instead of simply applying theories that bring unity and clarity, an archipelagic framework is interested in how "differences" might "interact, collide, and coexist" by "accident."[34]

The term "archipelagic" has resonances in Southeast Asian culture. First, in the scholarship of the region, Singapore and the Philippines are disciplinarily understood to belong to "island," "maritime," or "archipelagic" Southeast Asia. Second, the Philippines prides itself in being an archipelago comprising 7,100+ islands, depending on high or low tide. Also topographically archipelagic, Singapore's actual spatial configuration as an archipelago is often elided in prevalent media representations of it. What is commonly known to be Singapore is, in fact, a central island surrounded by peripheral, outlying islets such as Pulau Ubin, Pulau Semakau, Lazarus Island, Kusu Island, and St. John's Island. Furthermore, because of their historical origins as thriving port cities at the nucleus of important trading routes, the spatial environments and urban populations of both Manila and Singapore have analogously been shaped by diverse, trans-local flows. The shifting movements of these flows could be seen to map the amorphous contours of the archipelago.

Arguing that the normative political and cultural boundaries between them are provisional and contingent, Glissant advocates for reimagining regions as shifting networks of variable trajectories and temporalities, with a multiplicity of interactions and conjunctions.[35] Refusing their default systematization or categorization, Glissant's inclusive conception of the archipelagic enables the juxtaposition of seemingly unrelated objects within the same geographic location or historical period. While disparate at first glance, their archipelagic juxtaposition exposes a tenuous affinity, variance, or disparity that would disclose the complex interconnections and arrangements of colonial, local, national, regional, and global flows.

If Walter Benjamin reimagines the arcades in *The Arcades Project* as indexes of salient words, objects, and images in Paris during the nineteenth century, which have become forgotten despite disclosing the emergence of capitalist modernity, mass consumption, and media spectatorship,[36] I hope to use archipelagos as frames for excavating and tracing the relationships of seemingly disparate words, objects, and images in Manila and Singapore across the twentieth and twenty-first centuries. Through this approach, the archipelagos of affinities, variances, and disparities that become discernible through the juxtaposition of materials about glass windows, movie screens, souvenir postcards, and carnival rides in the print, audiovisual, and spatial cultures of a geographic and historical milieu can make visible the shifting networks of interconnections and arrangements among capitalism, modernity, consumerism, and spectatorship on different scales.

Between Arcades and Archipelagos

Few studies about Asia, East Asia, or Southeast Asia offer a comparative cultural history of the complex, entangled variations and transformations of capitalism, modernity, consumerism, and spectatorship. Most scholarship is more limited and intensive in scope, dwelling on a single consumer space, a single geographical location, or a single historical period. This book is divided into three main parts, each focused on the 1930s, 1960s, or 2000s. Parts I and II comprise three chapters each. While the first two chapters in each part vividly describe the geographic and historical milieus of either Manila or Singapore, the third chapter more closely juxtaposes the resonant spaces, words, objects, and images in their public cultures. Each chapter is dedicated to examining at least one important commercial and leisure space, whose representations in the print and audiovisual cultures of the milieu unveil its prevailing tendencies. Apprehending commercial and leisure spaces as focal points for critical analysis in the chapters, I examine distinct archipelagos of discourses, narratives, and images that are commonly associated with capitalist modernity, public life, mass consumption, leisure time, and media spectatorship. Like Walter Benjamin's theory of the dialectical image in *The Arcades Project*, my goal is "to discover in the analysis of the small individual moment the crystal of the total event."[37] Across various moments of transition, I aim to trace the entangled genealogies of capitalism, modernity, consumerism, and spectatorship in postcolonial Southeast Asian metropolises by excavating and mapping affinities, variances, and disparities among seemingly unrelated print and audiovisual media representations of popular commerce and leisure spaces.

Part I, "1930s Manila and Singapore," looks at the historical period when the Commonwealth of the Philippine Islands and the Straits Settlement of Singapore were under the colonial occupation of the United States and United Kingdom. While the neoclassical monumentality of the central public square of Raffles Place propagated ideals of empire and permanence, the Art Deco architecture on the main commercial street of Calle Escolta epitomized the norms of prestige and progress.

Chapter 1, "Walled Street of Modernity," analyzes literary representations of vaudevillian comedians and female shoppers struggling to harness sweeping modern forces through their encounter with glass displays in the retail boutiques of the Crystal Arcade, which were endowed with the vivid materiality of movie screens. Chapter 2, "Between Spaces of Imperial Languor," analyzes W. Somerset Maugham's short stories set in Singapore and Malaya to examine how expatriate officials consumed newspapers and postcards in their bungalow verandahs to overcome their languor and impotency from the ungovernable multiplicity and dynamism of the entrepôt economy. Chapter 3, "Spectacles beyond the Limits of Exhaustion," uses exhibition booklets, print advertisements, and editorial letters to explore sensorial immersion in carnivals and amusement parks and cooperative labor in ports and sporting clubs, which extended the productive capacities of entrepôt workers beyond their physical and social limitations.

Part II, "1960s Singapore and Manila," shifts the book's focus to the early stages of postcolonial development in Manila under Mayor Antonio Villegas and in Singapore under founding prime minister, Lee Kuan Yew. This historical period was characterized by the impassioned spectacles of mass protests and labor strikes as residents frequently gathered in popular movie theaters, coffee shops, and night markets. Whereas the infrastructure of Manila was overburdened by internal migrants, Singapore relocated its population to housing estates in its outskirts to confront urgent problems of congestion, violence, and unrest.

Chapter 4, "Temporalities of Development and Delinquency," describes how the discourses of the ruling People's Action Party against the emotional disruptiveness of rural villages and labor strikes was embodied in the *pasar malam*, or night market, which, despite being significant hubs of social life, found their creative informality regulated through the gradual, pragmatic adjustment of legal and medical codes. Chapter 5, "Panoramic Popularity in the Neon Streets," dissects how the conception of neon as virtual infinitude in Edgardo M. Reyes's Tagalog novel *Sa Mga Kuko ng Liwanag* evoked representations of youthful delinquency in Nick Joaquin's journalistic writings, which became contained by the self-service infrastructures of suburban supermarkets. Chapter 6, "Public Spheres of Postcolonial Fantasy," explores imaginaries of self-determination and metamorphosis in the genre cinema of iconic, controversial stars P. Ramlee and Joseph "Erap" Estrada, whose mythic personas, gossiped about in coffee shops, created fissures for innovative ideas about transforming the established order.

Under Part III, "Millennial Southeast Asia," Chapter 7, "Neoliberal Cosmopolitanism in the Tropical World City," concludes the book with Kevin Kwan's *New York Times* Best Seller *Crazy Rich Asians* and Glenn Diaz's multi-award-winning *The Quiet Ones* by looking at Manila and Singapore during the late 2000s and early 2010s when their domestic economies relied on their management of external, transnational flows of finance, information, and talent. The chapter contrasts the architectural typologies of shopping malls such as SM Megamall on EDSA and Ion Orchard on Orchard Road, whose outsourced axiomatic of previously separate commercial and leisure spaces incarnated the utopian normalcy of the world city in drawing the purchasing power of overseas investors and migrant workers with the buzz of elite prestige.

PART I

1930s Manila and Singapore

CHAPTER I

Walled Street of Modernity

In Manila and Singapore, the historical period of the 1930s was defined by the economic and geopolitical anxieties of the Great Depression and Pacific War amid a dynamic period of commercial, infrastructural, and artistic innovation. Under occupation by the declining and rising superpowers the United Kingdom and United States, these cosmopolitan port cities were important hubs in transoceanic shipping and airplane routes for the extraction, distribution, and exchange of global industrial supply chains, which allowed for the increased mobility of newspapers, movies, letters, and postcards between metropole and colony. Consuming stylish fashions in their luxury shops and department stores and immersive attractions in their amusement parks and movie theaters, urban residents negotiated diverse and contradictory modern flows that shaped the limits and possibilities of agency and collectivity.

Into the third decade of U.S. colonial rule, Calle Escolta, Manila's "Queen of the Streets," had developed into its thriving financial and commercial center, where flows of images, goods, and bodies converged. Albeit compact in dimension, being only half a kilometer long and twenty meters wide,[1] the Escolta epitomized the promise of this historical moment. Because of its long history as a hub for the galleon trade of silk and silver between China and Mexico, Manila was a pluralistic, multicultural environment with a mix of Spanish, English, Tagalog, Cebuano, Ilocano, Japanese, and Hokkien being spoken and overheard in public. As the model colony of the United States, the atmosphere of prestige and progress projected by its main street offered proof of the Philippine Islands' growing readiness for independence and self-determination. Exemplified by the commercial, administrative, techno-logical, and infrastructural changes introduced by state and business in the urban environment, modernity during this period became apprehended in the form of an inexorable, expansive, seemingly supernatural phenomenon that ordinary people appeared to lack the means to control or harness with their own autonomous capacities.

The Escolta's most striking commercial building was the multimillion-peso, fully air-conditioned Crystal Arcade. Financed by the Taverna Luna Incorporated, the family company of the heirs of T. H. Pardo de Tavera, an active member of the nineteenth-century anticolonial Propaganda Move-ment, it was designed by preeminent artist Juan Luna's son Andres Luna de San Pedro, an architect trained in France and Japan.[2] Many of the Escolta's prominent stores such as Sun Photo, Syyap Tailoring, and Sarabia Optical had relocated to the Crystal Arcade, which housed the Manila Stock Ex-change, the nucleus of the 1930s gold mining boom. Influenced by the latest architectural styles from Japan, France, Germany, and the United States, its interior was adorned with elegant Bavarian granite, Belgian leatherette, and Alsatian ceramic.[3] While its state-of-the-art boat-type foundation was built by Filipino engineer Jose G. Cortez to accommodate earthquake tremors, its basement featured drain pumps to manage the flooding from overflowing canals, which plagued Calle Escolta during the monsoon season. Beneath reflective, polychromatic glass walls, insets, and ceilings, its centerpiece was its majestic double staircase, which was a feat of modern engineering in the Philippine Islands that ascended from the middle of the atrium without vis-ible structural support. Extolled by local newspapers on its inauguration as "the last word in modernity,"[4] the Crystal Arcade exemplified the ability of vernacular innovations to transcend their tropical milieu.

Despite this atmosphere of dynamism and possibility, the repercussions of the global economic depression at the end of the prosperous "roaring"

The Tavera-Luna Building and Crystal Arcade, the only building of its kind in the Orient, as it appears. With this new edifice architectural art makes a long step forward in the Philippines.

FIGURE 1. Heralded in local newspapers, the Art-Deco Crystal Arcade represented a paradise of progress with its air-conditioned atrium and spectacular lighting. (Photo from National Library of Australia)

1920s continued to impact the everyday life of Filipinos into the succeeding decade, with their decreased purchasing power.[5] Anxieties about the future became magnified when the Philippine Islands were granted a definite path by the U.S. government toward national sovereignty with widening access to electoral democracy. Periodicals expressed the growing apprehension that the domestic economy would falter without the steady demand of American markets for duty-free Filipino products such as sugar, hemp, coconut oil, and copra. Filipino politicians and journalists debated whether the pre-independence period should be extended or political independence should be overturned.

In tracing the entangled genealogies of capitalism, modernity, consumerism, and spectatorship in popular commercial and leisure spaces in Southeast Asian cities, this chapter focuses on the built environment and media ecology of 1930s Calle Escolta as a main commercial street in a colonial port city in the early twentieth century. I explore three dominant tendencies I gleaned from the print and visual cultures of newspapers, advertisements, fictions, and plays during the 1930s: the equation of sanitation with capitalist modernity, the introduction of cinema as mass entertainment, and the emergence of women in public life. I start the chapter by dissecting the logic of *air-conditioned, sanitary modernity*, which transcendentally imposes a dialectic of sanitation and exclusion on the undesirable realities that are perceived to pollute its domain. Uncovering the affinities between glass windows and movie screens as innovations in the infrastructures of commercial and media exhibition, the chapter examines how the translation of the norms of air-conditioned modernity to the spatial landscape shaped the impact of practices of consumerism and spectatorship on social identity and value. Analyzing the figure of Kenkoy in Tony Velasquez's comics in the popular Tagalog-language *Liwayway* magazine, I explain how modern forces appeared to be imbued with the transcendent force of divine intervention when consumers of new products and styles struggled to manage them on their own without the awkwardness and embarrassment of *hiya*. Seeing consumerism as a means for negotiating modernity, I peruse English-language publications such as the *Tribune* and *Philippine Magazine* for representations of how Filipino women departed from the domestic cloister of the household to contribute their newfound purchasing power to the burgeoning consumer economy. Apprehended through the cognitive absorption of the cinematographic gaze, transparent technologies of glass windows endowed their products with images of vivid materiality and magical self-renewal. The chapter concludes by analyzing how Deogracias Rosario's Tagalog-language short story "Greta Garbo" discloses the shift in the basis of social distinction from material possession to celebrity mimicry.

The Divine Intervention of Air-Conditioned Modernity

With the occupation of the Philippines at the end of the nineteenth century by the United States, the spatial and social landscape of the archipelago was transformed. The colonial era under Spain from the sixteenth to the nineteenth centuries, corresponding with its decline as an economic and geo-

political empire, had been contrastingly marked by repetition and stagnation. Due to their inherent fragility, physical structures failed to transcend
the rhythm of recurrent catastrophes. Majestic state and church buildings
made of wood, stone, or adobe tended to be damaged or demolished by
typhoons, fires, and earthquakes.[6] The local population of the Philippine
Islands experienced time as an inevitable cycle in which newly built structures would eventually be destroyed through the agency of nature and the
sanction of God. Such catastrophes would be attributed by Catholic friars
in their homilies to the innately sinful thoughts and actions of natives.[7]
This cyclicality was echoed by the immobility of society as people stayed
bound to their given circumstances throughout their lifespans. As exemplified by the character of Sisa in José Rizal's seminal novel *Noli Me Tangere*,
most natives subsisted with scarce hope of ascending through the established
hierarchy, which was dominated by landowners and friars of Spanish descent.

Without the inertia of the earlier regime, the U.S. colonial government
contrastingly introduced technological and infrastructural advances commonly recognized as modern.[8] Assuming the force and veneer of divine intervention, it brought electricity to streets, buildings, and homes. It paved
and illuminated roads to ensure the quick and efficient movement of bodies
and goods. Under U.S. rule, wood, stone, and adobe structures were re-
made with iron, glass, and concrete.[9] In his historical montage of fin-de-
siècle Netherlands East Indies cities such as Batavia, Medan, and Soerabaja,
Rudolf Mrázek describes how modernity was made tangible and visible
through ubiquitous innovations in roads, vehicles, clothes, appliances, and
radios such that it became experienced as a relentless, transformative force.[10]
Echoing Eric Hobsbawm's emphatic account of modernization,[11] it was perceived as a sweeping, almost supernatural phenomenon whose possibilities
individuals could barely grasp. Such advances in the infrastructures and
technologies of production, energy, transportation, domesticity, fashion, and
communication expanded the parameters of existing modes of visual perception and spatial behavior by accustoming bodies to speed and change.[12] Under U.S. rule, Calle Escolta rose to prominence as the epitome of progress in
1930s Manila with its stylish façades, orderly interiors, and luxury imports.
As the new regime extensively and effectively renovated spaces, structures,
bodies, and practices with modern norms, Filipinos came to equate modernity with the United States.

The United States believed that its Manifest Destiny in the Philippine Islands was intrinsically tied to the cultivation of *sanitary, air-conditioned modernity* in the everyday life of the local population. From the onset of its rule in the last years of the nineteenth century, it strove to enforce strict standards of health and hygiene to prevent the physical and mental degeneration of bodies in the tropical milieu. Warwick Anderson writes that the U.S. colonial government regarded the cityscape of Manila, with its crude structures, faulty drains, and unpaved roads, as sordid and primitive. *Tiendas*, shops that opened to the road, were considered unsanitary and were ordered enclosed.[13] Native markets were rebuilt with reinforced concrete and were placed "under municipal supervision."[14] Health officials would regularly visit their premises to inspect to see if the vendors at these markets wore clean, unsoiled clothing, kept clean hands and trimmed nails, and used clean, white wrapping paper.[15] According to the logic of these government policies, only if public spaces of exhibition and exchange like stores and markets were made orderly and sanitary could they facilitate commercial and consumer practices that signified civilization and progress.

Driven by the entangled ideals of health, hygiene, order, beauty, and morality, the project of sanitary, air-conditioned modernity in Southeast Asian port cities during the early twentieth century represented the efforts of the colonial regime to exploit modern forces, even if these forces frequently eluded its complete control. Through the implementation of this project, aspirations and fantasies for civilization and progress became incarnated in the built environment and social practice. With evangelistic and pietistic intensity, both public and domestic spaces were refashioned according to its norms such that any reality that failed to comply with them could not be considered modern.

In 1930s Manila, the logic of sanitary modernity was exemplified by the innovation of air-conditioning, which was installed in many of the newly constructed and renovated buildings on Calle Escolta, such as the Capitol Theater, Heacock's Department Store, and the Crystal Arcade, during the 1930s. Aiming to promote modern ideas of health and hygiene, W. L. Blakemore, a British colonial official in Singapore, explained the workings of the technology in one of his radio broadcasts: "Air-conditioning actually comprises a number of processes and the first is the purification of the air in a room by removing from it not only all dust and dirt but also a considerable proportion of the bacteria and the odors arising from food and from the perspiring occupants of the room; in addition the fresh air which is introduced into the room is passed through filters to remove all dust and dirt and most of the bacteria."[16]

According to Blakemore's description, air-conditioning involves the "purification" of a circumscribed domain to make it more habitable for its occupants by "removing" contaminants like "dust," "dirt," and "bacteria" as well as filth, stench, and noise. Understood to be "the natural result of tightly closing all doors and windows with a view to rendering the room more or less air-tight," it requires the formation of a strict enclosure, from which outside contaminants are expelled. In this way, the technology of air-conditioning demonstrates the severity of the logic of sanitary modernity, which indiscriminately and ruthlessly cleanses the public spaces of the city of their impurities.

Mary Douglas argues that sanitation rests on enclosure, which strictly delineates and enforces a spatial and symbolic hierarchy between the interior of a circumscribed domain and its outside. According to Douglas, realities that do not fit the overarching pattern of this domain are deemed chaotic and recalcitrant "anomalies."[17] Regarded as detrimental and threatening to its order, they must be banished to the outside. Expanding on Douglas's ideas, I would add that a dialectical framework is imposed on diverse, contingent realities. For modernity to become established as a dominant presence in a circumscribed domain, an administrative or infrastructural configuration must classify, devalue, and expel all the realities that it considers to be a danger to the identity and stability of this domain. As the space is understood to contain them, the outside becomes the signification of these excluded realities, which modern forces have purified from the interior.

The project of introducing sanitary modernity has often coincided with that of delivering moral order to the city and its population. Douglas highlights the religious character of sanitation in that it resembles rituals that are meant to purge a spatial environment of its anomalous pollution.[18] When the arrival of the U.S. army in Manila turned the Escolta into a den of saloons, Governor-General William Howard Taft decreed these supposedly sinful establishments closed to restore its reputation.[19] Notably under the administration of Mayor Justo Lukban, a nationalist physician who participated in the Hong Kong revolutionary junta and cofounded the Nacionalista Party, systematic efforts were undertaken from 1917 to 1920 to transform Manila into a modern urban environment without vice and sin. Recreational activities like gambling, cockfighting, and prostitution, whose usage of bodies and finances was deemed immoral, were declared illegal and banished to its outskirts.[20] These governmental interventions pervaded the configuration and imagination of the public spaces of the Escolta as needing to be sanitary, lawful, and modern to be more conducive to business.

It is only with modernity that newness assumes a more secular form, even if it retains traces of its religious character. Defined by national development in the 1960s and neoliberal cosmopolitanism in the 2000s, it was shaped by evangelistic and pietistic religion in 1930s Manila. Historians write about how the U.S. government's doctrine of Manifest Destiny, which led to its colonial occupation of Puerto Rico and the Philippine Islands, was rooted in the belief of its divine exceptionalism.[21] Entwined with this belief was the missionary zeal to effect religious renewal in individuals.[22] As evident in its discourse, the U.S. colonial regime's endeavor to civilize the cityscape of 1930s Manila by eliminating its undesirable elements carried in it the messianic desire to cleanse the world of its sinfulness. As though authorized by the undiscriminating and uncompromising force of religious renewal, it strove toward the conversion of the entire social body at the exclusion of irredeemable, undesirable realities that might threaten it with contagion.

Exclusivity in the Commercial Street

Epitomizing this logic of exclusivity through its atmosphere of prestige, the Escolta first gained prominence from being lined with elegant shops that carried luxury goods imported from overseas. During the 1930s, the façades and interiors of its buildings and stores exemplified Manila's reputation as "one of the most progressive cities in the world" by espousing modern norms of architectural beauty, social behavior, and commercial exhibition.[23] Because the financial means for acquiring luxury goods was limited to members of the social and economic elite, many of the visitors to Calle Escolta frequented the Crystal Arcade, La Estrella del Norte, and H. E. Heacock Company simply to browse their alluring glass displays.

By the middle of the 1870s, Calle Escolta, the parallel Calle San Vicente, and adjacent Calle Nueva had gained prominence as commercial spaces

where imported products could be purchased retail.[24] The area of Calle Escolta grew famous for its *bazares*, shops carrying the European luxury goods
that the newly affluent Chinese *mestizos* and native *indios* keenly desired.
The largest Chinese-owned *bazares* were those of Chua Farruco and Velasco
Chua Chengco on Calle Nueva. They sold carriage ornaments, dinnerware
sets, kitchen stoves, Chinese silks, European cottons and yarns, Viennese
furniture, and Parisian musical instruments. These shops would have enormous backrooms, which were supposedly meant to store stocks but often
kept the most luxurious and expensive items.[25] Hidden from public view,
such goods relied on their concealment for their exclusivity. Akin to royal
and religious sovereignty, whose authority was opaque and impenetrable,
the commercial street gained prominence not only from what it offered but
also from what it withheld.

Historical accounts from the last decade of the nineteenth century describe how shops on Calle Escolta contributed to its atmosphere of prestige
by carrying imported goods from Madrid, Paris, Rome, Macao, London,
and New York. The Escolta's most prominent luxury shops included Botica
Inglesa, Perfumería Moderna, and La Estremeña, as well as La Estrella del
Norte and La Puerta del Sol, both of which continued to operate into the
1930s.[26] Personal narratives from the early years of U.S. colonial rule noted
the predominance of European establishments offering a variety of products
and services: Swiss jewelries, French millineries, Spanish tobaccos, English
emporiums, German chemists, and Spanish physicians.[27] Located not far
from Plaza Moraga on the southwest side of the Escolta since being founded
in 1870, La Estrella del Norte had long established itself as a prominent
source for luxury items from France such as jewelry, watches, and perfume,
as well as for being the first to introduce a bicycle and phonograph.[28] La
Estrella del Norte's newspaper advertisements highlighted its commitment
to selling "the finer things in life."

Calle Escolta's selection of luxury goods greatly appealed to Manila's social and economic elite, who liked to appear in public on special occasions
dressed in the latest Parisian fashions.[29] Listening to the military brass band
play while viewing the spectacle of sunset, members of the elite would regularly visit the Luneta at dusk in carriages decorated with European ornaments.[30] Displaying images of wealth and status, they presented themselves
to the gaze of other individuals to affirm their standing in the established
hierarchy. Contingent on the public visibility of material abundance on their

bodies, their prestige rested on their ability to demonstrate their ownership of luxury goods.

Anthony Reid writes that, in Southeast Asian cultures, social prestige was a crucial means for individuals who did not belong to royalty or aristocracy to ascend the established hierarchy.[31] Without the fortune of having inherited their wealth and status, merchants and migrants used the earnings they amassed to display possessions and perform activities commonly understood to bear the value of luxury and exclusivity.

The individuals who garnered prestige were those who had access to the backrooms where luxury goods were hidden. The value of their prestige stemmed less from their capacity to acquire ownership of material possessions than from their skill at flaunting these exclusive objects in public. Although the immediate visibility of luxury goods furnished the basis for prestige, the prominence of this visibility was magnified by their concealment from and inaccessibility to the majority of the population. The only reason prestige derived value from material possession was that, being stored in backrooms, luxury goods could be seen nowhere else in public than on the bodies of the individuals who owned them.

Public Figures of Transition

From the beginning of its rule at the turn of the nineteenth century, the U.S. regime established extensive public education and civil service systems that trained Filipinos in the more inclusive rudiments of modernity,[32] such as modern ways of visual perception and social behavior. Newspapers performed a similar function, serving as dictionaries and manuals of modernity by educating their readers about words, attitudes, objects, habits, and situations understood to be new or innovative.[33] Prominent national periodicals during the 1930s, like the *Tribune* and *Philippine Magazine*, were published in English, the dominant language of modernity in the Philippine Islands. Proclaiming that its audience was the "most wide-awake and progressive people in the Far East," the monthly *Philippine Magazine* contrasted modern consciousness and activity with the slumber of tropical inertia. Based on the content of its articles, the language of this claim implied that physical changes to infrastructure and technology must be complemented with an open standpoint toward novel and transformative ideas, practices, and relations. The Sunday edition of the *Tribune* devoted regular sections to modern science, youth, and women that promoted the norms of modern knowledge and behavior. Aside from espousing the virtues of reason and efficiency, they instructed burgeoning segments of the Filipino populace about the proper means by which they could negotiate the rapidly shifting circumstances brought about by modern forces.

Modern forces proved to be less manageable for individuals than for the government, which possessed authority over the resources of its territory. Displaying their own capacity for harnessing the possibilities of modern forces was one way for Filipinos to demonstrate their readiness for self-determination. Paul Kramer and Warwick Anderson write how, for the U.S. regime, Filipinos' innate capacity for mimicry was supposed to enable them to acquire sovereignty and modernity without delay. From the standpoint of colonial officials, however, because Filipinos were inherently primitive, they could never be fully assimilated into a state of civilization.[34] Any natural incapacity for order and hygiene would be compensated for by their possession of technological implements such as consumer goods, whose use they needed to repeat until it had become habitual and ingrained.

Believed to be controllable only by government and business in their construction of the infrastructure, architecture, and technology of the city, modernity was depicted in the print and audiovisual culture as rendering ordinary people incapable of harnessing its possibilities with their own autonomous capacities. Equipped with increased purchasing power as members of the growing workforce, urban residents could not avoid dealing with modern forces when inhabiting commercial spaces, purchasing imported goods, and adopting urban lifestyles. Although instances of modernity became discernible in the language they spoke, the fashion they wore, and the bearing they assumed, their personal encounter with it was troublesome and tentative, a situation that was culturally represented less by the adventures of heroic demigods than by the misfortunes of humorous caricatures. While seemingly frivolous, these comic figures of transition found in media representations supplied significant models of conduct that illustrated how awkwardness and embarrassment might be appropriate responses in dealing with modern forces.

One such exemplar of modernity was Kenkoy, the hapless, gangling protagonist of advertising artist Tony Velasquez's comic strip *Album ng Kabalbalan*, or "Album of Follies," which started being published in the popular Tagalog-language *Liwayway* magazine in the early 1930s. Promoted through the sale of toy merchandise, the character Kenkoy would be performed in a comedy skit on stage in vaudeville events at the Savoy and on radio during Esco Hour on KZIB.[35] Extending its reach across the archipelago, this comic strip would be reproduced in the vernacular languages Cebuano, Hiligaynon, Ilocano, and Bicolano for *Liwayway*'s sister regional magazines.[36]

Kenkoy represented the humorous awkwardness of the attempt to grapple with modernity. Exemplifying how consumerism involved an improvised fashioning of identity, his spontaneous response as a consumer and mimic of styles to the growing dominance of modern influences was expressed through an exaggerated physicality. He could be seen as the literary transfiguration of a vaudeville performer who incorporated an incongruous miscellany of styles into his appearance and demeanor. The clown archetype that Kenkoy typically invoked found itself thrown into an unfamiliar and disorienting situation whose norms he failed to master.[37] Attired in an untucked, oversized white cotton suit with his hair slicked back with pomade, Kenkoy spoke in broken English with cannibalized words like "*Bay-gali*," "*Beri*," and "*Wat-sa-mara*." His disjointed language revealed the difficulty in smoothly reconciling seemingly incongruous realities during this period. Episodes in the comic strip examined the tentative, everyday attempts of Filipinos to assimilate the novel social practices that U.S. culture disseminated. Coming at the expense of its protagonist, the comic strip's vaudevillian humor compensated for the humiliating awkwardness of these attempts at mimicry, which typically resulted in failure.[38]

Discourses of air-conditioned modernity that circulated in print advertisements promoted the capacity of consumer items to deliver the miraculous benefits of modernity to the everyday life of Filipinos. Embodied in the transformative products of technological innovations, the profound changes introduced by modern forces were commonly perceived to be supernatural and divine,[39] beyond the reach of ordinary individuals to generate without an interceding agency. While U.S. advertisements for consumer items during this period focused on social reputation and mobility,[40] local advertisements for Ivory soap in the 1930s offered to introduce the conditions of cleanliness, health, and happiness to consumers for only a few centavos: "A little thing like Ivory soap—bringing you the blessing of cleanliness, as the first aid to good health—plays an important part in your happiness and enjoyment of life. . . . Form the Ivory habit. Take advantage of the cleansing Ivory lather to keep yourself in the pink of physical condition. Ivory for bath, Ivory for face and hands—washes away more than dirt and the stain's impurities. It washes away the blues—makes life seem better and brighter."

In the advertisement, Ivory soap is transfigured into a sacred object whose "blessing of cleanliness" will bestow "good health" through faithful use. Although seemingly inconsequential because of its size and appearance, this product is presented with the supernatural capacity to purge undesirable elements such as germs and sorrows. It presents sanitation as the continuous process of eliminating undesirable elements from the bodies of people, which entails the simultaneous application of technological innovations and repetition of hygienic practices.[41] Because Filipino consumers might find modern realities to be unfamiliar and unmanageable, their adoption of them requires persistence. Only if they embrace as their habit the activity of washing their bodies with Ivory soap would they find the bliss of heavenly paradise on earth.

Warwick Anderson traces how the U.S. colonial regime's strategy for confronting the squalor of local realities shifted from spatial segregation to physical discipline. As the belief in the native body's natural resistance to germs was superseded by the concept that immunity could be cultivated and acquired,[42] the government began to intervene in the everyday life of the population. Training Filipinos to adopt hygienic practices, it subjected local realities understood to be private, domestic, or interior to the discipline of its public health policy.[43] Teachers in its extensive public school system instructed their students about the value of washing hands and wearing shoes and the danger of eating raw vegetables and spitting on the street.[44] In refashioning customs and habits, it aimed to mold weak, filthy, immature natives into productive, orderly, modern citizens.[45]

With infrastructural and aesthetic innovations in the consumption of fashion during the 1930s, the performance of sanitary modernity in the urban environment became a means for Filipinos in Manila to demonstrate their capacity for self-determination. In the main street of Calle Escolta, for instance, the predominantly female salesclerks who worked in the luxury shops negotiated the expectation of ridding their appearance and behavior of undesirable elements according to modern norms of commercial display.

Psychologist Jaime Bulatao explains how the normative social behavior of Filipinos appears to be rooted in *hiya*, which he defines as an overwhelming feeling of shyness, timidity, or embarrassment.[46] According to Bulatao, *hiya* often manifests in an unfamiliar and disorienting situation that is beyond the capacity of an individual to comprehend or control. Unable to cope with the perceived judgment of the public, this individual grows anxious and elusive almost to the point of paralysis. Building on this concept, I would suggest that representations of Kenkoy and soap in the public culture of 1930s Manila reveal how ordinary people experienced their encounter with modernity as a disorienting situation in which they confronted unfamiliar realities without having the knowledge or ability to do so. The debilitating experience of *hiya* kept them from experimenting with untested adaptations, whose awkward performance could easily result in embarrassment. As depicted in the exaggerated physicality of Kenkoy, modernity forced a transformation to their bodies that allowed them to manage unpredictable realities with their existing capacities.[47] They relied on the aid of consumer products and lifestyles to alter their appearance, behavior, and attitude. This refashioning of physical capacities included making the feeling of embarrassment more acceptable as part of their assimilation into modernity. As a transitional figure, Kenkoy demonstrated how embarrassment could be embraced in dealing with modern forces despite the possible awkwardness or failure of the encounter.

From Domesticity to Consumerism

Highlighting the complexities and possibilities of consumerism, the print culture of 1930s Manila likewise reveals a fascination with modern femininity as a site of transition and transformation as growing numbers of Filipino women performed salaried labor beyond the household. Contrasted with Kenkoy, who similarly adopted Western clothes and lifestyles,[48] they appeared to deal more adroitly with the relentless arrival of modern forces and changes. From being homemakers who routinely managed the cloister of secluded domestic space, women became workers and consumers who frequently navigated the dynamic public spaces of the city. For many businesses centered on mass consumption, this multitude of female shoppers with new purchasing power was a burgeoning target market. Features and columns in periodicals instructed their female readers about how to behave in social settings and engage in leisure practices by purging awkwardness and sentimentality from their bodies.

According to Denise Cruz, the stereotype of a traditional Filipino woman is founded on the character of Maria Clara in José Rizal's *Noli Me Tangere*.[49] Defined by *hiya*, she is depicted throughout the novel as being shy, genteel, mawkish, and docile, bereft of the composure and assurance of modern reason.[50] Accustomed to the cloister of feminine propriety, Maria Clara can only apprehend the contingencies of the world outside in affective terms. In most of her attempts to interact with the world, she is rendered inert by the onslaught of uncontrollable emotions. Echoing the ambivalent gendered agency of Victorian literary culture in the personification of Maria Clara,[51] traditional Filipino femininity was defined by its withdrawal to the private domain of domestic space, where reality would be more calm, forgiving, and certain for the self-fashioning of identity.

This normative understanding of vernacular femininity was echoed in Wilfrido Ma. Guerrero's 1940 English-language drama *The Forsaken House*, which portrayed the character of the mother as unconditionally subservient to the inflexible patriarchy. The playscript's notes describe the traits of the mother as those typical of a Filipino woman who was born and raised under Spanish colonial rule, when female education centered on the leisure activities of embroidery and dancing.[52] Her behavior, like that of her children, needed to conform to the prevailing norms of the time for her family to maintain a respectable standing in the established hierarchy. As depicted in Guerrero's works from this period, the spaces that could be occupied and the actions that could be performed were strictly circumscribed. Even in the apparent serenity of domestic space, the female voice remained mute.

Influenced by the conservatism of Spanish Catholicism, families invested less in their daughters' education, as they believed that women should be raised to become homemakers.[53] Women who desired to work needed to seek the permission of their husbands based on the common belief that their absence from the household would result in its degeneration. The laws of 1930s Philippines continued to reproduce these social norms. Because women had no rights to private property inscribed into law, their husbands possessed the legal freedom to sell familial assets without their consent.

Until they won the right to suffrage in 1936, their participation in the public sphere of politics remained limited.

Regular salaried labor created new social identities and roles for Filipino women outside the circumscribed domestic space of the household. Under Spanish rule, they were known to engage in limited trade, selling their wares along the roadside while squatting on the ground. They provided services as housemaids, seamstresses, milkmaids, teachers, and midwives.[54] When the colonial government established the tobacco monopoly in the late eighteenth century, large numbers of Filipino women were enlisted to work in cigar and cigarette factories in Manila because they were perceived to be more patient and careful than Filipino men.[55] Many new employment opportunities opened to women much later in the 1920s and 1930s, particularly in the modern service sector, where they worked as salesclerks, typists, stenographers, and bus conductors. The regular wages they derived from these jobs equipped them with the purchasing power to become prodigious shoppers, the foremost contributors to the burgeoning consumer economy.

Published in a 1935 issue of the *Graphic*, the article "The New Filipino Woman" elaborated on the terms of modern femininity.[56] Describing the current historical moment as an upheaval, it observed that newly employed women throughout the Philippine Islands were gradually overcoming their ingrained "social conservatism." Their greater purchasing power enabled them to navigate the complexities of domestic and public spaces with facility.

"Confessions of a Beautiful Shopgirl," a 1932 *Philippines Free Press* essay, was written by a young salesclerk at one of Calle Escolta's stores. The writer explained that the allure of the products she would encounter while strolling along the commercial street drove her to find a suitable job, which would grant her purchasing power instead of having to rely on the financial support of her husband. According to her account, her dealings with male customers who flirted and haggled with her taught her to conquer her "original shyness" or *hiya*—to become more "sophisticated" as a modern individual. This overcoming of the ingrained social conservatism of Maria Clara meant learning to employ personal relations, which had formerly dominated and debilitated her, to her own advantage as a commercial agent. To keep herself from being overwhelmed and bewildered according to the stereotype of women, she needed to skillfully manage the onslaught of flows in the marketplace. Instead of allowing herself to be reduced to an inert object of sexual desire, she appropriated their representation of her for her autonomous purposes, such that she would be able to possess her own objects of desire.[57]

Roberta Lee's Modern Etiquette column in the *Philippines Free Press* aimed to equip Filipino women with the know-how of modern sophistication. Offering advice about seemingly mundane matters such as answering phone calls and behaving at dinner parties, the author instructed readers about how modern Filipino women should act amid the onslaught of changes in technologies and lifestyles without being rendered inert. According to an article from the *Graphic*'s Home and Fashion section, training Filipino women to become individuals with modern sophistication was vital because of their integral role in the national economy.[58] In helping commercial establishments to flourish from the business they supplied, they had to be skillful and efficient consumers, adept in the art of shopping, which meant knowing what to buy, where to buy, and when to buy.[59]

These varied prescriptions suggested novel ways for bodies to refashion their relationship with their rapidly changing environment without becoming disoriented or paralyzed. Occupying the public spaces of the cityscape with adeptness, Filipino women unsettled and expanded the limits of what they commonly perceived to be capable of accomplishing.

Consuming Glass Displays

In 1930s Manila's print culture, the terms of modern femininity were defined by the public activity of shopping in the main commercial street. Newspaper accounts from the historical period would describe how urban residents visited Calle Escolta with the implicit purpose of gazing at the various items on display behind its many glass windows and counters. Meandering along the sidewalks of the Escolta, modern women were said to spend their leisure time outside the cloister of the household engaged in this new pastime of browsing. To browse, in this case, was to scan products on display without the immediate complementary action of purchasing them.

The pastime of browsing in the main street became possible when shops grew increasingly dependent on window displays to exhibit selections of their stock to attract customers. The first commercial structure in the Philippine Islands to feature a glass storefront in 1909,[60] Heacock's Department Store on the Escolta, used window displays to sell modern consumer products such as watches, typewriters, cameras, and radios in the 1930s. In Singapore, glass window displays were present in only a few establishments, such as the department store Whiteaway, Laidlaw, & Co. on Battery Road. Amid the profusion of urban flows in a thriving port city, store windows needed to be striking enough to command distracted pedestrians to cease their meanderings and view their displays even for a quick duration.

Prior to the invention of glass windows, shops had typically stored their stocks of merchandise deep inside the building, away from the eyes of passersby.[61] When the growth in industrial production and distribution increased the supply of goods in the eighteenth and nineteenth centuries, shops needed to devise innovative methods of attracting potential customers. Exploring trade opportunities in mid-nineteenth-century Manila, Robert MacMicking described his encounter with the multicultural *tiendas* of Binondo: "The great object of the Chinese shopmen appears to be, to show the most varied, and frequently miscellaneous, collection of goods in the smallest possible space."[62] At first, the conventional commercial practice was for shops to cram their windows, doorways, and frontages with a selection of goods being sold. As store windows increased in size and transparency, they allowed consumers a larger vista of the products being kept within their interiors, drawers, and backrooms. Shops would be lit from the outside with gas lamps, which would illuminate interiors whose halls and ceilings were covered with mirrors.[63] Inside, merchandise would be hung visibly yet haphazardly from architectural fixtures like pillars, railings, and walls, with the goal of drawing buyers through the sight of clutter.[64]

Newspapers and magazines in 1930s Manila described how the visual and aesthetic configurations of store window displays strove to capture the attention and curiosity of crowds in the busy public spaces of the city. Instead of simply showcasing products for sale, the "gleaming" windows and lights of Heacock's Department Store were described as having the goal of drawing customers.[65] The 1932 *Philippines Free Press* essay "Confessions of a Beautiful Shop Girl" highlights how female shoppers on the Escolta were allured by the clothes, cosmetics, perfumes, hats, and jewelry exhibited in its glass displays.[66] But their lack of purchasing power to acquire these products "frustrate[d] them."

The most prominent commercial building on Calle Escolta during the 1930s, Crystal Arcade, was designed to be not merely structurally utilitarian

FIGURE 2. Pedestrians strolling on the Escolta gaze at the glass window displays of department stores and retail boutiques. (Photo from University of Wisconsin-Milwaukee Library)

but also aesthetically unique in its modernity as a "New Paradise for Shoppers."[67] Faithful to the name of the building, its interior was a study of "novelty" in glass and lighting. Each story formed a "gleaming" wall of Belgian plate glass. Facing the street outside and the atrium indoors, store window displays were illuminated with lighting encased in x-ray reflectors. Insets of prismatic glass were built into the floor to further augment the radiance of the interior. Two resplendent glass skylights, designed by the German stained-glass company Kraut, were situated at the front and rear of its palatial atrium. Secured to steel frames to prevent them from falling during earthquakes, the skylights comprised small panels ringed by a rectangular, polychromatic band of diamonds and triangles. With a total cost of 180,000 pesos at the time, more plate glass reportedly had been used in the Crystal Arcade than in the rest of the Calle Escolta. Its cavernous interior was described as possessing a "fairy" quality because of the crystal linings on its walls and insets on its pillars, which were illuminated by indirect lighting.[68] Praised for its allure in drawing consumers, the magical, "fairy" quality of the Crystal Arcade's glass infrastructure and technology was said to drive away the "depression blues" by generating a sense of heavenly blissful paradise among them.[69]

Writing about commercial architecture in cosmopolitan Shanghai before the Pacific War, Weihong Bao describes how products exhibited in store window displays acquired a supernatural, "gleaming," "fairy" quality through the transformative transparency of plate glass.[70] Utilized for commercial architecture, transparent plate glass enabled window displays to isolate, frame, and emphasize the commodity as an object for public visibility and scrutiny. The physical dissociation of the viewer from the object behind the glass window caused the significance of its material properties to be diminished in favor of the magic of its visual attributes.[71]

Whereas the process of capitalist exchange had traditionally been cumbersome and protracted as a result of the clutter in which merchandise would be presented, the framing of window displays instilled order in the commercial arrangement. A modern form of sanitary, air-conditioned order was introduced when the window display wrested the commodity from the onerous circumstances of its labor production such that any evidence of these circumstances became purged from sight. Unimpeded by the clutter of merchandise, the focused gaze of the consumer was permitted to scrutinize and compare different products with greater clarity and discretion.

The "fairy" quality of the Crystal Arcade in attracting visitors suggested the element of fantasy involved in the design and illumination of glass window displays. The work of Arthur Fraser for the Marshal Field's department store in Chicago during the first decade of the twentieth century had epitomized its signature theatrical and picturesque aesthetic. To enhance their transparent desirability, shops would arrange their products in extravagant tableaus of lifelike mannequins and scenic backgrounds adorned with colored lighting, tinted glass, and silk and velour draping.[72] Analyzing the rise to prominence of the oil painting, John Berger highlights the heightened perception of materiality that accompanied the emergence of consumer capitalism. He explains how oil paintings became valuable acquisitions among members of the burgeoning merchant class because they represented for them the objects that lay within the grasp of their newfound wealth. Objects rendered through the medium of oil painting were more textured and tangible, and therefore more graspable, more capable of being acquired.[73] Marketed to the public through theatrical, picturesque store displays, products became endowed with an alluring aura of materiality. Defined by the physical dissociation between consumer and commodity, it was this potent aura of inaccessible materiality and not their distinct material properties that made products more desirable.

In addition to its theatrical, picturesque design, the supernatural, "fairy" quality of glass displays might have likewise derived from the spiritual significance associated with windows in a predominantly Catholic society. Writing about the stained-glass windows of Gothic cathedrals, whose majesty influenced the monumental architecture of department stores, Otto von Simson explains how the legibility of their spiritual significance relied on illumination from light, which appeared to originate from elsewhere.[74] Alluringly illuminated through the technical artistry of spotlights and backlights, store window displays could have been apprehended as revealing the possibility of divine transcendence offered by commercial products that were marketed early on using Christian Evangelical values of self-renewal.[75] Instead of merely deriving from the promise of heavenly bliss, as was the case in previous historical periods, the form of self-renewal and transcendence presented through the window displays of department stores and retail boutiques conveyed the transformative aura of miraculous material progress.

Between Prestige and Stardom

This form of self-renewal and transcendence based on material progress rested on the dissociation of social value from the bodies of individuals and its circulation in their spatial environment. In 1930s Manila, the print culture highlighted how many people frequented the shops on Calle Escolta with the primary purpose of browsing the products on display behind its glass windows and counters. However, like the female shoppers in "Confessions of a Beautiful Shop Girl," because they considered the goods sold on Calle Escolta to be expensive and unaffordable given their modest budget, they refrained from making any purchases. Buyers could opt to acquire items that resembled those sold on Calle Escolta at lower prices from the neighboring areas. Versions of most of these products were available at the *tiendas* of Calle Rosario, perpendicular to the western end of the Escolta.[76] Pedestrians searching for cheap *hecho derecho* or ready-to-wear clothes could find them on Pasillo de la Paz, adjacent to the Crystal Arcade.[77] From Calle Escolta, they could easily walk a few blocks northward to Calle Gandara for reasonably priced shoes.[78] If they desired even cheaper goods, they could travel farther north to Divisoria Market.[79]

Skillfully navigating between domestic and commercial spaces instead of being shy and docile, figures of women in the public culture demonstrated an ability to grapple with complex modern forces.[80] The instructions for modernity in newspapers aimed to shape women into efficient salesclerks and costumers by purging from their bodies the economically unproductive elements of inertness and unpredictability. Departing from the rigid identities to which traditional society expected them to conform, Filipino women learned to adopt an ambivalent stance that enabled them to straddle different roles.[81] While only the government was presumed to have the capacity for exploiting the possibilities of modernity, they intimated a nascent facility for doing so without reinforcing established binaries and hierarchies. Through their adroit encounter with modern forces, they revealed how urban residents could harness possibilities beyond the limits of necessity that had previously been attainable only through material wealth and social standing.

Writing about modern commercial and leisure practices in Shanghai before the Pacific War, Weihong Bao highlights the close link between glass windows and movie screens in terms of the allure they generated and the identity they facilitated.[82] Amid the rise of cinema as the dominant form of cultural entertainment in the cosmopolitan city during the 1930s, the mimicry of glamorous movie stars through their appearance became an important source of self-renewal and value.

Personifying the "perfect type" of the "*nagbabagong*" or "modern" Filipino woman, Monina Vargas, the protagonist of Deogracias A. Rosario's 1930 Tagalog-language short story "Greta Garbo," is, like Kenkoy, a headstrong consumer of the dominant images, idioms, and lifestyles circulating at the time.[83] Literary scholar Helen Lopez highlights how Deogracias Rosario is the principal Filipino writer from before the Pacific War whose work captures how modern femininity subverted traditional stereotypes through the consumption of cosmopolitan attitudes and fashions.[84] Featuring the climax of an extramarital affair, which supposedly typified the lifestyle of a modern woman during this period,[85] Rosario's "Greta Garbo" transpires inside a train headed for Baguio, a chilly highland resort city north of Manila, where the protagonist plans to elope with her lover, a celebrity aviator. As she awaits his arrival inside the train, the casual flow of her euphoric thoughts is interspersed with her increasingly anxious countdown to the train's imminent departure. The Tagalog narration is frequently injected with words and catchphrases borrowed from Castilian and American idioms that emphasize the easy admixture of global cultural norms in cosmopolitan Manila. The narrative's brisk, adjective-less sentences, evoking fleeting, fragmentary images like in a movie, seem to approximate the speed and spontaneity of modern urban life. Unlike Guerrero's plays, events are set not in a house, the conventional, interior domestic space of rest and reproduction, but in a train, the paradigmatic, modern public space of movement and progress.

The people whom Monina Vargas encounters can recognize her resemblance to Greta Garbo because Greta Garbo's Hollywood movies are popular in Manila. The short story captures the emergence of a form of identity and agency based on media spectatorship that involves the emulation of movie stars.[86] Espousing Garbo as her modern feminine ideal, Monina personifies the way that Garbo's onscreen characters transcend the necessity of given conditions by acting boldly and forcefully to realize their aspirations. In the first paragraph of the story, she uses her mirror image in her vanity case to refashion her appearance with the sanitary modernity of the beauty product of makeup into the white-skinned likeness of Greta Garbo. "*Aakyat sa Baguio si Greta Garbo!*," her unspoken assertion to herself that opens the story,[87] affirms her identity as the movie star. The short story describes how she would sign her letters and photos using the borrowed name of her idol. Like a guiltless consumer in the marketplace of love, Monina diverges from the stereotype of Maria Clara by exercising her newfound freedom as a modern woman to choose from a range of suitors without having the patriarchal will of her parents imposed on her.

While waiting for her lover, she glances intermittently at the pages of the *Tribune*, the most widely circulated English-language newspaper of the time, which reveals to her that her lover is already married. Although their romance started only a few months back, they have decided to elope, perhaps because the social proprieties and pressures of the era prevent them from being together. Their romantic relationship can only rely for its certainty on the imagined identities they are supposed to have assumed as Greta Garbo and her onscreen lover. The tenuousness of their relationship is captured in this extract of a near accident that reveals the fragile intimacy that results from ambiguous physical contact: "*Hesus!—ang pagitlang sigaw ni Monina, nguni't hindi lamang maalaman kung sanhi sa halik ni Octavio sa kanya o sa karitelang kaunti nang matumbok dahil tila 'zigzag' ang takbo ng automobil.*"[88]

To overcome the debilitating cloister of domestic space and the bewildering dynamism of the urban environment, Monina Vargas must refuse these options by choosing to occupy an ambivalent frontier beyond their domains. Instead of submitting to the normative role of a woman as a docile consumer of mass products, she insists on defining the terms of her own identity. Because her romance with her lover is illicit and secret, she must avoid being recognized in public as Monina Vargas. To save herself from the humiliation that would diminish her social prestige, she must cleanse from her appearance all traces of quotidian elements with the dualistic severity of air-conditioned modernity. She must adopt the name and guise of Greta Garbo, an illusory and tenuous identity that is based less on the daily persona of Monina than on a circulated image of stardom.

Rosario's "Greta Garbo" challenges the understanding about the relationship between consumerism and distinction described in Thorstein Veblen's seminal 1899 book *Theory of the Leisure Class* as being founded on social comparison and emulation. Expanding on Marx's ideas about capitalism in writing about the financial elite during the Gilded Age, Veblen explains how the acquisition and consumption of material possessions cannot be dissociated from the performance and perception of social distinction.[89] To elevate their standing in the established hierarchy, according to Veblen, individuals exhibit images of wealth and luxury. Occupying public spaces, they strive to be seen by others as the owners of commercial goods. Based on this conspicuous display, the social values of commodities and their consumers become determined by the mutual visibility of objects, bodies, and practices that conceal from public sight their undesirable elements. More than simply being derived from materiality, Veblen likewise suggests how the aura of prestige rests on the appearance of freedom from labor, utility, and necessity, such as when individuals demonstrate their capacity for expenditure beyond the daily requirements of physical subsistence and comfort. In the print and visual cultures of 1930s Manila, urban residents who obtained an aura of prestige were those who were recognized as having access to a scope of exclusive activity normally withheld from the majority of the population.

Rosario's "Greta Garbo" explores the transition in the basis of social distinction away from the possession of luxury toward the recognition of stardom. As a modern consumer, its protagonist, Monina Vargas, acquires fashionable beauty products that, bestowing anonymity on her identity, transfigures her appearance into the transcendent likeness of a celebrity, her idol Greta Garbo. Because she is a former Manila Carnival pageant contestant, her public image is shaped by the gossip that circulates about her in newspapers.[90] Perceived to be a carefree, modern woman, she is placed under suspicion for lacking femininity.[91] Pursuing an illicit romance with a secret lover, she is constantly worried about being recognized by other people. Instead of merely resting on her material accumulation, as Veblen argues, "Greta Garbo" hints at the shift to a form of distinction based on the accidental non-reciprocation and misrecognition of an image that circulates beyond physical presence through gossip and media.

Contrary to conventional narrative expectations, the actual climax of the short story is not the failed arrival of Monina's lover but the triumphant accident of Monina's misrecognition. As the dominant strand in the narrative is revealed to be not so much the unpredictable romance between the lovers but the indeterminate identity of the protagonist, the grave tragedy of unrequited love is elevated to the farcical triumph of personal fulfillment. As it is described in the short story, Monina's physical resemblance to Greta Garbo is supposedly lost when she tumbles from the train with the awkwardness of a vaudeville performer. Despite losing the accoutrements of her appearance, she is identified as Greta Garbo by a hovering newsboy, who earns a living from circulating the truths of national periodicals. While the newsboy's utterance may be laced with sarcasm, his affirmation of this identity in language lends it solidity. Instead of facing public humiliation, she experiences a minor embarrassment that compensates for the agonizing dispossession of her expected lover with the accidental acquisition of her desired identity.

This moment of unavoidable, accidental *hiya* actualizes the creation of a modern identity. In the short story, Monina Vargas strives to fashion her appearance into that of a celebrity to acquire more social prestige. But transgressing the norms of traditional Filipino society, she experiences *hiya* in fleeing from the public eye to elope with her secret lover. Her desire to remain anonymous in this instance is broken when her awkwardness in an accident leads to the misrecognition of her as Greta Garbo. In contrast to Kenkoy, Monina Vargas's ability to affirm her own identity is ultimately beyond her control. Ruled by dynamic forces that she cannot fully harness, her identity dwells in the realm of gossip and coincidence.

Rosario's "Greta Garbo" suggests that, in the main commercial street of 1930s Calle Escolta, social distinction seemed to derive its value not from material abundance but from arbitrary association. Because the commercial street was easily accessible to visitors, anyone who occupied its domain had the capacity to acquire an aura of distinction through accidental misrecognition. If they examined the goods available there but then purchased similar items elsewhere, then the significance of the commercial street for them did not derive from the opportunities for consumerism that it facilitated. It became significant for the social value that individuals unintentionally and coincidentally obtained from occupying its domain. Instead, the image of prestige circulated within this domain like an immaterial commodity that individuals could acquire just by being seen as physically present in this public space for a continuous or recurrent duration. Because they were publicly perceived to examine the luxury goods being sold there, they became misrecognized as having the financial resources to obtain ownership over these goods.

Social distinction in 1930s Manila seemed attainable only for those who possessed the financial means to obtain luxury imports. For the female workers equipped with a new purchasing power who would browse the glass displays of the Escolta, it radiated with the transcendent cinematographic possibility of an object nestled behind an impenetrable glass case. Even without their awareness, they already had been accidentally acquiring value through the simple act of inhabiting the space of the main commercial street for an extended duration of time.

Between Spaces of Imperial Languor

"Our Modern Age," an essay published in a Kuala Lumpur youth magazine, appears to resonate with the vibrant print culture of 1930s Manila when it emphatically captures the euphoria over the arrival of modernity in British Malaya: "The atmosphere of the present age seems to be saturated with modernism. Words that we know, terms that we are acquainted with, phrases that we hear of oftentimes, clauses that we can make use of and sentences that we can employ fail to describe this age of marvels. . . . On the earth, in the air, on the sea, under the sea are wonders innumerable. Almost every day brings us new thrills."[1] This account presumes that, because 1930s Singapore was a flourishing trading port where bodies and goods circulated with minimal legal and administrative regulation, its officials and residents unconditionally embraced and effortlessly harnessed the potential of external flows. Contrary to this assumption, however, the print culture of the Straits Settlement seems to reveal that the prevailing attitude toward modernity in the middle of the decade was less emphatic and more ambivalent.

If a U.S. colonial city such as Manila was distinguished by the inexorable, expansive force of air-conditioned, sanitary modernity, progress in Singapore Municipality under the British Empire was more slow-paced and tentative. While shaped by the Straits Settlements' vitality as an entrepôt, the perception of modernity in 1930s Singapore's print and visual media representations was permeated by the decline of the British Empire. This more languid form of modernity was evinced by the preoccupation, in the colony's most prominent newspapers the *Straits Times*, *Malaya Tribune*, and *Singapore Free Press and Mercantile Advertiser* in 1937 and 1938, with the installation of air-conditioning in public buildings such as cabarets, hospitals, and theaters, which was reported to have occurred later than that in Manila during the early 1930s. Letters and commentaries in these newspapers decried how British Malaya "lagged far behind" nearby locations such as the Philippine Islands and Netherlands East Indies in adopting modern innovations to infrastructure and technology.[2]

If the literary culture of 1930s Manila was defined by its negotiation of modernity through representations of local women leaving the household to become consumers, that of 1930s Singapore visualized white men arriving in the colony to serve as officials, which did not necessarily signify the arrival of progress. The ambivalence in the articulation of modernity in the latter milieu is discernible in the short stories set in British Malaya of W. Somerset Maugham, the most popular English writer in the interwar period, who contributed significantly to Singapore's global imaginary at the time.[3] Taken from two collections, *The Casuarina Tree: Six Stories* (1926) and *Ah King* (1933), these fictional narratives about the expatriate life of colonial officials and their spouses typically unfold in two contrasting locations, the mysterious jungle of Malaya and the teeming entrepôt of Singapore. Most of the critical and scholarly writings about Maugham's work dwell on the moral degeneration of white male expatriates from illicit romances and murders. This chapter analyzes the media ecology of 1930s Singapore's literature, newspapers, architecture, and postcards to uncover how the officials of government institutions and managers of mercantile agencies suffered from languor and impotency, which arose from their complex encounter with both the inscrutability of local conditions and the uncontrollability of modern forces. In the face of this governmental incapacity, I argue that technological and artistic innovations in the production and circulation of postcards and photographs provided a means for managing this complexity.

Juxtaposing 1930s Singapore with 1930s Manila, this chapter explores how the uncontrollability of capitalist modernity caused individuals to retreat to domestic spaces of private leisure and consumption, where visual representations mediated this dynamism. It starts by describing the bustling yet congested landscape of an entrepôt, whose multiplicity and dynamism the British colonial administration struggled to domesticate.[4] Looking at the depiction in Maugham's short stories of the domestic spaces of European expatriates, I examine the architectural typology of the bungalow verandah, which functioned as a spatial and temporal sanctuary where they consumed newspapers that dissociated them from the imminence of change from modern flows in the spatial environment of the port city. Analyzing the monumentality that the British regime established in the commercial square of Raffles Place to propagate its official ideals of empire, I explore how souvenir postcards reproduced these ideals through their photographic representation of empty public space devoid of the unmanageable vitality of local crowds.

The Landscape of the Entrepôt

Established as a trading port by the British East India Company in 1819, Singapore was intended to challenge the Netherlands' monopoly on trade in the region. By the late nineteenth century, the Straits Settlement flourished as the main entrepôt of exchange for raw materials and consumer goods among the United Kingdom, China, India, North and East Africa, Arabia, Siam, the Netherlands East Indies, and the Philippine Islands.[5] Envisioned as a laboratory for laissez-faire ideals, its colonial administration implemented liberal economic and immigration policies that insisted on the absence of taxes, quotas, and monopolies. Attributed as the main reason for its success as a port,[6] its statecraft rested on the ideology that the market would prosper only if freed from government control.[7]

Despite its slowing economy in the early twentieth century, the British Empire derived a significant part of its revenue from colonial Malaya's lucrative rubber industry, whose growth was a direct outcome of the United States' booming automobile industry when it was a rising industrial and economic power. At the beginning of the 1930s, Malayan rubber comprised more than 40 percent of the global production of rubber, accounting for approximately one-fourth of all Singapore exports.[8] Because the shipments of rubber from British Malaya and the Netherlands East Indies passed through Singapore's ports, the Straits Settlement supplied two-thirds of the world's rubber by the middle of the decade.[9] The prosperity of the entrepôt drew migrants from nearby areas of the continent with its prospect of a better livelihood.

If migration to Singapore primarily comprised migrants from Southern China, W. Somerset Maugham's Malayan short stories typically involve the arrival or return of expatriate officials from or to the metropole. The most popular British writer before the Pacific War, Maugham himself was a frequent visitor to Singapore who would stay at the luxurious Raffles Hotel on Beach Road, which, prior to reclamation, marked the coastal edge of Singapore's main island. From its languid vista, which lay a short distance from Collyer Quay, where transpacific steamships would dock to unload their passengers, the thriving bustle of the trading port unfolded. Echoing news articles and photographs from this historical period, Maugham's fictional narratives set in Singapore describe how colonial officials would encounter the diversity and profusion of its urban environment with astonishment and incomprehensibility: "Singapore is the meeting-place of many races. The Malays, though natives of the soil, dwell uneasily in towns, and are few; and it is the Chinese, supple, alert, and industrious, who throng the streets; the dark-skinned Tamils walk on their silent, naked feet, as though they were but brief sojourners in a strange land, but the Bengalis, sleek and prosperous, are easy in their surroundings, and self-assured; the sly and obsequious Japanese seem busy with pressing and secret affairs; and the English in their topees and white ducks, speeding past in motorcars or at leisure in their rickshaws, wear a nonchalant and careless air."[10]

This representation of a conventional street scene from Maugham's Malayan short stories highlights how urban residents of various races and languages would occupy the same public spaces while pursuing multiple itineraries according to divergent temporalities. The frenetic cadence of its lines evinces the unease among European expatriates about its Asian residents, whose cultures remained exotic and enigmatic to them. Located on the fringes of an incomprehensible world far from the comfort and stability of home, British colonial officials were seen to enter an ungovernable terrain of uncertainty and danger.[11] In Maugham's stories, which feature the standpoint of officials who struggle to preserve the social norms and expectations of their mother country, the fragile boundary between civilization and amorality is undone by their exposure to the contingency and complexity of the local tropical milieu.

This boundary between civilization and amorality rested on the segregation of the domain of expatriate life from the environment through which the local population fluidly moved. As initially delineated in the 1822 Plan of the Town of Singapore, the districts of Chinatown, Kampong Glam, and Little India were designated for the respective occupation of Chinese, Malay, and Indian residents. Whereas the British regime had established these districts to limit the social interaction and moral contagion between Asians and Europeans, who lived to the west of the town, diverse ethnic and linguistic communities formed around sites of labor and worship at its center. If European expatriates tended to cloister themselves in the Tanglin, Claymore, and Lower Bukit Timah districts, Asian migrants ended up mingling with other ethnicities they normally would not have encountered in their places of origin. A large majority of the migrants to Singapore from Southern China were Hokkiens, most of whom settled on Amoy and Telok Ayer streets around the Thian Hock Keng temple. Teochews, being mainly dockworkers, gathered in nearby Boat Quay, South Bridge Road, and Circular Road. Cantonese dominated Temple, Pagoda, and Mosque streets, where they operated blacksmiths, potteries, haberdasheries, restaurants, and bakeries.[12] Whereas Tamils, Malayalees, Sindhis, Bengalis, Gujeratis, Hindustanis, and Punjabis from South Asia concentrated in the vicinity of Serangoon Road and Kampong Kapor, Malays, Hadramis, Bataks, Minangkabaus, Bugis, Banjarese, Javanese, and Boyanese from British Malaya and the Netherlands East Indies clustered around the Sultan Mosque near the Kallang and Rochore rivers. The small Eurasian community of mixed European and Asian descent resided around the area of Queen Street and Waterloo Street.[13] Aspiring to manage this seemingly incomprehensible diversity, longtime colonial officials in Maugham's stories pride themselves in their familiarity with local languages and cultures while distancing themselves from a more immersive practice of vernacular customs, which they assumed that other expatriates regarded as "undignified."[14]

An outcome of the global flows of goods and bodies that concentrated there because of its thriving laissez-faire economy, the multiplicity of the entrepôt posed a problem for the British regime. Describing with vividness

the complexity of their urban setting, W. Somerset Maugham's short stories encapsulated the typical response of expatriate officials to this situation, which contrasted with their comfortable experience of their mother
country. Confronted by a profusion of unfamiliar realities that resist easy
comprehension, they display an anxiety over the British regime's capacity to
govern its territory. "Everything was new to him. . . . He stood at the corner
of a busy street and wondered at the long line of rickshaws and the little
men between the shafts running with dogged steps. . . . He peered into the
Chinese shops in Victoria Road where so many strange things were sold. . . .
He was confused. He thought it would take him years to find his bearings in
this multi-colored and excessive world."[15]

Narrated from the standpoint of a young, newly arrived museum taxidermist surveying his immediate surroundings for the first time, this extract
from "Neal MacAdam" reveals his detachment from the local tropical milieu. Differing from the familiar world of the metropole, which was characterized by its routineness and stability, public life in the colony consisted of
numerous encounters with "strange" realities. In the extract, the experience
of "new[ness]" in the urban setting of Singapore Municipality is depicted not
as an opportunity for transformation but as a threat to security. The young
white male expatriate is bewildered into incapacity by the local milieu, despite his claims to possess a functional understanding of the Orient from
having perused the novels of Joseph Conrad. As a museum taxidermist, he
proudly fashions an image of himself as being equipped with the superior
knowledge and education to domesticate its multiplicity with the same facility at curating a museum glass display out of fossilized remnants. "Confused"
by the "multicolored," "excessive" diversity and complexity of this alien milieu, colonial officials are portrayed as lacking the ability to deal with the
affairs of the trading port.

Evident in the rationale of the British Empire, the discourse of imperial
conquest extols the capability and resolve of the colonizer to liberate the
uncivilized, ignorant, and helpless native population from their primitive
conditions of existence.[16] Colonial ethnographies, travelogues, and etiolo-
gies portray local residents and their communal spaces as being indolent and
unproductive toward industry.[17] Abdul JanMohamed argues that fictional
narratives about colonial situations have a tendency to be founded on a fixed,
Manichean dichotomy that emphasizes the weakness and inadequacy of na-

tives against the vitality and superiority of colonizers without affording them any potential for self-determination.[18]

Establishing the foundation for imperial rule, these binaries are present in the works of W. Somerset Maugham set in the South Pacific, such as in the anthologies *The Moon and the Sixpence* and *The Trembling of a Leaf*,[19] in their opposition between the languid Orient and dynamic West. In contrast to local Asian residents, European expatriate officials and managers considered themselves to be adept at recognizing and managing the demands of different situations.[20] Exposed to the bewildering contingency of urban flows in Singapore Municipality, however, the British regime was faced with an administrative and epistemological impasse in its effort to govern its territory with order and efficacy. Defined by constant struggle over the public identity of the built environment, the colonial government's attempts to introduce the norms of sanitary modernity to urban spaces and infrastructures met resistance from the local population.[21]

Imperial Monumentality

Looking at the everyday spaces, practices, and objects of expatriate life that helped maintain its veneer of civilization, Maugham's stories set in Singapore dwell on the contrast between the fixity of empire and fragility of its rule. Most commercial activity in the Straits Settlement during the 1930s was concentrated in two districts on opposite banks of the Singapore River: the area of High Street and North Bridge Road north of the river and that of Raffles Place and Battery Road south of the river. The many retail stores on High Street and North Bridge Road were lodged in the nondescript shophouses that lined their thoroughfares. Housing the offices of the most important firms and banks, it was Raffles Place that constituted the spatial heart of the Straits Settlement from which financial and commercial flows radiated, where the norms of empire were reproduced.

Before the Pacific War, Raffles Place was a rectangular plaza encircled by majestic, monumental buildings with a large central area reserved for parked automobiles and rickshaws. According to photos from historical documents and souvenir postcards, a road ran around the plaza, in between the ground floors of buildings and parked rows of vehicles. The combined presence of

FIGURE 3. In this postcard, the monumental architecture of the department store John Little & Co. in Raffles Place espouses imperial ideals of order, elegance, and civilization. (Photo from National Archives of Singapore)

several department stores and luxury shops within the enclosure of Raffles Place added to its exclusive atmosphere. Located on the east side, parallel to Collyer Quay, the department stores John Little & Co. and Robinson & Co. were renowned for supplying local and expatriate residents with imported British products. With branches across the Straits Settlements and the Federated States, John Little & Co. was the sole distributor in British Malaya of A. B. Jones & Sons chinaware, Walker & Hall's cutlery, Hedges & Butler wine, Bird's custard, J. A. Hunter & Co. meats, Smith & Wellstood's stoves, Coleman lamps, and Burroughes & Watts billiard tables, most of which had gained their prestige in the Victorian era as exemplars of British craftsmanship.

According to architectural historian Lai Chee Kien, the public squares of British colonial cities were constructed to project the symbolic domination of the empire.[22] Conveying imperial values of order, elegance, and civilization, the array of buildings in Raffles Place aimed to establish an official ideal of public life. Epitomizing the norms of imperial beauty, many of these monumental edifices were built in the ornate Victorian Eclectic style by the prominent architectural firm Swan & McLaren during the post-war economic boom of the 1920s. With their proud cupolas, arches, and striations, the elegant uniformity and monumentality of such structures rendered imperial norms legible and consumable in a dynamic entrepôt. Writing about spatial culture in the British Raj, Thomas Metcalf explains that colonial architecture needed to be designed in a manner that evoked the British Empire's confident authority and effective governance.[23] Unlike municipal buildings in Selangor, which incorporated Oriental motifs, those in Singapore were unabashedly neoclassical in aesthetic. This preference for classical styles highlighted the enduring quality of empire because the symmetry of classicism was supposed to signify eternal order.[24]

Monumentality refers to the quality by which a physical structure establishes a prominent and reverberant presence within a domain through a concatenation of its visual appearance and cultural significance. Monuments must be legible enough to be an arbiter of social value and distinct enough to be a reference for spatial orientation.[25] Their architecture must emerge from the congestion and multiplicity of the surrounding urban environment, which threatens to submerge and marginalize them. Their design must be striking and memorable such that they linger as indelible images in the consciousness of pedestrians.

State monuments are designed to function as highly visible symbols of sovereignty.[26] According to Lewis Mumford, monumental architecture emphasizes "the assurance of stability and security, of unrelenting power and unshakable authority."[27] Because the colonial government could not penetrate and influence every domestic space, where social identity is conventionally produced and maintained, it needed to rely on commonly viewed and utilized buildings to reinforce the norms it wanted ingrained among the local population. The objective visibility of these norms in monumental architecture was intended to ensure their validity and permanence. Even if they might have been designed to exude prominence and attract clientele, commercial buildings that emulated the appearance of state monuments performed a similar function. Monumental structures fortified the immutability of empire amid the imminence of flux. The visual stability that these buildings presented amid the stark diversity of languages, bodies, and cultures enabled individuals gazing at them to situate themselves against their surroundings by supplying them with a more manageable, rational frame of perception. With this frame of perception, the residents of the colony would ideally aspire and strive to attain a higher plane of progress in the hierarchy of civilization.

If public life became unsettled as a result of the congestion and mobility of the municipality, monumentality reestablished public life. Amid the burgeoning practice among the Asian residents of Singapore Municipality to appropriate public spaces for their own autonomous purposes,[28] monumentality fulfilled the desire of the British regime to promulgate its own rigid ideal of public life based on imperial norms of order, elegance, and civilization. Monumentality did not operate with the opaqueness of the palace or the church, which exuded authority from within their enclosure without disclosing their entire appearance. Instead of remaining opaque, authority now relied on its objective visibility, which rendered its presence incontrovertible and unconquerable. By filling the range of vision, monumentality kept the eyes of observers concentrated on the façade such that the impression prevailed that the identity of all its contents had been made exterior and public. The importance of this visibility was highlighted by how the outlines of monumental buildings were lit at night, with the façades of the most prominent structures fully illuminated. By insisting on its monopoly over public life through the visibility and objectivity of its monuments, it divested the local Asian residents of their capacity to participate in the appropriation of urban space.

Languid Modernity

The incapacity of colonial rule was shaped by a fin-de-siècle sensibility that was discernible in the inert wariness of British expatriates toward the diverse flows of the port city. Rooted in the supposed physical and moral degeneration concomitant with the decline of empire, it was articulated in the configuration of their domestic spaces, which withdrew them from the unmanageable contingency of public life. In W. Somerset Maugham's short stories set in Singapore and Malaya, spaces and objects like bungalows, verandahs, and newspapers function as private sources of sanctuary, comfort, and relaxation that afford them escape from the tumult and difference of the local milieu.

Based on the racial segregation of Singapore Municipality, colonial officials and mercantile managers resided in the Tanglin district, which spread out from the western end of Orchard Road. Early into British rule, secluded villas were first constructed west of the main town, where nutmeg, gambier, and pepper plantations were located.[29] The dominant typology of a colonial residence in the tropics, which dated back to the establishment of spice plantations in British Malaya, was that of a black-and-white, one-story bungalow that sat in solitude atop a hillock, enclosed by a large, manicured garden like that of an English country estate.[30] Originally built to house the owners of plantation estates, the tropical bungalow provided the spatial configuration for the homes of colonial expatriates. With black timbered sections and white rendered walls, bungalows were commonly referred to in Singapore as "black-and-whites." Beneath a high hip roof with short ridges, the ground floor of these structures was typically made of brick, on top of which rose a timber frame.[31] Designed in the Palladian style, their architecture aspired to reproduce traditional English values of elegance and status,[32] akin to the monumental buildings in Raffles Place. As the principal private space for foreigners in an alien milieu far from the comfort and security of their mother country, the tropical bungalow epitomized the isolation and languor of colonial expatriate life.[33]

Colonial discourses and narratives typically framed unfamiliar local realities as an enigmatic and uncontrollable threat.[34] Shaped by the predominant Victorian anxiety about spatial boundaries,[35] British officials and managers in the Straits Settlements believed that exposure to its Asian residents, who for them were naturally disorderly, resulted in physical and social disease.[36] According to this colonial etiology, the contagious degeneracy of expatriates' physical and moral character would then lead to the collapse of the entire civilization.[37]

In Maugham's Malayan stories, the colony is imagined to be a dangerous terrain where the limits of European civilization and morality are repeatedly transgressed through adultery and violence. In "The Door of Opportunity," which narrates the inability of colonial officials to respond to a local uprising, Chinese are portrayed as irrational rioters whose violent actions cannot be quelled. Despite the desire of white protagonists to learn more about indigenous culture, they unquestioningly presume the local population to be guilty of witchcraft in "P&O" and murder in "Footprints in the Jungle," betraying their fear and anxiety about contagion. In the print culture of the time, intimate interactions with native inhabitants, which violated strict racial boundaries, were believed to foment vice among the expatriate community. One of the tropes of social breakdown far from the metropole was that of an extramarital affair that, marked by violent outbursts and fights between British gentlemen, ended with an incensed lover killing the perpetrator. In the aftermath of a tenuous romance with his superior's carefree spouse, the eponymous museum taxidermist in "Neal MacAdam," for example, finds his imperious categories of Enlightenment knowledge and Victorian morality, which maintained the semblance of order in his public life, helpless, undone by illicit savagery.

Given this enigmatic and uncontrollable threat, the tropical bungalow's architecture of enclosure was designed to reduce contact between its homogeneous expatriate community and the disorderly local population. Its servants' quarters and kitchen, where members of the local Asian population lived and worked, were detached from the main house. Zoning laws segregated the serene, sprawling enclaves of bungalows from the squalid, congested districts of shophouses such that their residents would be kept from inhabiting the same public spaces.[38] Meant to provide seclusion and sanctuary for its residents from the local environment,[39] the architecture of the bungalow was designed to resemble that of a home in Victorian England.[40] Planted along the perimeter of the property, dense vegetation functioned as the organic intimation of a fence, which ensured isolation and security.[41] The long driveway, which wound around the slope of the hillock before bringing guests to the car porch at the front of the house, heightened the sense of privacy and status. The bungalow's spatial configuration was meant to protect its residents from the degeneracy that ensued from contamination.[42] Perceived to originate from outside the circumscribed domain of civilization, vice, violence, and delinquency resulted from the breakdown in strict racial and moral categories.

Likening it to a fin-de-siècle sensibility, W. Somerset Maugham's short stories depict the languor and impotency of expatriate officials who are faced with the unmanageable problems of colonial rule in an alien milieu. Historical scholarship reveals that many of the colonial officials and mercantile managers based in Singapore and Malaya were young bachelors who were enticed by the prospect of adventure in an exotic foreign land. The belief was prevalent among them that imperial conquest provided a marker of vigorous masculinity. In Late Victorian England, a posting in the colony was an opportunity to revitalize the strength and courage that had supposedly gone lacking during the late nineteenth century decline in Britain's economy.[43] In the figures of District Officer Alban in "The Door of Opportunity," Assistant Resident Cooper in "The Outstation," and the eponymous museum taxidermist in "Neil MacAdam," these youthful bachelors are portrayed as arriving in the colony abounding in vigor and "exuberant joviality,"[44] with the confidence that they would have little difficulty administering the territory according to the British Empire's ideals of civilization. With overbearing assurance about his knowledge and civilization, the protagonist of "Neil McAdam" is described as radiating with the heartfelt optimism typical of youth: "He had brown curly hair with a peculiar shine in it; sometimes when the light caught it, it glittered like gold. His eyes, large and very blue, shone with good humor. . . . It was his ingenuousness, his candor, and the freshness with which he confronted the world."[45] According to Maugham's imaginary of expatriate life, it was this fragile naiveté about the complexity of the local milieu, however, that caused young bachelors like him to lose their hold on civilization as they slipped into despondency, alcoholism, or suicide.

Against the backdrop of the bustling, diverse entrepôt of Singapore, colonial officials are contrastingly rendered in Maugham's stories as being afflicted by an acute degeneration of their physical and mental capacities.[46] Concerned with the encounter of expatriates with the local environment, these narratives highlight the stark disparity in outlook among government officials and plantation managers between idealistic arrivals and exhausted old-timers. For example, in "The Door of Opportunity," the visage of the Governor, who must confront a local rebellion, embodies the psychological burden of colonial rule over three decades: "His hair was grey, his face, his eyes; he looked as though the tropical suns had washed the color out of him . . . he looked tired and depressed. Even his voice was grey."[47] Brought about by the recalcitrance of the Asian population, the "strain [of being] an empire builder" disclosed itself through the tentative and listless demeanor of European expatriates.[48] Captured in Maugham's work, their experience of the colony was pervaded by this fin-de-siècle sensibility, which was characterized by an inert wariness toward its unfamiliar, diverse realities.

As a private sanctuary, bungalows insulated British expatriates from the ominous urban flows of the thriving entrepôt economy by recreating the pleasant lifestyle of the mother country.[49] Tropical bungalows were patterned after suburban English homes, which were originally built to provide refuge against the pollution, overpopulation, and crime of rapidly industrializing cities. Located in the exclusive Tanglin district, these homes were furnished in elite fashion with imported British necessities and ornaments acquired from the department stores in Raffles Place. The members of the expatriate community in Malaya considered such consumer items to be vital because of the significance that British material culture during the Late Victorian and Edwardian periods gave to the decoration of domestic space.[50] Through the identities and lifestyles they made possible, these products enabled expatriates to cope with the solitary experience of exile. Amid the teeming multiplicity of the entrepôt, which threatened to unsettle established social norms, they filled the domestic spaces of expatriates with objects that produced solace and stability through a taste of home. By reproducing norms of spatial configuration and social behavior from the mother country, the use of such objects permitted colonial expatriates to retain aspects of their

FIGURE 4. Tropical bungalows and verandahs furnished colonial expatriates with a private sanctuary to withdraw from the contingency and multiplicity of the port city. (Photo from National Archives of Singapore)

everyday life before their relocation. Creating a domain of languid comfort, it allowed them to withdraw from the onslaught of diverse, contingent forces that threatened to transform their existence.

Ideally, a British home provided relaxation and regeneration for its residents through the palliative effects of nature.[51] Through an architecture of enclosure from the local milieu, the tropical bungalow helped generate an experience of languid comfort for those unaccustomed to the Malayan climate. Geographers explain how the hill stations of Baguio and Buitenzborg enabled colonial officials in the Philippine Islands and Netherlands East Indies to recuperate their energy and vitality in the face of their supposedly debilitating conditions.[52] Urban historian Michael Pante describes how hilly suburbs were a favored residence for expatriates in Manila under U.S. occupation because of their cool, fresh air far from the congestion and bustle of the city center.[53]

The Temporality of the Verandah

The typology of the tropical bungalow in Singapore and Malaya was designed to manage the difference of the local tropical milieu. Architectural conventions such as high ceilings were meant to alleviate the debilitating effects of hot and humid air.[54] However, the most important innovation of the bungalow was the verandah, which was a roofed, open-air area that, encircling the structure, created a sanctuary where residents could unwind.[55] In Maugham's "The Door of Opportunity," the verandah is depicted as a vital private space that requires careful curation, decoration, and maintenance to generate a semblance of order and comfort with an image of home from the mother country distinct from the local milieu. Adjacent to the interior of the house while exposed to its outside, the verandah offered a secure feeling of intimacy with its natural surroundings,[56] which cultivated attitudes and practices of leisure and repose that contrasted with the unrelenting restlessness of the trading port. After an enervating workday, the predominantly male residents were said to recline in the comfort of a rattan chair in their verandah to write letters or read newspapers while sipping tea or whisky.[57] It was in the verandah that expatriates learned about changes to the affairs of the world without having to immerse themselves in these complex realities.

Lulled by the soothing pleasures of the verandah, they relied on the mediation of newspapers, like six-week-old issues of the *Illustrated London News*, for
a form of relation to the tumultuous world beyond their enclave.

Newspapers are significant objects in Maugham's stories "The Outstation" and "The Door of Opportunity," where they act as sources of solace, civilization, and stability. The aged character of Resident Wallaburton
in "The Outstation" exemplifies how longtime officials developed a daily
habit of reading through old newspapers, such as the *Times* and the *Observer*, shipped from Britain. Affording them temporary reprieve from the
ungovernable diversity and dynamism of the local milieu, this habit created
"the illusion of living at home . . . [as] a tie to civilization."[58] Although these
newspapers "kept them abreast of what was going on in the world," however, they simultaneously "emphasized their exile."[59]

Contrary to literary scholar Eddie Tay's compelling argument,[60] the reading of old newspapers from London did not necessarily represent the failure
of expatriate identity to find solidity. This routine practice of everyday life
could instead be understood to be another type of failure: that of colonial
rule. Such a failure might have arisen from the refusal of officials to engage
with the dynamic flows of their territory, either because they stubbornly
awaited orders from the metropole or haughtily misrecognized the culture
of the population. In "The Outstation," the Resident cherishes his daily habit
of numbering and arranging old newspapers from the metropole to maintain
a semblance of order and civilization amid the onslaught of modern forces.
Instead of acting as a public source of information for expatriates like him,
newspapers offered them a private means of stability. Reliant on the tenuous capacity of words to create a picture of events from the immediate past
of a distant location, such expatriates apprehended the world beyond their
enclave as transpiring in a realm outside their grasp.

Mediating the relationship between colony and metropole through news
reportage, advertising, and travel writing, the visual and spatial composition
of newspapers such as the *Illustrated London News* presented the affairs of the
world as radiating from the imperial center of London. This layout supposedly positioned readers with an imperial gaze that subdued the cacophony of
diverse voices.[61] In the *Illustrated London News* during the 1930s, for instance,
the week's summary of international events of "topical interest" was reported
through regular photo collages with titles like "The Camera as Recorder,"
"From the World's Scrap-Book," and "Personalities of the Week: People in

the Public Eye," featuring scenes from the different parts of the British Empire. Such photo collages tended to dwell on topics of human interest like scientific innovations, criminal trials, tragic disasters, and sports matches. Without furnishing much detail about their complex circumstances, this genre of pictorial reportage would have the effect described by Stuart Hall of constraining the scope of knowledge.[62] Through the delimited frame of the news capsule, an apparently newsworthy event is refashioned into an enthralling spectacle devoid of conflict that can easily be consumed by the listless reader.[63] Expatriate readers were made to relate to the outside world with benign detachment as though its prevailing conditions had been purged of their direct consequence. Instead of developing a blasé attitude, which Simmel famously argues would protect their physical and mental capacities,[64] this example suggests how they might have sought refuge from the contingency and multiplicity of their surrounding environment through the media technology of print capitalism.

Unlike 1930s Manila, consumerism in 1930s Singapore did not necessarily equate with the adoption of an emphatically modern lifestyle and identity. With scarce reportage on the affairs of the colony, the daily editions of Singapore's most widely circulated English-language newspapers before the Pacific War highlighted the detachment of their readers from local reality. Print advertisements in the *Straits Times* and *Malaya Tribune* recurrently emphasized how the consumer goods they promoted would bring their users not so much modernity as comfort. The provision of comfort swathed individuals in an experience of timeless withdrawal from the concerns and anxieties of the world.

For expatriates, bungalow verandahs were liminal sites of temporality that lay between the time of work and the time of repose. In their soothing embrace, the urgency of time was suspended, creating the ideal environment for leisurely consumption. Enclosure was fundamental to colonial rule not only because it excluded locality but because it also marginalized change. In the urban milieu of the entrepôt, expatriates were bewildered and debilitated by the onslaught of modern forces, which divested them of their passion and energy.[65] Based on their characterization in W. Somerset Maugham's short stories, they were inclined to surrender to the "force of circumstance," to quote the title of one such work. A line from the same narrative reads, "At their feet, with a mighty, formidable sluggishness, silent, mysterious, and fatal, flowed the river. It had the terrible deliberation and relentlessness of destiny."[66] Wearied by their incapacity, these expatriates resigned themselves to the inevitability of time and progress.

In the public culture of 1930s Singapore, a languid form of modernity appeared to prevail. In contrast to sanitary, air-conditioned modernity, which forcefully segregated interior from exterior to cleanse bodies and spaces for the arrival of progress, this languid verandah modernity remained isolated from the movement of time. Despite its seeming opposition to the dynamism characteristic of modernity, this tendency could be seen as one version of modernity because it arose as a response to modern flows. If modernity is understood to be an encounter with external forces, then its languid form assumed a detached standpoint from which it torpidly gazed at the tumultuous world that extended beyond its circumscribed enclosure without embracing its looming influence. Whereas the logic of air-conditioned modernity imparted the tenor of an accelerating present, that of languid modernity proffered the glimpse of a hesitant future.

Rosalind Morris argues that the officials of an empire in decline tend to be beguiled by fantasies of beginning anew,[67] but in the case of Singapore's British expatriates, there was a denial of the possibilities for commencement, a listless surrender to the inert space of verandah modernity between reverie and implementation, between fantasy and action. The inability to deal with the immediate demands of a complex situation undoes the fragile veneer of civilization in "The Door of Opportunity" of the new District Officer, who considers himself to be "superior" because of his elite class and education but struggles to quell the local uprising. The persistent, tacit awareness prevailed that, because the forces of modernity could not be controlled and exploited, embracing them would only hasten the demise of the comfortable conduct of life that expatriates had long enjoyed. Instead of being a site of spatial refuge for imperial reproduction, a reprieve from the chaos of local realities, the tropical bungalow became a site of temporal refuge for imperial survival, an enclosure of time, a sanctuary from the inevitability of modern upheavals.

Photographic Spaces of Civilization

If the print and visual cultures of verandah newspapers encapsulated the secluded private life of British expatriate W. Somerset Maugham's short stories, the colonial regime's ideal of public life was inscribed in souvenir postcards, which expatriates would mail to their friends overseas, of 1930s Singapore Municipality's monumental architecture. While Maugham's fictional narratives set in British Malaya describe the trading port of Singapore as being typified by the ungovernable congestion and multiplicity of bodies, documentary photographs project the image of an orderly domain that was at best a fantasy. Gathered as part of the official record of their territory, the photographs produced by officials and the postcards circulated by expatriates disclosed the aspiration to overcome the incapacity of the British Empire to manage the complex affairs of the Straits Settlement.

With technological and infrastructural innovations to photography, printing, and transportation in the early twentieth century, the popularity of postcards grew as tourists and expatriates mailed them to overseas addresses as souvenirs of their travels.[68] Postcards of Singapore Municipality from before the Pacific War would feature sites such as Raffles Place, Collyer Quay, South Bridge Road, and Battery Road, which were important because of their commercial or cultural significance to the spatial environment. Many of these postcards focus on the monumental architecture of public buildings or the exotic details of places of worship. Inscribed with the phrase "Greetings from Singapore," these postcards depict the sites of residence, labor, and exchange frequented by its local Asian residents as being wracked with congestion and disarray. Concretizing the colonial perception of local public spaces, the pictures of vernacular religious rituals found in such postcards fill the frame with the innumerable bodies of participants. Spread haphazardly across the frame of the postcard, these bodies give the impression that they are not susceptible to order.

Susan Stewart explains how postcards reduce a diverse and contingent reality to a miniature object that is more manageable and consumable.[69] Refashioning physical space within their delimited frame, postcards could be compared with the news capsules found in the *Illustrated London News*, which rendered historical conditions more comprehensible by truncating their particularities. Managing the complexity of reality through the fixity of an image, they foregrounded the attributes of a geographical location that the sender wished to convey to others as part of his experience of the world. Defined by the clarity and detail in recreating distant landscapes,[70] these portable visual representations of colonial territory would serve as symbolic proof of conquest of the alien milieu.[71]

Colonial postcards disclosed the effort to contain the dynamism of the urban environment through the rational objectivity of documentary photography. Imposing on their viewers a standpoint of detachment from the local milieu, they featured photographs that had been taken with a transcendent standpoint from above that attempted to include the entirety of a given reality within the boundaries of the frame. Postcards of local sites could be juxtaposed with those of colonial sites, which illustrated the efficacy and authority of the state. In the crammed photographs of the residential areas of the Asian population, vernacular domestic space became equated with the decrepit exteriors of shophouses, whose throngs of occupants loitered along the unpaved road that ran between them. The exteriors of shophouses were typically captured on camera from a slanted angle to highlight their haphazard profusion.

The print culture of English-language newspapers and memoirs reveals how Singapore was known overseas as the "Cesspool of the East" or "Singalore." Chinatown, where a large majority of its migrants from Southern China concentrated and resided, was commonly understood to be its heart of vice and disease, a sordid, depraved zone of crime, gambling, prostitution, violence, and opium addiction. The district was packed with shophouses that had a width of sixteen to eighteen feet and a depth of three to four times this width.[72] On the first and second floors of these shophouses, windowless rooms were divided into small cubicles no larger than two double beds, where a family as large as seven lived. Because their cavernous interiors opened to the outside only through the front door on the ground floor, the louvered windows on the upper floors, and the air well in the middle section, shophouses provided little sunlight or fresh air for their inhabitants.[73]

Because Singapore's entrepôt economy was founded on physical labor, government and business became unsettled by fear and anxiety that the vice and disease supposedly prevalent throughout its urban environment would jeopardize trade by contaminating, enfeebling, and destroying the bodies that inhabited them.[74] In the 1930s, it became imperative for the municipal commission to refashion the Straits Settlement into a healthy, disciplined, virtuous, and sanitary domain where labor was productive and trade was prosperous.[75] To realize its plans for the colony, it strove to render visible and public the private domestic spaces, hidden from surveillance, where vice and disease were commonly thought to be fomented.

The British colonial government in Singapore needed to monitor the Asian population's activities, which it suspected to be sordid, criminal, and diseased when conducted behind closed doors.[76] The technological innovation of the photographic camera enabled reality to be recorded as documentary evidence for government action. Suspecting the private domain to be a site of reproduction, the municipal authority operated according to the notion that if the local inhabitants were left to the secrecy of their enclosed spaces, then their inherent maladies would rapidly and extensively propagate through contagion. By characterizing private spaces with clutter and obscurity, the camera insinuated they required cleansing so that the unruly bodies inhabiting them could be subjected to the supervision of a governing authority.[77]

Despite colonial rule being characterized by determination in the face of anxiety, its impotency was disclosed in one of the photographs that supplemented W. J. Simpson's seminal 1907 *Report on the Sanitary Condition of Singapore*. Here, the camera attempted to document the bleak, congested interior of a shophouse in Chinatown. In the foreground of the photograph, a gangling man wearing loose white garments is seated on a stool to the left of the frame. His face has been penciled in. Behind him, spectral figures, engulfed by the darkness of the background, peek from barely visible doorways that line a dim, narrow corridor. Due to the inability of the photographic technology of the time to operate in poorly illuminated spaces, the corporeal form of their actual bodies fails to be captured on film. Resisting the effort to invade their private domain, they withhold their corporeality from being turned into official evidence of the presumed sordidness of local realities. The outlines of their bodies have been roughly drawn with pencil to signify their presence for the purposes of governance, but the use of pencil sketches to fully capture them in a photograph puts the veracity of this presence under doubt. Unsettling the categories of documentary and administrative truth, these spectral figures inhabit an interim space between existence and erasure. Nestled in the ambiguity of their visual presence, they refuse to be given a public character according to the terms of the state.

Contrasted with this image of congestion and disarray, the souvenir postcards of foreign tourists and expatriate officials characterize the sites of municipal authority and commercial capitalism as vast and empty spaces devoid of the presence and movement of crowds. In photographs of prominent sites such as Collyer Quay and Queen's Place, the landscape of the entrepôt is presented as an orderly and sanitary vista with only a handful of bodies scattered across the expanse of the frame. Vicente Rafael analyzes how documentary photographs commissioned by the U.S. colonial government organized native Filipino subjects according to a hierarchy of civilization and progress that aimed to realize its project of sanitary modernity to bring order to their unmanageable difference.[78] The visual representations of colonial public space in souvenir postcards of Singapore epitomized the state's perception of the Asian population as dispersed and languid amid the majesty of empire. This fantasy of control divested local residents of the experience of public life by effacing it from their delimited frame. Colonial postcards exhibited an inclination toward the exteriority of the local milieu, whose objective visibility would subject it to control. Akin to monumental architecture, the postcards signified the aspiration to establish eternal order in the urban environment of the Straits Settlement by creating an immutable image that would endure amid the unrelenting restlessness of transformative modern forces.

Faced with the persistent recalcitrance of the local Asian inhabitants amid the growing impotency of empire, British expatriate officials withdrew to their leisurely domestic sanctuaries, where they could deal with the unmanageable affairs of the world through the delimited frames of verandahs, newspapers, and souvenir postcards. In establishing imperial norms of order and civilization, colonial authorities relied on monumental architecture and documentary photography to refashion the private and public spaces of the municipality. Beneath the majestic façade of empire thrived the contingency and multiplicity of urban forces in an entrepôt, which disclosed its failure as an unattainable ideal.

CHAPTER 3

Spectacles beyond the Limits of Exhaustion

The immense popularity of carnivals and amusement parks on the urban periphery distinguished the public cultures of mass leisure, entertainment, and spectatorship in the thriving colonial port cities of Manila and Singapore during the historical period of the 1930s. Established by the U.S. government as an orderly version of the rowdy local fiesta that promoted its ideals of sanitary modernity and industrial progress, the Manila Carnival on Wallace Field was an annual event with commercial exhibitions, beauty pageants, and military parades staged for two weeks before the start of the Lenten season in the predominantly Catholic territory. Operated by diasporic Chinese entrepreneurs, the New World and Great World amusement parks on Jalan Besar Road and River Valley Road featured movie theaters, restaurants, cabarets, social dances, boxing matches, and carnival rides that, opening daily in the evenings, provided sources of recreation, pleasure, and revitalization to the multicultural workers of Singapore's entrepôt.

Writings about the annual Manila Carnival, which commenced in 1908 shortly after the inauguration of the democratically elected Philippine

Assembly, tend to focus on spectacles of either its military parades as a site of colonial modernity or its beauty pageants as a source of national identity,[1] which exemplified the ascendancy of the United States as an imperial and industrial power. Most scholarship about Singapore's amusement parks before the Pacific War dwells on how they furnished venues for recreation and cosmopolitanism where the diverse communities of the Straits Settlement would converge and interact.[2] As boisterous commercial and leisure spaces in port cities, however, I would argue, 1930s Manila and Singapore's carnivals and amusement parks were less sanctuaries for comfort and relaxation than central to the workings of the entrepôt economy in producing the hierarchy and mobility essential for the global and intraregional transport, distribution, and exchange of industrial goods.

In a vibrant trading port, these innovative consumer spaces could be situated as part of a larger media ecology in relation to similar consumer spaces that prevailed in the urban environment at the time. Print announcements and advertisements about the Manila Carnival and New World and Great World amusement parks in the most widely circulated publications in the Philippine Islands and British Malaya during the 1930s such as the *Tribune*, *Manila Daily Bulletin*, *Philippines Free Press*, *Straits Times*, *Malaya Tribune*, and *Singapore Free Press and Mercantile Advertiser* would be juxtaposed with columns, news, and letters about their many amateur sporting clubs. As important sites of public leisure and mass entertainment in colonial port cities, the economy of amusement parks should be understood in relation to the culture of sporting clubs, which likewise flourished during this period, given their analogous management of the labor, diversity, and mobility of residents. In contrast to colonial social clubs, which, like tropical bungalows, furnished European expatriates with the norms of identity and stability of the metropole in the company of their fellow white men, local sporting clubs allowed Asian professionals to experiment with modes of physicality and cooperation for a nascent political community.

The chapter's first sections focus on the attractions and spectacles in the Manila Carnival and New World and Great World amusement parks by looking at their contrasting modern spectorial experiences of pleasure and progress. While carnivals and amusement parks relied on technological innovations in transportation, electricity, and lighting that enabled their attractions and rides to operate into the evenings, they incorporated the industrial logics of systematization, mobility, and marketing into the exhibition and arrangement of their spectacles. After dissecting Fredric Thompson's 1908 concept of carnival spirit, this chapter analyzes the sensorial immersion of carnival rides and boxing matches, whose spectorial experiences exposed urban residents to thrilling, innocuous forms of violence and death. Most film theories dwell on the dissociation between spectator and spectacle, particularly the way it induces docility and atomization through the cognitive absorption of the cinematographic gaze. Tracing the entangled genealogies of visual perception and media spectatorship amid the rise of capitalist systems of production and distribution, media historians highlight their shift toward a more embodied physiological configuration.[3] The abundance and variety of spectacles in 1930s Manila and Singapore's carnivals and amusement parks were designed to generate both cognitive absorption and sensorial immersion among their crowds that would revitalize and extend their labor and productivity for the work regime of the entrepôt economy. I conclude the chapter by discussing how, instead of instilling practices of docile spectatorship akin to the mass sports spectacles staged by the colonial government, local sporting clubs cultivated physical and collective activities that prepared the Asian population for future conditions of sovereignty and self-determination in the face of their limited access to democratic participation.

Manila Carnival and Industrial Progress

One of the largest public events under U.S. colonial occupation in the early twentieth century, which aimed to promote its ideals of civilization and progress, the sixteen-day Manila Carnival would be typically staged on Wallace Field east of Luneta Park with its entrance facing the monument to the U.S.-backed national hero José Rizal. Enclosed by *sawali* or interwoven bamboo slats, the Manila Carnival featured an array of attractions and spectacles that provided diversion and reprieve from the work regime of industrial production and distribution. Founded on ideals of order, hygiene, and morality, the sanitary modernity of the Manila Carnival had been initiated by the U.S. regime to supplant the perceived filth, unruliness, and backwardness of local fiestas, which it feared as a threat to social order and a source of mass insurrection.[4] Over four decades of U.S. rule, its function changed

as the Philippines Islands moved toward the political and economic autonomy of Commonwealth status. With an annual attendance in the hundreds
of thousands, the Manila Carnival's spatial configuration was designed to
manage the supposedly dangerous energies and passions of Filipino crowds
by channeling them into the norms of consumption for commercial goods
produced in the United States and ideals of progress for colonial subjects
aspiring for national sovereignty.

As the United States' premier colony in the Asian region, the Philippine
Islands served as an exclusive site for the extraction and manufacturing of
agricultural crops such as copra, sugar, and hemp for export to U.S. markets. Through the various public institutions it established, the U.S. colonial
government sought to educate the Filipino population about the commer-
cialization of industrial products.[5] Formalizing the collaboration between
colonial and local elites, the Manila Carnival was intrinsically linked with
the promotion of industry and business. From 1921 until the Pacific War,
the Manila Carnival's director was Arsenio Luz, president of the Philippine
Chamber of Commerce, who, as a journalist, had worked in different capacities for Spanish- and English-language publications such as *El Renacimiento*,
La Vanguardia, *El Ideal*, and *Philippine Herald*. The founder of the Boy Scouts
of the Philippines, Luz was the first director of the Manila Hotel and first
president of the Rotary Club. As an active member of media companies, state
institutions, and social clubs that contributed to the formation of Manila's
vibrant public sphere in its nascent democracy, his resume of competencies
and achievements illustrated how the modernity of Filipino bureaucrats and
entrepreneurs proved their readiness for self-determination.

In its print culture of exhibition booklets and newspaper advertisements,
the Manila Carnival presented itself as a blissful reward for submitting to
the toil of the industrial work regime that enabled urban residents to "forget
life's bitter aspect." Its carnival grounds featured an abundance and variety of
attractions and spectacles such as skating rinks, beer gardens, funhouses, fortune tellers, snake charmers, two-headed calves, Ferris wheels, and bumper
cars that immersed visitors in a spectatorial experience of euphoric reprieve.
At the entrance, visitors could purchase masks, horns, and confetti for use
inside.[6] The sides of the enclosure were lined with concessions that led up to
an auditorium at the far end of the carnival grounds, facing a palm garden.
On each night of the carnival, the auditorium hosted a different ball, culmi-

nating in a Coronation Night that crowned the Carnival Queen; the balls generated enormous popular interest from Manila's residents.[7] Brochures for the 1930s editions of the Manila Carnival conveyed the expectation that these public events would allow the community to transcend the despondency and languor from the global economic recession: "It is the purpose to make of this festival a truly never-to-be-forgotten period of revelry mirths and laughters; of funs, frolics, dancing and all sorts of amusements; of riotous colors and exquisite and fantastic shows and sights; . . . in short, of all those things that are devoted to the sunny side of life."[8]

Staged at Wallace Field next to the Rizal Monument, facing Manila Bay, the Manila Carnival permitted leisure practices that were legally prohibited within the territorial borders of the city. Implementing its ideal of sanitary modernity to purge the spatial environment of immorality, crime, and violence, the Manila city government had banned cabarets, cockpits, and brothels from its jurisdiction. Businesses reestablished these unlawful commercial and leisure spaces right outside Manila's city limits, not far from the terminuses of its *tranvía* streetcar system.[9] In the print culture, the rural districts that constituted Manila's outskirts beyond the reach of *tranvía* lines were commonly called the "ends of the earth,"[10] defining the boundaries of civilization and modernity during this period. Immediately north of Santa Cruz, where Calle Escolta was located, the district of La Loma was described in newspaper accounts as a breeding ground for contagion from delinquency and depravity, where muggings and gunfights were daily routine.[11] Illustrating how the logic of sanitary modernity dualistically expelled undesirable realities to the outside of a circumscribed domain, the collective imaginary of 1930s Manila pictured the urban outskirts as a sordid, inscrutable, and menacing zone where the violence and danger of sinful, illicit, and corrupting practices had been exiled and were believed to thrive. Incorporating the exuberance of cabarets within its enclosure,[12] the Manila Carnival offered a temporary reprieve not only from the onerous labor of capitalist production but also from the intractable morality of sanitary modernity.

As a site "where fun and frolic go hand and hand with commerce, industry, and art,"[13] the Manila Carnival was the hybrid of an amusement park and a world exposition that signaled the incorporation of social life under industrial capitalism.[14] Because it generated enormous popular interest, the Manila Carnival was often utilized as a public stage by the colonial government to launch important initiatives. Its annual commercial handbook supplied comprehensive details about agricultural and industrial production in the Philippine Islands with entries about various manufacturers, importers, and wholesalers of textiles, hats, baskets, and soap, with the first pages dedicated to key industries of sugar, hemp, tobacco, and coconut. The Manila Carnival's entanglement of trade and spectatorship was typified by its five main parades, which would pass through the city-state's important public spaces Plaza Goiti and Rizal Avenue: the opening-day parade, the business and industrial parade, the military parade with U.S. soldiers and scouts, the civic-educational parade with public school teachers and students, and the floral parade featuring the Carnival Queen.[15] Although beauty pageants are said to have been a main attraction of the carnival, which propagated ideals of femininity and whiteness as a measure of sanitary modernity,[16] its many commercial exhibits could be seen to celebrate material progress more prominently according to the norms of industrial productivity and mass consumption. At the Manila Carnival, revelry would usually be subordinated to industry, which dominated the first four to five days, with the staging of pageants, wearing of masks, and throwing of confetti prohibited until the last three to four days.[17]

On the cover of the 1932 Manila Carnival Handbook, a weary yet smiling farmer waves at the giant masked spirit of revelry in the heavens, formed from the smoke of industrial factories. As one its goals, the Manila Carnival claimed to reimagine how "spiritual and physical relaxation" can contribute to the trajectory of "moral and material progress."[18] Secularizing beliefs of religious transcendence based on norms of industrial productivity, the language and iconography of carnival brochures depicted prosperity as a supernatural deity whose intervention would transform the supposed disorder and savagery of the local milieu. Echoing the logic of exhibition in world expositions, the Manila Carnival organized and displayed the diversity of industrial goods from across the archipelago according to a hierarchy of civilization.[19] The trajectory of progress was further exemplified by the recurrent promise of organizers that next year's event would be grander and more meaningful than the previous one. With each staging, the carnival grew more explicitly commercial and pedagogical in orientation, with trade fairs, industrial exhibits, and military parades of greater scale.[20] Amid the granting of political autonomy to the Commonwealth of the Philippines

FIGURE 5. On the cover of the Manila Carnival Handbook, the carnival spirit smiles down on the primeval local landscape as a transcendent figuration of industrial progress. (Photo from National Library of Australia)

in the mid-1930s, the carnival shifted from its preoccupation with romantic narratives of chivalrous royalty toward an interest in economic issues about industrial production. With attractions such as the Sugar Place, Tobacco Emporium, Rice Center, Hemp Tavern, Copra Castle, Hall of Mines, and Temple of Commerce and Industry, the Manila Carnival hosted booths and pavilions featuring the various regions and products vital to the incipient national economy. While distributors were taught how to market their merchandise to different areas of the archipelago, investors were acquainted with the sites of important agricultural and mineral resources. In the Manila Carnival's assemblage of parades and exhibits, the diversity and complexity of the archipelago's tropical milieu became subordinated to the transcendental, regimented logic of air-conditioned modernity, which was defined less by imperial civilization and permanence than by commercial and technological innovation.

Sensorial Profusion in the New World

While the spectorial experience in the Manila Carnival subordinated mass entertainment to air-conditioned modernity and industrial progress, that of Singapore's New World and Great World amusement parks promoted physical mobility and sensorial immersion to enhance entrepôt labor. Singapore's amusement parks were called in the Malay language *taman hiburan*, which literally meant "park of entertainment." Exemplified by Coney Island in New York and Great World in Shanghai, amusement parks were fenced enclosures with an assemblage of spectacles including carnival rides, boxing matches, *bangsawan* performances, and movie theaters, and were designed to attract and captivate a wide range of the population. Residing in cramped shophouses with insufficient sunlight, ventilation, and sanitation, its Asian residents spent most of their time outside work and home in the Straits Settlement's many public spaces seeking euphoric reprieve. Whereas the Straits Settlement's exclusive commercial streets, department stores, luxury hotels, and social clubs catered to an affluent minority, its popular amusement parks, New World, Great World, and Happy World, targeted its diverse majority.

Located on the outskirts of the municipality, far from its daily congestion and bustle, the parks advertised their capacity to supply entertainment attractions and leisure activities that were "out of the ordinary." Contrary to the assumption that they were exceptional, they should be understood instead as otherwise in that they furnished routine public spaces for a wide majority of the population. While Manila's carnival was a two-week annual event, Singapore's amusement parks were open from dusk until midnight all year, unlike their prototype, New York City's Coney Island, which operated only during the North American summer months of June to September.[21] Frequented throughout the year, Singapore's amusement parks functioned less as an alternate world of momentary fantasy than as a vital component of everyday life.

Unlike amusement parks in the United States, notably Coney Island, which was situated at the distant terminus of several trolley lines,[22] those in the Singapore Municipality were central to the social life of the residents because they regularly hosted both private and public events such as family gatherings, wedding celebrations, and trade fairs. Relying on thousands of electric lights to illuminate their grounds at night, these amusement parks allowed public activity to continue long after the workday had ended, thereby reconfiguring the routine of everyday life. Despite their location on the periphery of town, Singapore's amusement parks could be said to possess centrality not only because they formed part of the routine of the port city but also because they recreated some of its bustle. The experience of exhilaration found in these parks derived from the immersion in crowds and mobility of bodies that they facilitated, conditions that were associated with urban modernity but devoid of its supposed disorder.

The New World Amusement Park was described in historical accounts as being the busiest and most boisterous of Singapore's amusement parks. Spanning four hectares, its grounds were sprawled between Jalan Besar and Serangoon Road on the edge of Little India. Inaugurated on August 1, 1923, it was built by its Straits Chinese proprietors Ong Boon Tat and Ong Peng Hock close to the Serangoon Road Race Course to draw on the crowds who constantly gathered there.[23] Tracing some of their origins to the nearby port of Malacca, the Straits Chinese were a typically educated and affluent Anglophone ethnic community with mixed Chinese and Malay heritage who drove business in cities such as Penang and Singapore.

In 1930s Singapore, the New World's admission fee was 10 cents, a price affordable enough for the typical Chinese laborer, who earned $10–20 per month.[24] The cost was steeper for the Tamil workers who were hired to construct and repair the roads of the municipality because they received only 50–60 cents in daily wages.[25] Extolled in its advertisements as "the pioneer park of all Malaya," the New World promoted itself as the "First in Conception and the First to study the needs of, and cater for, First-Class Amusements for all classes" with a business strategy of inclusivity for mass consumption, which would appeal to the Straits Settlement's diverse communities.

Originating as a Temporary Exhibition and Recreation Ground, the New World was opened partly as a result of the success of the 1922 Malaya Borneo Exhibition in Telok Ayer.[26] It was closely patterned after the indoor amusement centers of Shanghai, the paragon for mass leisure and entertainment in Singapore during this historical period. Shanghai's vibrant amusement centers, such as the Great World Entertainment Center on the junction of Yan'an and Xizang roads, featured six stories of theaters, cinemas, funhouses, restaurants, roof gardens, puppet shows, wrestling matches, acrobatic performances, shooting galleries, gambling stalls, and fortune tellers.[27] By incorporating a wide range of attractions, these innovative public spaces reshaped pleasure into an exhilarating experience of abundance and variety.

Appearing to be haphazard in its spatial configuration, architectural blueprints of the New World Amusement Park that were submitted to the colonial authority for official approval reveal a systematic order produced to generate enjoyment.[28] Visitors to the New World during this period could enter the main park grounds on Jalan Besar through one of two adjacent portals, which stood between two sets of ticket booths that encircled a bandstand. The left portal directed visitors to the Sunlight Hall, which, with a maximum capacity of 1,400 seats, was home to the acclaimed City Opera with its *bangsawan* and *kroncong* performances.[29] The right portal led to the Moonlight Hall, which would stage vaudeville shows and boxing matches. Continuing from the Moonlight Hall on the right, along the iron fence that enclosed the park, visitors passed an indoor cabaret and an open-air cinema. A tea garden and a beer garden were situated on the opposite side of the cinema from the cabaret. On the left part of the enclosure, another open-air cinema followed the Sunlight Hall. Past the hall and the cinema, visitors were treated to carnival rides, such as the thrilling Ghost Train and the more relaxing Merry-Go-Round, that supplied different degrees of excitement. To the right of the Merry-Go-Round, the Twilight Hall faced the back of a towering pagoda. Behind the Twilight Hall toward the right sat the popular New World Restaurant. At the far end of the park, the Solar and Luna halls bordered Serangoon Road. In addition to staging concerts and operas, the park's array of halls featured Filipino vaudeville acts, Javanese *wayang wong* performances, and international boxing matches. Distributed across different parts of the enclosure, commercial stalls sold an assortment of goods including toys, clothes, and knickknacks. Food kiosks offered popular hawker specialties such as congee or rice porridge, *satay* or skewered meat with peanut sauce, and *kway teow* or stir-fried noodles with dark soy sauce.[30] By organizing the abundance and variety of its spectacles, the amusement park heightened its visitors' immersive experience of entertainment and pleasure. The exuberance of different attractions situated in close proximity never impinged on each other's spectacular experience but combined to enhance the carnival spirit of the entire park.[31]

Anticipating the configuration of shopping malls, Singapore's amusement parks represented an innovative typology of consumer space at the time in which traditional forms of leisure and entertainment like theater performances and social dances were arranged within the same enclosure as modern forms of leisure and entertainment like motion pictures and carnival rides. Presented alongside each other, these disparate realities were afforded equal value without being submitted to a hierarchy of technological progress or cultural sophistication. Amusement parks resembled international expositions in how they strived to encompass the entirety of the world within their enclosure through their multiplicity of spectacles. While evoking the impression of organic randomness, their spatial configuration organized their contents so that they could be encountered as a series of consumable experiences that gradually intensified the exhilaration of visitors seeking reprieve. Drawing on the multiplicity and mobility of the modern urban environment, however, they ended up shaping the physical and perceptual movement of bodies into the necessary mode of labor for the workings of the colonial entrepôt economy.

Carnival Spirit

The spatial configuration of the carnival and amusement parks in Manila and Singapore during the 1930s appears to exemplify the blueprint of Fredric Thompson, the impresario behind the popular Luna Park on Coney Island. In his 1908 essay "Amusing the Million," Thompson attributes the success of his amusement park to the production of a "carnival spirit" within its circumscribed domain. According to Thompson, the amusement park should be "designed to give the natural, bubbling animal spirits of the human being full play, to give people something fresh and new and unusual, to afford them respite from the dull routine of their daily lives."[32] Contrasting the routine of everyday life with the exceptionality of the amusement park, he writes that people could be seen as overgrown children who seek opportunities for play outside their oppressive work regime. Harnessing the common desire for play, Thompson explains that the "gaiety" of the amusement park is not spontaneously produced but must be carefully orchestrated through a multiplicity and arrangement of spectacles. In this sense, Thompson's conception of "full play" could be understood as the suspension of the "routine" norms of functionality and productivity that prevail outside the amusement park in exchange for a comprehensive sensorial immersion in a momentary world of entertainment and pleasure.

For Thompson, interest and excitement about the carnival and park must first be magnified by circulating compelling images and narratives of their spectacles among the public, which was evident in the Manila Carnival and New World and Great World amusement parks' many announcements and advertisements in the Philippines, Singapore, and Malaya's newspapers. Every element within the enclosure should be designed with the goal of enhancing its carnival spirit. The visual attributes of the architecture should evoke a sense of allure and dynamism. The continuous introduction of "new" and "unusual" attractions throughout the carnival and park grounds should keep visitors in a perpetual state of mobility and euphoria. In Thompson's blueprint, the immense pleasure of the carnival spirit is generated only when its spatial and temporal experience has become suffused with the immersive logic of spectacle.

Thompson's blueprint for the typology of the amusement park resonated with Bakhtin's seminal theory of the carnival in that both their conceptions imagined momentary enclosures of diversion and revitalization beyond the established hierarchy where people could mingle without regard for the prescribed norms of identity or collectivity.[33] Echoing Bakhtin, the rationale for the Manila Carnival in its brochures describes how, in marking the changing of the seasons, the carnival is meant to celebrate the dialectic of change, dynamism, and renewal that encompasses negation and affirmation, as well as destruction and creation. While, for Bakhtin, the carnival is recuperative of the lost life for the marginalized classes in an insurmountable established order, for Thompson, the carnival could be understood to restore the lost vitality of individuals wearied by the dominant work regime.

In the carnivals and amusement parks of Manila and Singapore during the early twentieth century, delinquent practices and lifestyles that had been adjudged to be illegal and exiled from the city became permissible in the amusement park. Whereas Manila's city government had banned sinful vices such as gambling, prostitution, and cockfighting from its borders, Singapore's municipal administration had prohibited hawking and idling from its streets and verandahs.[34] In this way, delinquent, fugitive modes of modernity that were perceived to be dangerous and corrupting were allowed to re-emerge in an innocuous form of play in an enclosure designed for momentary pleasure and reprieve. If these illicit practices could be understood to occur beyond the bounds of prosperity and legality, their innocuous forms in the carnival and amusement park not only allowed a "respite" from "dull routine" but extended the limits of permissible activity.

The Experience of the Spectacle

The antecedents of Singapore's amusement parks in the metropole, the English pleasure gardens, were created to function as a sanctuary from the sordidness of the rapidly industrializing Victorian city.[35] The amusement parks of Singapore Municipality during the 1930s did not necessarily grant people complete physical reprieve from the hectic conditions of the modern urban environment because they depended on large crowds and mobile flows for their success. Serving less as sanctuaries from than extensions of the established order, they offered not so much a reversal of dominant norms than a restoration of enervated bodies. As a public space with as much centrality as educational, industrial, and religious institutions, the amusement park correspondingly propagated official norms of collectivity, behavior, and spectatorship among its visitors.

Collectivity and spectatorship in 1930s Singapore became shaped in the New World and Great World amusement parks through assemblages of spectacles that juxtaposed carnival rides, *bangsawan* performances, boxing matches, and movie screenings. Highlighting the link in the logics of carnival and spectacle, Fredric Thompson explains how spectacles must be designed and orchestrated to heighten the spatial and temporal experience of the carnival spirit. In an amusement park, visitors are presented with an abundance and variety of attractions that suffuse the atmosphere with their exuberance and gaiety. To maintain their interest while enticing them to return, the park must constantly incorporate thrilling novelties— "something fresh and new and unusual." To draw the widest majority, Thompson adds, shows should be "diversified" so that their "appeal" becomes "universal."

Writing about the performances of the Netherlands East Indies theater company Komedie Stamboel, Matthew Isaac Cohen notes that public events during the late nineteenth century were called *tontonan* or "spectacle," a derivation of the Batavian Malay word *nonton*, meaning "to observe."[36] For people at this early moment of modernity in Southeast Asia, a spectacle was something that demanded to be witnessed and observed with a sense of astonishment. Capturing an individual's attention for a duration of time, this astonishment entailed a degree of physical detachment between the spectacle and its observer. Gaining potency through its visual apprehension, it transformed the individual momentarily gazing at it into a spectator completely absorbed in its reality. Incapable of averting this attention under this state of cognitive absorption, the spectator was led to abandon any ongoing activity or movement, being withdrawn from the normative flow of everyday life.

In the entangled logics of spectacle and carnival in the amusement park, however, the experience of gaiety was defined not just by cognitive absorption but by a restless dynamic of mobility and immersion that governed the physical and perceptual movement of bodies throughout its enclosure. Highlighting its distinction from theatricality, which rests on a singular, alluring image, Thompson explains that spectatorship in the park is defined by "full play." To intensify play among its visitors, carnival shows should be "short" while rides should have "speed." In other words, "everything must be on the 'go.'" Visitors should not be permitted to stay idle in one location but be induced to move constantly throughout the park. Through this induced motion, the dynamism and multiplicity of 1930s Singapore's urban environment as a port city would be incorporated and systematized in the spatial configuration of the amusement park. The sensorial profusion from an abundance and variety of spectacles corresponds to the "full play" that Thompson envisions—the capacity of the amusement park to present a seemingly infinite array of spectacles that would cause the reverberation of the carnival spirit to dominate its enclosure.

Contrary to the dominant understanding of modern consumer spaces, the amusement park did not cause isolation and withdrawal in individuals but fostered participation and immersion in crowds such that normative social relations became reconfigured. Without formal squares or plazas built into their spatial configuration, amusement parks did not permit visitors to linger in place.[37] Pursuing random itineraries, bodies loitered and meandered according to the prescribed spatial configuration of the park grounds. They drifted along to the flow and rhythm of other anonymous bodies, which were pulled in different directions by the various attractions organized within the enclosure. If each spectacle operated by seizing the attention and energy of individuals, the arrangement of spectacles in a carnival propelled them to shift their attention and location from one spectacle to another without surcease. Even if individuals became absorbed by a particular fantasy, its grip on them was fleeting because the park's configuration stimulated movement and dynamism. Although the performance of a spectacle gathered bodies in the same public space, different spectacles attracted different sets of bodies, forming multiple crowds. Due to the momentary duration of each spectacle, permanent crowds never formed. Moving from attraction to attraction in circuitous itineraries, crowds swelled, dispersed, and dwindled. Caught in this shared, sensuous experience, these meandering crowds constituted a tenuous community whose potential stayed unrealized.

Immersion on the Threshold of Death

In addition to inducing physical motion to generate a carnival spirit, the spatial configuration of 1930s Singapore's amusement parks encouraged sensorial immersion. The shared experience of sensorial immersion was evident in the spectatorship of the amusement parks' boxing matches, one of the most successful forms of mass entertainment at the time, which was said to be even more popular than the *bangsawan*.[38] Featured boxing events would normally be staged at the open-air New World Arena, which was located at the left end of the New World Amusement Park near Serangoon Road. Spectators could pay fifty cents, one dollar, two dollars, or three dollars to sit at one of the 2,500-seat arena's tiered sections.[39] Local newspapers reported on the latest news about professional fighters who originated from within the region and around the world: Y. C. Song from Singapore, Young Johnson from Ipoh, Neil Hemchit from Malacca, Rough Joe Diamond from Batu Pahat, Arthur Suares from India, Mohamed Thajudeen from Ceylon, Nai Boon Mah and Nai Som Pong from Siam, Mohamed Fahmy and Fattah Hassan from Egypt, Ventura Marquez from Mexico, Aimé Raphael and Eugene Huat from France, Young Gardner from the United Kingdom, and

Al Rivers from the United States. Promoters in British Malaya appeared to favor talented, charismatic fighters from the Philippine Islands, such as popular champions Young Frisco, Joe Bautista, Battling Sima, Max Santos, Con Cordero, Johnny Mortell, and Ignacio Fernandez, who formed an early part of a lineage of Filipino global entertainers, together with Borromeo Lou and Canuplin.

Singapore's most famous boxer before the Pacific War was Ignacio Fernandez, a Filipino migrant whose matches would headline the New World Arena in the New World Amusement Park. As Singaporean and Malayan champion from 1936 to 1938, Fernandez was renowned for his "iron jaw" and "wicked right."[40] Characterized by "piston-like jabs" and "dynamite left hooks" that were powerful enough to knock out opponents without having to rely on his signature right, Fernandez's fighting style was described as being "beautiful to watch" because of its "mechanical grace."[41] Originating from Silay in Negros Occidental in the Central Philippines, he gained fame as Asia's bantamweight, featherweight, and lightweight champion during the 1920s. While fighting in the United States' boxing circuit, his most legendary bout was an early-round knockout against future champion Al Singer in Madison Square Garden in 1929,[42] which was elevated to myth in newspapers with conflicting accounts about the speed of the knockout. A victim of financial mismanagement by his handlers, he was forced to return to Asia on the cheapest passenger steamship ticket. Although no longer as powerful, Fernandez grew in reputation as a boxing idol in Singapore; many of his main events were covered in the local newspapers, and he entered the city's popular memory. Articles published in the 1970s and 1980s reported how fans from around the world would visit or correspond with him in his retirement home in Singapore.[43] During an election campaign in the 1960s that helped establish his position of authority over Singapore's national sovereignty, founding prime minister Lee Kuan Yew referred to him in a public speech as an example about the importance of continually striving by needing to avoid being knocked out when too complacent.[44]

In a less cited extract from his seminal book *Discipline and Punish*, Foucault uncovers the relationship between cognitive absorption and sensorial immersion as he hints at the link between spectacle and carnival. Writing about the public punishment of criminals who violated the laws of the sovereign, Foucault describes the spectacle as a ritualistic, ceremonial event that resonates with the carnival spirit's elements of sensuousness and revitalization: "With spectacle, there was a predominance of public life, the intensity of festivals, sensual proximity. In these rituals in which blood flowed, society found new vigor and formed for a moment a single great body."[45] Foucault's conception of spectacle expands its parameters beyond the cognitive absorption in an object that is solitary and docile to the sensorial immersion in an experience that is collective and dynamic. Overcoming the physical detachment between object and observer, the irresistibility of a spectacle's allure derives from the vigor of this performance, which, in turn, invigorates its spectators. The close proximity of bodies in the crowd causes their energy and enthusiasm to spread through contagion.

Despite the popular fervor that boxing matches generated, spectators would remain detached from these spectacles because they did not bear the bodily consequences of the violence on display. Superseding this physical detachment, the contagious excitement of the crowds combined with the gripping intensity of the fighters caused cognitive absorption of the spectator to transform into emotional immersion. According to Joyce Carol Oates, who wrote a book about the sport, the spontaneous, naked display of vulnerability, pain, and mortality allowed spectators to form an immediate, intimate bond with this spectacle.[46] Oates writes, "Boxers are there to establish an absolute experience, a public accounting of the outermost limits of their beings; they will know, as few of us can know of ourselves, what physical and psychic power they possess—of how much, or how little, they are capable."[47] Through the unrestrained spectacle of the boxing match, the fighters publicly demonstrated how the capacities of the human body could be pushed to their limit. The visibility of this violence suggested how the exceeding of physical necessity often occurred on the threshold of death.

The immediacy of sensorial immersion in the amusement park's spectacles was likewise exemplified by thrilling carnival rides such as Merry-Go-Rounds, Ferris Wheels, Ghost Trains, and Dodgem bumper cars. Their speed and mobility reproduced the dynamism and energy of the urban environment but without its disorder and transformation. Such carnival rides were adaptations of modern forms of transportation like the automobile, airplane, and motorboat, but for the purposes of recreation.[48] To be able to immerse spectators in a consumable moment of exhilaration, they divested the technological innovation of vigorous motion from its prescribed function of transporting bodies from one location to another. Dissolving the physical detachment between spectator and spectacle, the potency of carnival rides rested on the direct participation of individuals in their pursuit of vigorous motion.

The logic of the carnival ride challenged the conventional theory of spectacle because it displaced the centrality of cognitive absorption. In the workings of the carnival ride, less emphasis was given to visual apprehension than to immersive experience as the object of the spectator's gaze was displaced onto the rapid change in scenery. Strapped to the carriage by a safety belt, the spectator was physically transported by its technology, which dictated the prescribed movement along a trajectory while determining the scenery within sight.

As opposed to the spectacles of theater or cinema, the spectorial experience of carnival rides rested on the mobility of the spectator. This could be seen in relation to the importance of the mobility of the spectator in minimalist art, on whose reception the work is based in its durational experience. Writing about the theatricality of Judd's minimalist art, which entails a shift in the model of spectatorship from docile absorption to fluid interactivity, Michael Fried explains how it replaces the object of representation, which grounds the meaning of realist painting, with the encounter with "objectlessness" or "endlessness." Without a fixed object for the gaze to concentrate on, meaning becomes derived from the circumstances of the encounter, which shape the evolving responses of the viewer throughout its duration.[49] In the case of the carnival ride, the constant need to readjust the gaze to the quickly changing scenery is what immerses the spectator in the experience. The spectator is captivated by the seeming endlessness or infinitude of the instantaneous experience, which transpires far beyond the normal limits of human activity. For the spectator, the experience of time feels distended as a comprehensive image of apprehended space saturates this singular moment.

Visitors to the amusement park found the carnival ride to be thrilling because it enabled them to participate in an innocuous form of danger.[50] It was through the controlled danger and violence of immersive spectacles such as boxing matches and carnival rides that 1930s Singapore's amusement parks reproduced the delinquent, fugitive modernity that had been banished from their domain of sanitation and civilization for the sake of recreation and reinvigoration. In contrast to boxing matches, which presented a spectacle of violence from its fighters, it was the mortality of the spectators that was exposed to the threat of violence. This immediate threat to their bodies made spectators aware of the parameters of their capacities. However, because of technological innovations in the construction of the carnival ride, the danger that confronted them could not possibly result in pain or injury. Their encounter with the limits of human activity occurred on the threshold of death, which renewed their experience of life.

Entrepôt Labor

The Great World Amusement Park's official newsletter promoted the efficacy of the carnival attractions and spectacles presented within its enclosure in delivering euphoric reprieve: "As one strolls through the park, troubles are forgotten, the mind is refreshed and stimulated, and one's interest and motivation in work are rekindled."[51] According to Frederick Olmstead, the architect behind Coney Island, its spatial configuration of leisure and entertainment was designed to alleviate the anxiety and discontent of urban life.[52] One of the amusement park's main attractions was nighttime performances of the *bangsawan*, which experienced its heyday of popularity in the Straits Settlements during the 1920s and 1930s.[53] Said to be favored by the local inhabitants over silent movies, which they contrastingly called *wayang mati* or "dead theatre,"[54] *bangsawan* was advertised in newspapers for its recuperative function in easing "torpid minds" and "worries" with "comfort."[55]

In 1930s Singapore, the amusement park provided a revitalizing source of diversion for visitors without leaving them in an idle condition of languor. Instead of sheltering them from the flux of the modern urban environment, I would argue that its carnival spirit complemented the workings of the entrepôt economy by preparing consumers for their return to the work regime. The amusement park's process of delivering individuals to an instinctual, childlike state could be understood as an integral aspect of the euphoric reprieve it offered. In this process of self-renewal, the park's array of immersive spectacles momentarily suspended the norms of productivity of the work regime so that bodies could continue to exert energy without losing their intensity. The danger of rest was the possibility of decreasing momentum, which, I would suggest, needed to be maintained at a robust level of "endlessness" in a bustling port with ceaseless flows.

Connected with global shipping and airplane routes through which sugar, hemp, copra, timber, tin, and rubber were distributed, both Manila and Singapore thrived as ports during the 1930s. A vital node in the global supply chain of U.S. industrial capitalism, Manila was a major port in the transpacific routes of steamship companies Canadian Pacific, Pacific Mail, and Nippon Yusen Kaisha, which transported passengers, mail, and cargo to and from San Francisco, Vancouver, Honolulu, Yokohama, Kobe, Nagasaki, Shanghai, Singapore, Calcutta, and Hong Kong with a travel time of a week-and-a-half.[56] Located in Manila Bay, Pier 7 was fitted with the most technologically innovative infrastructures for transporting bodies and goods through transpacific steamships, which were meant to illustrate the progress of the United States' model colony.

Diverging from this picture of industrial and technological progress, the entrepôt economy of Singapore was defined by the labor of dockworkers as conduits of mobility and exchange. Logistical operations at the trading port were managed by the Singapore Harbour Board, which relied on the labor supplied by private contractors such as the Cantonese Labour Syndicate, Tanjong Pagar Labour Company, and Indian Labour Company. Archival photos from the first half of the twentieth century, which visualize Boat Quay as being packed with lighters, document how it actively functioned as a wharf for transporting goods. In the late 1930s, dockworkers would typically be hired daily at a rate of 50–90 cents per shift.[57]

Before the invention of the science of logistics, capitalist distribution depended heavily on the contingency of manual labor. Writing about the history of logistics, Deborah Cowen highlights the importance of the body to logistics, which must discipline it because of the perception of working-class bodies as being unruly and irrational.[58] Expanding the definition of work, logistical labor produced the fuel of the economy and physical and spatial motion, which in Singapore had less value as a harbinger for modernity than as an impetus for trade. The labor of circulation transformed the value of goods in a port by enabling them to be rapidly transported across distant geographic locations without disruption,[59] without which exchange could not occur. A combination of special capabilities like strength, agility, concentration, and stamina was required to be able to transport large and heavy

FIGURE 6. The logistical labor of dockworkers at Boat Quay transported goods for the commercial exchanges of the trading port. (Photo from National Archives of Singapore)

quantities of items as quickly and efficiently as possible and without damaging them and reducing their value.[60]

By momentarily shifting their concentration away from the discipline of the work regime and toward the pleasure of the carnival spirit, "full play" in the amusement park allowed the bodies of visitors to be revitalized according to their own perceived terms. In contrast to the department store, whose enclosure was founded on labor's concealment,[61] the amusement park rendered visible and palpable the exertion and dynamism of labor but within circumscribed bounds. Instead of granting reprieve to individuals from the physical activity and motion that prevailed under the work regime, the park maintained an optimum level of exertion. Regulating the capacities of bodies through the abundance and variety of immersive spectacles arrayed in its economy of carnival, it harnessed the multiplicity and mobility of the modern urban environment while subduing their transformative force.

The euphoric reprieve experienced in the amusement park diverged from the languid comfort found in the tropical bungalow. The dynamic modes of cognitive absorption and sensorial immersion it provided to its visitors restored and extended the potential of their bodies for vitality and mobility. It purged visitors of their torpor by permitting them to expend energy without submitting this exertion to the established norms of rationality and functionality. According to the carnival spirit of the amusement park, the exertion of labor became "endless" and pleasurable because it was not measured against the demands for productivity and efficiency of industrial production and entrepôt circulation. Instead of defining the movement of flows based on commercial objectives, its assemblage of spectacles allowed each body to meander according to its own individual trajectory and velocity. By keeping visitors at a constant state of physical activity, the park tested the limits of their capacities for increased productivity. Despite the lack of explicit constraints on the scope of their activity, visitors to the outdoor park were not afforded complete rest from the heat and humidity of the tropical environment, which could leave them fatigued.

Democratic Experimentation in Sporting Clubs

The media ecology of the Manila Carnival and the New World and Great World amusement parks during the 1930s encompassed not only cultural shows but also sports matches outside their enclosures. To diminish the popularity of undesirable vices such as gambling and cockfighting, the U.S. regime introduced physical exercise and competitive sports such as baseball and boxing to the population of the Philippine Islands to promote proper values of discipline, resoluteness, courage, justice, and cooperation needed for modern sovereignty among local residents perceived to be barbaric and rowdy.[62] The rule-based competition in sports spectacles such as baseball games and boxing matches, which would be staged in Manila's famed Art Deco Olympic Stadium and Rizal Memorial Baseball Stadium, instilled a sense of fair play in spectators.[63] With their emphasis less on absorption in mass spectatorship than immersion in collective activity, the administrative innovations of amateur sporting clubs in Singapore that proliferated during this historical period allowed the Asian population to experiment with practices of self-determination and democracy.

Just like in other cosmopolitan Southeast Asian port cities, amateur sporting clubs proliferated across British Malaya as a complementary yet alternate site of leisure and entertainment to the amusement parks. Comprised mainly of middle-class male Asian professionals, these local versions of the more exclusive social club extended the workings of the amusement park in modulating the productivity of labor for the purposes of economic growth. Nurturing a mode of physical culture based on agility and cooperation, particularly against the tendency toward the docility of mass spectatorship, they made possible identities and collectivities that would be appropriate to future conditions of political sovereignty.

News about amateur sporting clubs dominated the pages of the English-language *Malaya Tribune*, the "Independent" and "Progressive" "People's Paper," which the Asian population liked to peruse. A regular section called The Club Verandah appeared in the mid-1930s focusing on news about social and sporting clubs. The column Club Diary in the *Malaya Tribune* would list the activities of clubs such as performances and fundraisers, together with attendance requirements and dress codes. The list of clubs whose athletic, social, and artistic activities were reported in local periodicals covered a wide range of designations and significations. With at least forty of them founded by the first decade of the new millennium,[64] it included the Amicable Athletes Association, Amateur Sporting Association, Anson Athletic Association, Playfair Athletic Union, Solar Athletic Union, Asian Athletic Club, Straits Bachelors Physical Culture Association, Balestier Friendly Athletic Party, Bendemeer Athletic Club, Upper Serangoon Recreation Club, Union Sporting Association, Siong Boo Athletic Association, Chinese Companion Athletic Association, Sincere Lads Badminton Party, Juvenile Football Club, Sime Darby Sports Club, Straits Union Football Club, Telok Ayer Epworth League, Straits Chinese Epworth League, Paya Lebar Epworth League, Lion City Club, Post Office Club, Lotus Club, St. Joseph's Old Boys' Association, Ai Tong Old Boys' Association, Chinese Association, Chinese Friendly Association, Thong Nghee Kok Association, Beng Choong Kok Association, Siew Sin Sia, Malay Recreation Club, Malay Teacher's Association, Overseas Telegraph Chinese Staff Association, Malay Public Servants Cooperative Credit Society, Singapore Short Hand Writers' Association, Young Men's Christian Association, Young Women's Christian Association, Chinese Christian Association, Straits Chinese Reading Club, Chinese Students Literary Association, Mayflower Musical & Dramatic Association, Malay Musical Association, United Chinese Musical Association,

Lunar Athletic and Musical Party, United Chinese Amateurs, Silver Star Minstrels, Merrilads Musical Party, and Gaylads Minstrels. The prevalent interest in collective activity even spread through social contagion beyond the cities, with reports of young residents of *kampongs* establishing informal clubs in ramshackle huts.[65] Newspapers explained how clubs addressed the common "desire" for "new" forms of association by "bring[ing] together persons interested in a certain thing or subject."[66] By the middle of the decade, 1,500 formal sporting clubs were in existence throughout the Straits Settlements of Singapore, Malacca, and Penang.[67] The public dissemination of knowledge about their events through newspaper announcements, columns, and advertisements enabled members of different clubs to keep apprised of each other's activities, which cultivated a common consciousness of their shared dynamism.[68]

In their configuration, local sporting clubs resembled European social clubs, the principal site for producing expatriate identity, community, and standing. The late nineteenth and early twentieth centuries were the heyday of the social club.[69] When not relaxing in the sanctuary of their bungalows, the European residents of Singapore Municipality liked to spend their leisure time in the prominent Singapore Club and Tanglin Club, which dated from the 1860s. After a long day of mingling with their mercantile firms' diverse workforce, the more exclusive social club afforded them the pleasure of being in the company of people with the same race, gender, and language who shared similar values, beliefs, and habits.

Originally formed in response to the strict racial and gender hierarchies of the elite social clubs, more inclusive amateur sporting clubs multiplied during the 1920s and 1930s, when the fever for collective activity accompanied the rise of the professional class. Teams were formed among the membership to compete in interclub and interstate tournaments in football, tennis, ping-pong, badminton, and many other interactive sports spectacles. Unlike those in the amusement park, which similarly cultivated the physical culture of strenuous motion and activity, these sports matches were collective spectacles for them not just to gaze at but also to participate in. By immersing themselves in them, they not only expanded their physical abilities but learned about cooperation and organization. As clubs frequently held leisure and entertainment activities such as parties, picnics, and dances,[70] Su Lin Lewis argues that these public venues for social interaction helped constitute business and community networks.[71] "By tak[ing] the place of other institutions, both athletic and social," the club became the principal hub of public life for the local population.[72] If the European social clubs acted as cloisters of languor and repose, the Malayan sporting clubs served as workshops of dynamism and development, where new modes of identity and sociality were explored and fashioned.

Multitudes of locals were first introduced to sports in schools that the colonial government and local philanthropists instituted. The sporting clubs they joined as professionals aspired to cultivate their physical culture, especially as an alternative social practice to vice.[73] Considered to be an important site of social identity and cohesion for the rising middle class in England,[74] sports were understood to be character-building,[75] cultivating self-control and courage in civilized individuals.[76] Espousing the physical and social ideals of Victorian masculinity,[77] sports fostered in their participants the virtues of selflessness, integrity, perseverance, responsibility, loyalty, cooperation, magnanimity, and authority.[78] Civilized individuals were expected to possess the know-how to govern their usage of energy. Valued for their recuperative function, athletics and exercise were seen as capable of restoring lost energy to the body.[79] As extreme play was said to result in the depletion of energy, sporting clubs trained their members in how to regulate its expenditure without wastage or overexertion.[80]

Developing robust physical and social bodies for the purposes of public life, sporting clubs became venues of possibility for the transformation of character and collectivity.[81] Letters in Singapore's newspapers highlight how clubs were both "sporting body" and "social institution" that provided both "physical" and "mental exercise" for those who "desire for culture." [82] A May 1934 article from the *Sunday Times* argued, "Sport influences us to act honestly, correctly, to be gentlemen. Together with our body our mind becomes stronger. Our brain becomes more elastic; it offers more resistance, it moves quicker, and it is more readily responsive."[83] Cultivating practices of fairness and teamwork,[84] competitive team sports instilled in club members norms for the healthy conduct of relations with other people. Instead of treating the tumultuous world outside as a threat that required order, it taught participants how to behave in the presence of crowds with composure and initiative. Its goal was to form a vital harmony among physique, cognition, and sociality.[85] As the body was reconfigured, the mind would become stronger and more agile in dealing with the troubles and contingencies of modern life.

Amateur sporting clubs in British Malaya furnished venues for the Asian population to practice self-government in a Crown Colony where political activity was restricted. As a successful model of U.S. imperialism, the Philippine Islands had been granted a definite path toward independence leading up to commonwealth status in the 1930s. To accommodate the recalcitrance of the Filipino elite while tempering the influence of the Catholic Church, the U.S. government gradually introduced limited suffrage. As early as three years into its occupation of the archipelago, the colonial regime staged elections for municipal officers and provincial governors who wielded authority over law enforcement, public works, and taxation.[86] Elections were held for the National Assembly in 1907 and bicameral legislature in 1916, which afforded the local population a degree of participation in democratic governance.

For the legitimacy to operate, amateur sporting clubs in British Malaya were required to secure an exemption from registration under the colonial government, which taxed associations that were not oriented toward the public good.[87] As evidence of civic responsibility among the local population,[88] sporting clubs were a more acceptable form of association than secret societies and trade unions, which it deemed to be recalcitrant and subversive. Because political activity among Asian residents was illegal during this period,[89] the modes of physical productivity and social organization that were performed in Singapore's sporting clubs created a nascent democratic space. A rare practice for the Chinese migrants in the municipality,[90] sports provided an opportunity for the English-speaking Straits Chinese to demonstrate their readiness for self-determination.

Intended to provide a sanctuary for collective recreation and relaxation, the sporting club unfolded as a workshop for self-improvement, where local residents experimented with the rudiments and responsibilities of sovereignty. An article that appeared in a July 1925 issue of the *Singapore Free Press* tentatively defined the amateur social club as "a sort of defense alliance tacitly concluded between a number of individuals, all moving in the same sphere of life, against the troubles and perturbations by which humanity is assailed."[91] A regular column, Around the Clubs, published in the Sunday edition of the *Malaya Tribune*, advocated for sporting clubs to act as vehicles for mutual aid among members of the Asian population,[92] based especially on their lack of opportunities for participation in governance.

Another article proclaimed, "The Club has the power to make a success of such institutions where independent bodies would fail."[93] Defining the contours of progress according to the multiculturalism of popular forms such as the *bangsawan*, articles and letters in the *Straits Times, Malaya Tribune*, and *Singapore Free Press and Mercantile Advertiser* about the proliferation of local sporting clubs debated gender and racial issues tied to enlightenment and progress in expanding membership to include Chinese and women.[94] Highlighting how clubs in British Malaya could serve as venues for modern expression, the print culture offered a public sphere for club members to challenge the established order by exploring areas for change through their collective activity.

Club activity featured elements of democratic rule. Members were tasked with drafting the club's constitution with its own rules of conduct and association. Operating like small modern governments, clubs held meetings, collected dues, and elected officers.[95] They fostered models and practices of cross-cultural interaction and intellectual exchange.[96] Through membership and involvement in amateur sporting clubs, locals were afforded the political capacities formerly restricted to expatriates and ratepayers. In training their bodies to be adept in sports or the arts, their bodies were made adaptable for cooperation and organization with other bodies. By acquainting them with new modes of sociality and community, this form of physical culture prepared the Asian residents of 1930s Singapore Municipality for the prospect of political sovereignty.

Under the colonial occupation of the United Kingdom and United States before the Pacific War, governments and businesses in Singapore and Manila introduced sanitary, air-conditioned modernity to their cityscapes that cleansed perceived sources of social and moral contagion from their public and private enclosures. Through the visual apprehension of window displays in commercial streets and carnival attractions in amusement parks, spectorial experience shifted from the cognitive absorption of the cinematographic gaze to the sensorial immersion of the urban environment in a bustling trading port. In 1930s Manila, both carnival and sporting events promulgated the U.S. government's industrial and imperial authority, which intimated that only it possessed the capacity to harness its elusive transformative potential of modern forces. If 1930s Singapore's amusement parks revitalized and extended the physical culture of local workers beyond the limits of their exhaustion, its sporting clubs afforded them an exceptional democratic space for collective activity that was prohibited in the Straits Settlement. Exploring new opportunities to practice their readiness for self-determination and sovereignty in the commercial and leisure spaces they frequented, the residents of these Southeast Asian port cities grappled and experimented with divergent temporalities of modernity that, amid the wake of a global recession and the threat of a world war, offered the tenuous promise of an emergent national community.

PART II

1960s Singapore and Manila

Temporalities of Development and Delinquency

Marked by the anxiety and turbulence of Cold War geopolitics and postcolonial development, Southeast Asian cities during the 1960s were shaped by the fervor of protests from students and workers amid the rise of cinema as mass entertainment. After slowly recovering from the destruction and trauma of the Pacific War, the residents of Manila and Singapore became preoccupied with the difficulties and possibilities of postcolonial independence. While the Philippines acquired its sovereignty from the United States in 1946, Singapore obtained semi-autonomy from the British Empire in 1959 and independence from the Malaysian Federation in 1965. Beset with persistent problems of congestion, unemployment, and unrest in the face of allegations and rumors of communist influence, national governments under the People's Action Party in Singapore and the Liberal and Nacionalista parties in Manila strove to implement their visions of urban renewal to refashion the spatial environment for the sake of economic and material growth. This youthful desire for revolutionary transformation reverberated across the subregion, with labor strikes and mass demonstrations on the streets of Singapore, Bangkok, Jakarta, and Manila challenging the authority of state and capital to dictate the terms of productivity, identity, and community.[1] The 1960s are commonly described in critical scholarship as a historical period characterized by the rise of mass consumption. In the wake of the thriving Philippine and Malayan movie industries during this period, urban residents in 1960s Manila and Singapore immersed themselves in the spectatorship and discussion of popular vernacular representations of delinquent rebels and monstrous metamorphoses that visualized the possibilities of the seemingly entrenched established order's upheaval.

Historians describe the Singapore of the 1950s and 1960s as being defined by its pluralistic public life.[2] Even the official historical accounts endorsed by the Singapore government highlight its vibrant political culture, which was characterized by a multiplicity of visions and demands about its crucial trajectory of development being passionately articulated through protest or in Parliament.[3]

On the assumption of power by the People's Action Party in 1959, its finance and defense minister Goh Keng Swee blamed the laissez-faire doctrines of British colonial rule for Singapore's lackluster economy, overcrowded housing, inadequate education, and high unemployment, which had stayed unresolved since the early twentieth century.[4] Its founding prime minister, Lee Kuan Yew, asserted that such seemingly insurmountable problems needed to be confronted by a radical transformation to the spatial and social landscape that required collective sacrifice from its citizens. Speaking about the changes to capitalist distribution and exchange crucial for prosperity in his landmark 1972 speech "Singapore: Global City," Culture and Foreign Minister S. Rajaratnam declared, "We cannot, as before, live by importing and re-exporting their raw produce. . . . Nor can we, as we do now, by selling them cheap textiles, shoes, slippers, chocolates, and things of that order. . . . We can no longer be the Change Alley of South-East Asia."[5] Resonant in the print culture of local newspapers and tourist guidebooks, Change Alley was a small, yet teeming passageway ensconced at the heart of Raffles Place, Singapore's main business and commercial district, that workers and residents would frequent in their daily routine. Representing the ruling People's Action Party's official discourse of development, what Rajaratnam's statement implied was that Singapore needed to reimagine its configuration and reputation as a bazaar in the world market by shifting away from the creative informality of entrepôt trade to the factory regimentation of industrial manufacturing.

As the newly independent government relocated Singapore's population from the congested city center to public housing estates in its remote urban outskirts, an emergent type of night bazaar called the *pasar malam* flourished as the provisional source for basic necessities. Proliferating as the autonomous initiatives of itinerant hawkers for livelihood, they quickly became important hubs of social life that captivated the collective imaginary of Singaporeans in the immediate post-independence period. Regarded as a threat by the state despite their social significance, these street markets embodied a divergent form of delinquent, fugitive modernity whose informality, creativity, and collectivity subverted the ruling People's Action Party's linear, overarching vision of sanitary, air-conditioned modernity. By the middle of the 1960s, the government implemented a "Keep Singapore Clean" campaign that summoned the collective sacrifice of the local population to eliminate "filth" and "squalor" from the spatial environment. Such undesirable realities encompassed buildings and drains perceived to be unhygienic, as well as hawkers and markets considered to be disorderly. In its narration of the official Singapore Story, the Singapore Broadcasting Corporation's 1980s documentary *Diary of a Nation* equates the first images of the "Keep Singapore Clean" campaign with street hawkers and markets as disruptive sources of filth and squalor that needed to be purged for the sake of development into a global city. Because the regime of industrial production required mass labor to become operative and efficacious, the air-conditioned modernity of the government depended on all the physical bodies and material resources that it could direct and exploit.

Looking at the transition between regimes of capitalist exchange and mass consumption, the chapter starts by revisiting the intertwined microhistories of Singapore's *pasar malam* and Change Alley, which have scant scholarship about them despite captivating the popular imagination of Singaporeans as hubs of social life during this important historical moment of transition. Situating this discussion against the backdrop of Singapore's initial stages of nationhood, I analyze the flexible statecraft of its newly independent government as it appropriated the emergency regulations of the British colonial regime to accommodate and refashion all the contents of its territory according to a new logic of sanitary, air-conditioned modernity. Analyzing the public speeches of Lee Kuan Yew about the disruptive spectacles of street markets and labor strikes, the chapter uncovers the People's Action Party's discourse about the danger of emotional contagion to national development. It concludes by discussing how the Keep Singapore Clean and Operation Hawker Control campaigns disciplined itinerant hawkers into responsible citizens by gradually adjusting the parameters of legal and medical codes along its prescribed trajectory of industrial productivity and civic responsibility. Characterizing the transience and excitement amid the initial stages of national development, the once common presence of night markets, which, coinciding with the Singapore government's efforts toward rapid economic and material growth in the 1960s and 1970s, disappeared after their prohibition as the first shopping malls began to be erected in the late 1970s.

The Heart of the Entrepôt

By 1963, the number of street hawkers in Singapore was estimated at 40,000, only one-fourth of them licensed.[6] Visible in archival photographs from the 1960s, the radiance and boisterousness of the *pasar malam*, the itinerant night markets that many of them constituted, suffused the dark, empty surroundings of the newly constructed public housing estates. At the end of the workday, from seven to ten in the evening,[7] crowds of residents from the nearby housing estate would gather at these rudimentary street markets to spend their leisure time as part of the new routine of their everyday life. Exemplifying the commercial informality and mobility of itinerant hawkers, assortments of goods would be displayed atop cloth blankets spread out on the ground under the illumination of fluorescent lamps and incandescent bulbs. Independent Chinese vendors typically dominated the stalls,[8] which carried a wide variety of items with negotiable prices including clothes, fabrics, silverware, chinaware, radios, and Japanese novelties.[9] At the many makeshift food stalls, families dined on fried noodles and skewered meats. As frequent customers, residents developed close relationships with merchants, who relied on these personal bonds for business.[10] From this popular activity an imminent community was formed in the early years of national sovereignty.

FIGURE 7. The radiance from the *pasar malam* punctuated the vast emptiness of the new public housing estates on the urban periphery. (Photo from National Archives of Singapore)

The innovative typology for commercial exchange, mass consumption, and social life of the *pasar malam* was defined by Change Alley, the principal shopping area of 1950s and 1960s Singapore, which had grown entrenched in the popular imagination over the first half of the twentieth century. Adjacent to Collyer Quay and Raffles Place, Singapore's financial and business hub, Change Alley was a cramped, bustling passageway formed from the narrow space between two commercial buildings. Commonly contrasted by shoppers with Raffle Place's prestigious Robinson's Department Store, which gained prominence as a sanitary, "casual," and air-conditioned enclosure with fixed prices for its exclusive items, Change Alley was famous for being a more boisterous, "faster," and more multicultural space with negotiable bargains for basic goods.[11] Distinguished by its teeming multiplicity, Change Alley was christened the "Street of a Thousand Faces," a nickname that was supposed to capture Singapore's identity as an international port city with its concentration of global flows of multiracial and multilingual merchants and consumers. The pervading image of Change Alley as a street market in the public culture derived its allure from its association with dominant notions about the exuberant atmosphere of the bazaar and the dynamic practice of bargaining.

As with the experience of the *pasar malam*, browsing through Change Alley's multitudinous stalls became a cherished habit of everyday life such that many Singaporeans considered their day to be incomplete if they failed to visit the passageway at least once.[12] Maximizing the limited space allotted, stalls featured seemingly endless stocks of items crammed onto wooden tables and makeshift racks. Archival photos of Change Alley reveal that wooden posts supporting the structure of every stall carried shirts and bags of different sizes, colors, and shapes in haphazard tiers. Amid the deluge by waves of anonymous bodies trudging through the passageway, the abundance and variety of items kept any single object from instantly gaining prominence in the eyes of consumers. As market stalls offered no fixed prices, consumers needed to be equipped with the cognitive and linguistic agility to vigorously negotiate the price of an item with the vendor, as a former shopper described: "The one thing about Change Alley was that you had to bargain. You had to know how to bargain . . . everybody goes there being prepared to use every device they know to bargain and in fact that was like a sport."[13] Described as a strenuous competition over the provisional price of a mundane object, the creative informality of bargaining was perceived to be a skilled interplay between seller and buyer whose contingency and flexibility reciprocally produced and shaped its exchange value.

Nicknamed "Shopper's Paradise," Change Alley had garnered fame as a commercial space where any item from around the world could be obtained at an affordable price through personal negotiation. Because Singapore was a trading port that imposed no taxes, quotas, or duties, the prices of goods were known to be lower in the city-state than in their country of manufacture.[14] Prices were said to be even cheaper in Change Alley. As early as the 1930s, Change Alley had already been recognized in the public culture as Singapore's version of the colonial metropole's Petticoat Lane,[15] its principal site of the *jual murah* or "cheap sale,"[16] where basic necessities could be purchased at low prices. Even then, assorted "odds and ends of necessities," including soap, toothpaste, shirts, sarongs, towels, rubber shoes, cottons, silks, razors, pens, eyeglasses, canned goods, drinks, fresh fruits, and curry puffs,[17] would be sold in Change Alley's stalls.[18] By the middle of the 1960s, stalls with names like Oriental, Albert Store, Idea Silk, Alley Photo, Haiyen Trading, Fairy Shoes, Poh Seng, Jit Seng, Koh Heng, Hong Sheng, Hua Hua, Mohammad Tamby, Nihalchand Ramchand, and House of Russian Goods offered a wider range of goods,[19] which expanded to include batiks, rugs, souvenirs, watches, sunglasses, umbrellas, costume jewelries, leather goods, electronic goods, and bootleg tapes.[20] The bazaar atmosphere of Change Alley was said to feature polyvocal transactions in diverse tones, dialects, and accents as the merchants of Chinese and Indian ethnicity could speak in a variety of languages such as English and Malay to entice potential customers.[21] In oral history interviews, Change Alley is repeatedly characterized as being "shoulder to shoulder."[22] Describing Change Alley as an "unforgettable experience," tourists likened it to a "beehive" with a "hundred yards of humanity jostling each other just to keep moving."[23] Writing about the open-air *pasar* in Java and Bali, Clifford Geertz highlighted its vivid amorphousness and fluidity: "Goods flow through the market channels at a dizzying rate, not as broad torrents but as hundreds of little trickles, funneled through an enormous number of transactions."[24] While resonating with the materiality of its sensorial profusion, the popular image of the bazaar as a memorable "beehive" of "humanity" disclosed its infinite commonality as a shared activity in a pluralistic trading port.

Itinerant bazaars flourished in 1960s Singapore because of the dearth in steady employment and income for the majority of the population.[25] The legal basis for their operation had been earlier furnished by the colonial government's Hawkers Code of 1950, which declared the right of every inhabitant in the territory to the use of vacant public space for the sake of their subsistence.[26] Advocating for illegal economies as vital means of livelihood in Peru, the developmental economist Hernando de Soto explains that the informality of the bazaar becomes exigent for urban residents without adequate access to housing, education, and employment.[27] Instead of requiring customers to journey far to its site of operation, this emergent type of commercial space incarnated the spatial mobility of Singapore's entrepôt economy by making supplies available to residents in their remote public housing estates. Emulating and enhancing the rhythm of periodic markets, *pasar malams* traveled daily from one area to another across Singapore. Their pattern of movement could be traced to that of the itinerant hawkers who would accompany the performances of Chinese *wayang* troupes as they toured various parts of the island.[28] With autonomous, informal modes of creativity, mobility, and sociality, this bazaar epitomized the sense of dynamism and possibility of the historical moment.

The government classified hawkers as either "itinerant" or "stationary," with the latter divided into "day" and "night," the prescribed time of their legal operation. But such categories proved to be fluid, as hawkers easily moved between them according to the demands of the situation.[29] Whereas the government felt threatened by this informality, businesses aspired to tap into its potential for commercial profit. Night markets drew large crowds of people because the retail stores concentrated in the city center normally closed on weekdays at five and on Saturdays at one in the afternoon. Because of the immense popularity that *pasar malams* were commonly understood to have, the owners and managers of the retail stores in the city center contemplated extending their operating hours into the evenings. To improve on their decreased earnings, these commercial spaces attempted to establish regular stalls, such as sales outlets for local shoe manufacturers, at the night markets.[30] The news article highlights how retail stores were beguiled by the possibility that joining a night market would enable them to exploit the purchasing power of its typical mass of consumers. *Pasar malams* derived the force of their popularity from the imagined endlessness of the crowds that were believed to congregate in their domain with frequency. Influencing perception and practice, the force of their popularity compelled stores to alter their temporal and spatial patterns of operation, to "modernize" their business strategy.

Although their spatial configuration resembled that of the open-air Malay bazaar, the most widely circulated English-language publications in British Malaya did not apply the term "*pasar malam*" to the night markets of 1960s Singapore at the outset. For example, a news article from the April 7, 1960, issue of the *Straits Times* referred to the highly popular weekly bazaar in Woodlands by the generic name "Woodlands Saturday market."[31] Only several months after, newspapers changed its common nomenclature to "Woodlands Fair," likening it to a "Little Change Alley." When night markets first started appearing across the island, they seemed to represent a uniquely new phenomenon that the public culture initially lacked the linguistic means to articulate. Confronted with a vaguely familiar phenomenon that could not be ignored because of its immense significance, newspapers eventually settled on the most suitable loanword, "*pasar malam*," to indicate its presence. The adoption of this name, which denoted a different type of commercial space that was comparable in form, affixed its emergent reality with meanings about informality associated with that commercial space.

Despite its seemingly rudimentary character, the *pasar malam* of 1960s Singapore could be understood to be modern because its emergence was an immediate response to conditions that ensued from the drive for modernization. In contrast to the government's systematic master plan for sanitary, air-conditioned modernity, it was a form of incipient, delinquent, or fugitive modernity that represented a divergence from modern conditions with its paradoxical, informal embrace of traditional configurations. Arising from the instability of transition, the existence of the *pasar malam* reveals the complexities of large-scale development, which creates openings and opportunities for ordinary people to improvise based on their given conditions and resources. If modernity is taken to denote a concentration of flows, such as those of bodies, finances, and technologies, then the *pasar malam*, instead of being a rudimentary antecedent that originated from a primordial stage of capitalism, could be interpreted as the inescapable surplus from Singapore's stages of development that eluded and complicated the latter's overarching, linear trajectory.

In line with the slippage in its naming, Deborah Kapchan conceives of the bazaar as a dynamic site of transition and transformation that constitutes an autonomous form of incipient modernity.[32] The anthropologist Victor Turner would regard the spontaneity, creativity, informality, and newness characteristic of the *pasar malam* of 1960s Singapore to be attributes of liminality, which he defines as the ambivalent interim state in the passage from one set of conditions to another.[33] As evident in attempts by news articles to make sense of its presence, the *pasar malam*'s fugitive, paradoxical quality rested on its provisional, interim status, which unsettled epistemological norms by allowing incongruous conditions to intermingle without formalizing. This interim state of informality is a moment of both uncertainty and possibility as social formations experience an open process of redefinition, where the scope for transformation exceeds the limits of the imagination.

Strike Contagion

In the discourses of news reports and public speeches, itinerant hawkers, who resisted government efforts at official regulation, were perceived to generate disorder, congestion, "noise," and illegality. Despite the vibrancy, conviviality, and transience of social gatherings at night markets, the state worried about the danger of "contagion" in which the heightened emotions of the moment would suddenly provoke the crowds to explode into mass protest. Based on this perceived threat of uncontrollable civil unrest, the spectacle of spontaneity and intensity of the crowd, which demanded immediate action, was regarded as detrimental to its vision of order and progress.

Because the established formal systems of national sovereignty and industrial capitalism failed to accommodate popular aspirations for sufficient living and working conditions, the urgency of these aspirations caused their expression to be transplanted to the streets of the city. Over 250 strikes were staged in Singapore in the early 1960s up until its separation from the Federation of Malaysia in 1965.[34] At the height of the Malayan Emergency in the mid-1950s, unionists and students would frequently stage demonstrations to publicize their demands for better compensation, freedom, and education.[35] On May 13, 1954, nearly one thousand students from Chinese middle schools demonstrated against the plan of the British colonial government to draft them into military service in the war against the Malayan Communist Party (MCP). Amid the upsurge in dissent, the state arrested members of the University Socialist Club at the University of Malaya on the 28th of the same month for publishing in the underground magazine *Fajar*.[36] The following year, students joined again with unionists in a strike against the Hock Lee Bus Company to call for shorter hours and higher wages.[37] These mass protests continued early into the succeeding decade, when students from the University of Singapore, Nanyang University, Singapore Polytechnic, and Ngee Ann College would rally against the People's Action Party's plan to shift the medium of instruction of the middle-school system from Mandarin to English for the purpose of global competitiveness.[38]

The popular fervor for protest from students and workers spread and led to the organization of white-collar employees such as department store salesclerks, public health professionals, and movie theater projectionists, who called for better working conditions. The most widely circulated newspapers of the time, such as the *Straits Times* and *Malaya Tribune*, visualized demonstrators with the spectacle of fierce determination and passion etched into their faces and bodies as they locked arms in solidarity. Through their ardent use of slogans and placards, mass protests aspired to generate awareness and support for their cause through their public communication of grievances about prevailing living and working conditions. Throughout the early 1960s, the Singapore Association of Trade Unions (SATU), Singapore Business Houses Employees' Union (SBHEU), and Singapore General Employees Union (SGEU) would call for an accumulation of labor strikes, sit-downs, go-slows, and walk-outs from white collar employees.[39] Immediately following a September 1961 picket by salesclerks at Robinson's Department Store,[40] storekeepers, electricians, carpenters, and artists at Shaw Brothers' main office and distribution center demonstrated for a $20–25 increase in monthly wages.[41] Starting in late December of the same year, four hundred employees at fifteen Shaw Brothers movie theaters went on strike for six weeks to demand their accumulated backlog of overtime pay. News photos highlighted how striking crowds were constituted by ordinary employees of different races and genders, some of whom wore dresses or slippers while performing their walk-outs and sit-downs. Cognizant of the spectacle of the strike, which could produce emotional affinity and public sympathy for their

FIGURE 8. Striking public health professionals express their multicultural solidarity against the established work regime. (Photo from National Archives of Singapore)

urgent cause, one of the protest signs declared, "Now Showing. . . . Sit Down Strike."[42]

In 1960s Singapore, efforts by the People's Action Party to regulate street hawkers and markets through limited licenses and balloted spaces resulted in strikes. In May 1966, two hundred *pasar malam* hawkers at Mountbatten, Guillemard, and Tanjong Katong protested the new balloting system, which they claimed restrictively delineated and distributed hawker pitches, by standing at their pitches "without doing any business."[43]

The labor strike is a sudden withdrawal by employees of their coopera-tion with management in business operations.[44] Disrupting the productivity of the work regime and the routine of everyday life, the strike is meant to compel state or capital to yield immediately to the demands of protestors.[45] Emphasizing the intrinsic value of labor power, the efficacy of the strike as a mode of collective action rests on its stoppage of the processes of industrial manufacturing,[46] which would reduce capital accumulation.[47] The spectacu-lar, rhetorical force of the strike is derived from the impassioned solidarity of the crowd, which stems from its tight physical density and contagious emotional intensity. Echoing the vigorous behavior that they witness from the others gathered close to them, participants of the strike quickly assimi-late their bodies to the energy of the crowd.[48] Formed by the synchronous mobilization of a collective action for an extended duration, the spectacle of infinite commonality from the large size and intense emotion of the crowd then elicits popular sympathy from onlookers.

Founded by former members of the People's Action Party in 1961, the Barisan Socialis threatened the PAP's monopoly on power during the early part of the decade in the period before postcolonial independence. Resting on the support of students and unionists from the predominantly Chinese population, the more radical Barisan Sosialis insisted that Singapore's mem-bership in the Malaysian Federation be unconditional, without constraints on the political and economic rights of its citizens.[49] The government blamed the strike's disruption of the economy on its organization by the Barisan Socialis. To diminish the threat that the strike posed to his party's control of the government, Prime Minister Lee Kuan Yew denounced the Barisan Sosialis for being a communist front whose actuations derived not from reason and foresight but from instinct and emotion.

Emphasizing its technical expertise and political experience to direct Sin-gapore along a continuous, linear trajectory of development, the People's

Action Party condemned the Barisan Sosialis for being ruled too easily by the emotion and contingency of the present situation. While the leaders of the Barisan Socialis were adept at gathering and mobilizing individuals by rousing their passions, Lee Kuan Yew claimed that collective, large-scale endeavors driven by passion inevitably failed because this passion quickly dissipated.[50] Powerful orators like Lee Kuan Yew's main political rival, the eloquent and charismatic Lim Chin Siong, supposedly beguiled with spectacular words of intense emotion, which were alluring because of the transformative force they carried. According to the 1961 report of the United Nations Technical Assistance team led by Dr. Albert Winsemus, chief economic adviser to the Singapore government during its period of rapid growth, the mass protests they staged were shortsighted in that they fought for the immediate subsistence of their members without working for the long-term prosperity of the entire population.[51]

Lee Kuan Yew echoed this idea about the collective sacrifices needed for rapid, linear growth in his 1967 speech to the Singapore Employers' Federation, "For Singapore, It Must Be Up and Up," when he condemned protests for diminishing "discipline" and "efficiency."[52] Envisioning a trajectory of development for Singapore's first ten-year plan, the United Nations teams' report proposed shifting away from the established entrepôt trade to bolster the laggard manufacturing industry, which would increase employment and productivity especially with the imminent closure of British military bases on the island.[53] According to the report, the availability of jobs in the manufacturing industry had decreased by almost 20 percent as a result of "unsatisfactory industrial relations, resulting in unrest, low productivity, and irrational wage demands."[54] Based on its logic, the rapid linear growth would be attainable only when the seemingly irresolvable antagonism between government and labor had yielded to conditions of "industrial peace."

Echoing the findings of the United Nations report about the disruptiveness of the strike, Lee Kuan Yew's thinking bore the influence of the seminal yet controversial theories of Gustave Le Bon, which presumed that the crowds formed by the students and unionists of 1960s Singapore were driven entirely by passion and immediacy. Devoid of reason and intentionality,[55] crowds tended to be swayed by external ideas instead of being able to negotiate their impact.[56] According to this provocative notion, any regime that rested on emotion for its authority would be forced to submit to the demands of this emotion regardless of their soundness. Such a notion resonated with the dominant discourse about crowds during the period of emergence of mass society and democratization of national politics. This discourse stated that managing the formation of the crowd was key to the speed and success of mass industrialization, which required the containment or dismissal of its irrational desires and energies.[57]

Lee Kuan Yew shared the misgivings of Le Bon, who regarded membership in a crowd as a threat to the preservation of the established order because it enabled individuals to realize large-scale endeavors that they never would been able to accomplish alone.[58] Le Bon's prejudices against the crowd disclosed its transformative potential. For Le Bon, the capacity of revolutionary crowds to undermine and overturn the established order came from their disregard for the legibility of dominant norms of propriety and reason.[59] Propelled by their impatience for change, they refused the pragmatic exigencies of development that the state attempted to communicate to the population. Because membership in a crowd was anonymous, individuals who were assimilated into crowds became more willing to forgo their inhibitions, which would have constrained their more overtly antagonistic and seditious actions.[60] Without much concern for the future,[61] their actions failed to consider the range of long-term consequences, especially for the productivity of industry and the welfare of the community. Because its agency enabled its members to exceed the necessity of given conditions, the crowd represented both promise and danger.[62]

Sanitary Modernity and Civic Responsibility

Adjudging protestors to be unruly and recalcitrant, the Singapore state experimented with different political and economic mechanisms to resolve the crisis of civil unrest to implement its overarching plan for rapid development. In response to the mass protests of 1955, the newly autonomous government enacted emergency regulations such as the Preservation of Public Security Ordinance, which granted it the authority to monitor and detain individuals perceived to be disruptive to social order for up to two years. The following year, Chief Minister Lim Yew Hock, in collusion with the British colonial regime, arranged for the prohibition of organizations and expulsion of students believed to be communist fronts.[63] Introduced by the People's

Action Party in 1963, the Internal Security Act authorized the closure of militant publications and arrest of opposition politicians.[64] Expanding the terms of emergency regulations, the Internal Security Act justified the intervention of sovereign power to confront threats not only to "public order" but also to "essential services." Such "services" were defined as consisting of commercial activities and business operations crucial to the productivity and efficiency of government and industry. Within the scope of this law, individuals identified as threats to public order and essential services were subjected to constant surveillance and banned from speaking in public.[65] Fearful of the influence of external forces, the government feared that the social and emotional contagion of protest would inevitably result in revolution akin to Cuba or China.

Chua Beng Huat argues that the People's Action Party successfully maintained its popular support for development by continually invoking an imaginary of crisis in which the survival of the whole national community could only be addressed through collective sacrifice.[66] Aiming to garner the consent of the population, this discourse of a perpetual emergency bemoaned Singapore's isolation as an island and its lack of a hinterland given the perennial threat from neighboring Southeast Asian nations Malaysia and Indonesia. Because development in Singapore under the People's Action Party commenced amid the backdrop of the Malayan Emergency, in which the declining British Empire waged war against the specter of the Malayan Communist Party, Ping Tjin Thum asserts that its logic pervaded postcolonial rule even after its official cessation.[67] Suspending legal norms for the intervention of sovereign power, the institution of emergency regulations in 1948 was originally meant to subdue dissent and establish stability. First enacted to contain the threat of the communist insurgency, emergency regulations in the 1960s became directed at creating a suitable spatial environment to speed up economic growth. Intervening on behalf of the welfare of the entire population, the official declaration of a perpetual state of emergency legitimated the government's refashioning of urban space and mass labor according to the trajectory and temporality of linear, rapid growth.

By the middle of the 1960s, the Singapore government began to implement Operation Hawker Control as a form of air-conditioned, sanitary modernity to address the emergency posed by these undesirable realities to public order. To ensure that its ambitious plans for development would be realized without impediment, the People's Action Party initiated Operation Hawker Control in accordance with its "Keep Singapore Clean" campaign, an extensive "cleanup" program launched in October 1968 to improve order and sanitation in the cityscape by revaluing and subordinating delinquent labor with greater utility in line with the linear progression of industrial capitalism.[68] Circulated through the local news media, official photos showed Prime Minister Lee Kuan Yew vigorously helping neighborhoods sweep and hose away litter from the streets.[69] Over 350,000 posters, stickers, and pamphlets were distributed in various public spaces across the island, including housing estates, factories, markets, bus stops, restaurants, movie theaters, and coffee shops, for several months. Maps and charts were set up by the Health Ministry in an Operations Room to monitor the cleanup campaign, which had deployed 4,000 team members to conduct surprise inspections.[70] The government enlisted teachers to promote the change in habit in their classrooms. It organized competitions with prizes for the cleanest spaces in Singapore. Encompassing the entirety of the island, Health Minister Chua Sian Chin described the civic responsibility behind the cleanup program as a "long and arduous" "crusade" for citizens, whose collective activity "requires all the stamina to endure and persist" as a robust national community.[71]

This same vigorous, persistent crusade to bring development by radically refashioning the city through sanitary, air-conditioned modernity was visible in Manila under the administration of Mayor Antonio Villegas. Appointed to the office with the sudden demise of his predecessor, Arsenio Lacson, from a stroke in 1962, Villegas served for the rest of the decade until losing reelection a year before the proclamation of martial law, after which his family migrated to the United States. Under his urban renewal program, which he christened "*Punyagi sa Kaunlaran*" or "Striving for Progress," Mayor Villegas aspired to beautify, order, and control the cityscape by paving roads, planting trees, building parks, covering drainages, burying wires, and eradicating slums. To eliminate congestion and pollution from the streets of the metropolis, he directed unruly jeepneys to be halted and smoke-belching vehicles to be impounded. To free the sidewalks for the movement of pedestrians, he insisted on the strict enforcement of the law forbidding the use of sidewalks for illegal parking and automobile repair. Villegas decreed that smoking was illegal in public spaces such as stores, restaurants, hotels, clubs, factories, buses, elevators, and cinemas. Regarding it as a "public nuisance" to a modern city, he prohibited the cacophony of horns and loudspeakers. Calling it a fire hazard, he banned packed "Standing Room Only" movie theaters from admitting more spectators. Mayor Villegas's slogan of air-conditioned modernity, "*Sumunod sa batas nang tayo'y maligtas*,"[72] emphasized the liberating transformation that yielding to his vision of progress would deliver.

In Lee Kuan Yew's English, Malay, and Hokkien speeches launching the "Keep Singapore Clean" campaign, he envisaged the liberating transformation of Singapore as a "home" and "garden" for all. Disclosing the intrinsic entanglement of the ideals of order, health, morality, and beauty characteristic of air-conditioned modernity, this vision of progress did not only mean relying on the government to institute a spatial environment that would be uncompromisingly sanitary, orderly, and secure. In an anthology of his news and opinion writings in the *Straits Times*, Cherian George uses the metaphor of air-conditioning as pervasive and essential to refer to the centralized political and social control and management exercised by Lee Kuan Yew and the People's Action Party over its population and environment to deliver material well-being and comfort, from the initial stage of national sovereignty onward.[73] The image of air-conditioning recurs throughout speeches of Lee Kuan Yew during the 1960s, where its installation in factories and rooms is taken to be a sign of progress that a modern city must strive to achieve throughout its domain.[74] Pursuing the dualistic, evangelical logic of air-conditioned modernity in 1930s Manila, the state strove to unconditionally banish negative realities outside its circumscribed domain for their innate corrupting influence. Faced with the island's scarce resources, however, air-conditioned modernity in 1960s Singapore sought to utilize all the elements of its domain as an inclusive "home" and "garden" for the purposes of industrial production and economic development. Instead of expelling them to a marginalized outside, the state adopted the evolutionary, utilitarian logic of 1960s air-conditioned modernity by seeking to incorporate discontinuous and recalcitrant pockets of informal social and economic activity to harness their creative capacities.

When colonial regimes attempted to enforce their policies, they had done so with severe and uncompromising violence. Their principal goals were to consolidate authority and propagate civilization, not so much to nurture the native population.[75] Exemplifying Foucault's genealogy of the art of government, this approach shifted away from the explosive, arbitrary violence of sovereign power when states, particularly those of newly independent nations, began to give importance to the welfare of their people.[76] Instead of supporting the economy of the metropole, they developed their own local economies to ameliorate and elevate the conditions of life within their territory. Without resorting to violence, threats to the established order were addressed through the design of programs for improvement,[77] which would appeal to popular support. As Benedict Anderson famously writes, these governments imagined the entire population as constituting a national community whose bodies and aspirations they strived to accommodate and cultivate as a whole, regardless of the immediate sacrifices and unavoidable consequences.

In his 1967 speech "The Raison d'Être of Singapore's Progress," Lee Kuan Yew highlighted that every resident must recognize that they are an "important wheel" in a "well-oiled, well-maintained machinery."[78] From the transcendent standpoint of the People's Action Party, according to Goh Keng Swee in a 1975 speech to the trade union of Singaporean dockworkers, the lack of "discipline" of mass labor resulted in the low "productivity" of the national economy.[79] During the electoral campaign, the People's Action Party had positioned itself as a political organization whose mobilization and advancement of mass labor would be corollary to its modernization of the island city-state. In his speech "Why I Believe in Socialism," delivered at the 1966 Socialist International Congress, Lee Kuan Yew highlighted the importance of the culture of "human resources" as an essential factor for economic growth.[80] In a speech, he insisted on the importance of "an efficient labour force," which would bring about "industrial development"; "more industrial development brings about more employment, more productivity, more happiness, more of the good things in life that can be paid for."[81] Divested of their proclivities for passionate impatience or comfortable idleness, their energies for collectivity were channeled into a definite outcome of factory work and not squandered through a purposeless, delinquent sociality.

With subsequent amendments to the law, Lee Kah-Wee describes the narrowing space for popular illegalities in Singapore during this historical period, which was justified for the collective discipline of nation-building.[82] Recognizing that the population was sympathetic to the livelihood of market vendors with a strong emotional attachment to their significance in social life, the government turned to the legibility of administrative and juridical mechanisms that would innovatively avoid the negative impact that public confrontation and violence could have on local support and foreign investment. Starting incrementally in 1965 and 1966 with the goal of continuously revaluing and reorganizing mass labor for industrial production, the Ministry of Health's Hawkers Department required every hawker to apply for an operating license. Approving only a limited number of applications, its model was an earlier cleanup campaign from the 1930s, which succeeded in reducing the number of hawker licenses by 10 percent each year until the number had been halved.[83] With a fee of six dollars, an approved license entitled a *pasar malam* hawker to use a pitch of twenty-four square feet at a designated location for three months.[84] The short validity of each license obligated hawkers to submit themselves periodically to the authority of the state for its permission to operate. Narrowing the sphere of action of street hawkers through gradual, minute adjustments of ordinances, these innovations by the state reclassified and domesticated their creativity and recalcitrance by repeatedly validating its authority and formalizing its legality under the rationale of sanitation.

Issued in March 1966, a New Hawkers Code established the basic illegality of hawking. From then on, for hawking to qualify as a lawful activity, it required the authorization of the state, which was determined by a restrictive set of criteria. To regulate all commercial movement and behavior on the island, the New Hawkers Code aimed to circumscribe the spatial and temporal legibility of public markets and stalls. According to this code, *pasar malam* hawkers could ply their trade only from five in the afternoon to eleven in the evening. Prohibited from congesting opposite sides of the same road, hawkers were not allowed to set up their stalls within four yards of fire hydrants, within ten yards of road junctions, or within fifty yards of markets, hospitals, schools, police stations, or places of worship. All forms of hawking were banned from sidewalks, drains, stairways, five-foot ways, and bus routes. Hawkers needed to obtain the permission of the government if they wished to change the selection of their goods or the position of their stalls. They were forbidden from erecting permanent structures of any size or shape. This narrowing in the legible codification of the law turned the urgent issue of urban poverty from a public spectacle of sympathy into a technical problem of illegality.

To be able to retain their license, hawkers were required to pass stringent medical examinations. The Environmental Public Health Act of 1968 ordered hawkers to maintain their bodies, clothes, implements, and spaces in a perpetual state of cleanliness. Public health inspectors from the Hawkers Department's Special Squad were tasked with enforcing the law by regularly examining the conditions of hawker stalls. By law, hawkers needed to ensure that the food they sold never touched any surface or object that was considered dirty. Instead of disposing of their rubbish in nearby drains, they were expected to collect and discard it in bins, which they themselves had to furnish. Through minute adjustments in existing medical and legal codes that gradually disciplined hawkers, the government aligned their social behavior with its legible, modern image of public order and stability, which was a prerequisite for foreign investment and national development.

Celebrating the success of its master plan in bringing legibility to development, the PAP Tenth Anniversary Celebration Souvenir featured an essay by Culture and Foreign Minister S. Rajaratnam that describes its statecraft and governmentality: "It is because the Party has the capacity to recognize hard facts and form its theory from them and not the other way around. It is pragmatic. It is sincere and dedicated about its ultimate goals, but it is prepared to change its strategy though not its basic objectives in the light of changing facts." Rajaratnam asserts that the People's Action Party's visions and policies have great efficacy because of their flexibility and pragmatism to adjust to shifting local, regional, and transnational conditions, which it cannot always control. Borrowing Rajaratnam's terminology, Chua conceives of this flexible statecraft as Singapore's distinctive mode of pragmatism, which has exemplified the People's Action Party's administration of the island city-state since postcolonial independence. As an "*ad hoc* contextual rationality that seeks to achieve specific gains at particular points in time and pays scant attention to systematicity and coherence as necessary rational criteria for action,"[85] this "instrumental rationality" of non-ideological pragmatism entails prioritizing legible policies and ordinances that would drive economic growth for national development at the expense of structures that are not directly beneficial to it.[86]

Throughout the 1960s, the People's Action Party continued the implementation of the 1958 Master Plan, which was first enacted in the run-up to independence. Made legible through maps of the different districts in city, the 1958 Master Plan had visualized, categorized, and demarcated the spatial environment to address urban problems of congestion, housing, and unrest.[87] James C. Scott explains how the state is able to perform its functions and enact its plans with increased rationality and effectiveness when it enhances the *legibility* of its territory.[88] As a requisite of modern governance, the condition of legibility refers to the administrative order, clarity, and formality of a spatial environment. Legibility is first inscribed through a *master plan*, a strategic blueprint that preexists the physical changes it proposes. Through the legibility of the master plan, contingent and informal realities are rendered visible so that they could be classified, manipulated, and organized based on its social and economic goals for the domain.

Writing about national development, Ernest Gellner describes its entanglement with industrial production as systematic teleological processes based on a pragmatic instrumental rationality. Gellner argues that a nation oriented toward industrial production is driven by the principle of "continuous improvement" through "sustained and perpetual growth."[89] Because it has limited resources at its disposal, a legible master plan enables it to formalize and organize the necessary changes to the landscape into achievable, incremental stages of development. With its implementation typically conceptualized over successive five-year periods, the long-term realization of a master plan for development rests on its continual renovation and renewal based on the success of each set of changes. Instead of having a direct, singular action, Tania Li adds that development entails minute or gradual adjustments or interventions, which may sometimes be complementary or contradictory.[90] According to Chua, this pragmatism is part of a crisis approach to governance, which involves "pre-emptory interventions," in which the government can make a radical shift in policy in response to a crisis that could lead to collapse.[91] In Singapore's case, as its policies were constantly amended or replaced to suit the demands of market forces, these mechanisms and strategies often ended up being incongruous with those of previous policies. The form that air-conditioned modernity assumed in 1960s Singapore differed from that of 1930s Manila in that, instead of being defined by dualistic ideals of sweeping evangelistic sanitation, it was shaped by pragmatic interventions of incremental economic development that adjusted to the demands of the crisis regardless of ideology.

The Danger of Bazaar Exchange

Delegitimating antagonistic feelings against the government through the formal codification of the law, the pragmatic implementation of Operation Hawker Control and the New Hawkers Code encouraged responsible citizenship by enforcing disciplinary norms of behavior and emotion. In a 1967 speech preceding the People's Action Party's Keep Singapore Clean campaign, "The Future of Singapore Depends Heavily upon Its Cleanliness," Lee Kuan Yew proclaimed the importance of "social responsibility" and "group discipline" for producing a legible image of hygiene, legality, control, and well-being that would entice foreign capital to invest in its economy.[92]

In exchange for an operating license, hawkers were obliged to act like "responsible Singapore citizen[s]." This prescribed identity of civic responsibility meant that they were "not to endanger traffic," "not to be a menace to public health," and "not to break law and order."[93] More than merely tidying and beautifying spaces for the sake of national progress, the cleanup program aimed to reorganize and revalue the bodies that inhabited them so that the citizens who contributed to its order and sanitation would be instilled with "social consciousness," "discipline," and "civic responsibility."[94] If citizenship was defined by the access to rights and resources in exchange for submission to the authority of the state, under the New Hawkers Code, being "responsible" as a "citizen" was equated with abiding by the official norms of public conduct. Both striking and littering were described as "antisocial" activities by "incorrigible" individuals. In designating "indiscriminate hawking" as a "menace," the code suggested that unregulated behavior was harmful to society and illegal in character. Reinterpreting informality, the government believed that *pasar malams* incited crime because the market vendors remorselessly applied their know-how to subvert legality and propriety for the sake of their livelihood. Although hawkers were believed to spread physical disease as a result of their lack of sanitation, according to Lee Kuan Yew, their threat to development rested on their potential, through emotional contagion, to engender the social disease of mass unrest.[95]

More than that, the informality and discontinuity of the bazaar were seen to be insufficient attributes for the overarching system of industrial production, which relied on the cooperative labor of citizens working without disruption. The People's Action Party's idea of the *pasar malam* as detrimental to sustained linear progress echoes the writings of Geertz and de Soto about the creative informality of the bazaar. According to Geertz, who highlights the contribution of bazaar exchange to social life, large-scale development can succeed only if its discontinuity and unpredictability are superseded in favor of the systematicity, rationality, and stability of industrialization.[96] Extolling capitalism as the panacea to underdevelopment and poverty, de Soto adds that informality can fuel the creativity and dynamism of entrepreneurship while cautioning about the need to transcend it for a "new formality," which would renew its economic system once it has achieved its purpose.[97]

Bargaining as "inter-play" had been described as the "life-blood" of the bazaar of Change Alley.[98] Loosely coherent and vaguely defined, the economy of the bazaar was marked by contingency and chance because of its reliance on the creative inter-play of bargaining. The bazaar merchant often improvised when interacting with customers as the prices of products changed depending on the circumstances of the sale. Without the guarantee of formal mechanisms and verified ideas,[99] market vendors were known in Singapore's newspapers to be "skilled businessmen" because they possessed an immediate instinct for the needs and backgrounds of customers.[100] Instead of gradually cultivating a healthy market for his goods, the bazaar merchant needed to wait for a suitable opportunity where he was able to give his best effort at selling his goods.[101] Quickly adjusting his sales techniques to match the customer, he enticed the customer with persuasive language while the customer responded in turn with feigned interest until both of them settled on a provisional price. Because of this variable negotiation and performance of feigned interest, uncertainty and pretense defined the commercial and social activity of bargaining.[102] According to the People's Action Party's disciplinary discourse of responsible citizenship, urban residents were expected to sacrifice such creativity, informality, and contingency for a more stable, overarching system of industrial progress.

Tourist guidebooks, which aimed to provide travelers to Singapore with an enjoyable visit to the emerging global city, portrayed the consumable experience of Change Alley as being strange and thrilling because of such innocuous dangers.[103] Unfamiliar with the norms of bazaar exchanges and bargaining practices, tourists were advised to be judicious and not hasty when purchasing products. Lying on the cusp of danger, this unfamiliarity was the source of the thrill. According to these guidebooks, they should guard against unscrupulous salespeople, paid by commission, who try to offer them incredibly cheap bargains. Before deciding on a purchase, tourists should compare the prices from various stalls to ensure that they are obtaining the best price for the product. Without having developed personal bonds with sellers, they were advised to carefully examine and evaluate the appearance of trustworthiness of the merchant and his stall. They were expected to scrutinize every product they intend to buy to see if they possessed genuine trademarks.[104] Mistrust was highlighted in these guidebooks as an inevitable attribute of the bazaar, even as being the source of its sense of menace and adventure. Whereas this image of the bazaar was effective in drawing tourists to the island, it propagated the idea of Singapore as an uncivilized space of sin where primitive and illegal practices were permitted to flourish.

In its master plan for national development, the People's Action Party's eventual goal was to expunge the presence of hawkers and markets from Singapore's streets and verandahs by transplanting them to indoor structures called "hawker centres" and "food courts" with adequate facilities for electricity, water, and sanitation. Over the next decade, the number of approved hawking licenses was gradually reduced in successive, incremental stages until the last *pasar malam* had been eliminated from the urban environment in 1978. Constituting an interim form of creative informality and delinquent modernity amid the relentlessness and uncertainty of rapid economic and material growth, *pasar malams* represented the endless possibility of historical transition, which the pragmatic governmentality of the People's Action Party permitted to flourish momentarily before curtailing them once the initial stage of development had been achieved with a new formality. As the final night markets and itinerant hawkers became prohibited from the urban environment, the first shopping malls were erected in the new main commercial street of Orchard Road, indexing a shift in the regimes of capitalist exchange and mass consumption from industrial production to neoliberal globalization.

CHAPTER 5

Panoramic Popularity in the Neon Streets

By the 1960s, Manila's main commercial street had shifted from Calle Escolta to the nearby Rizal Avenue as it became the central hub of mass consumption and social life in the expanding metropolis. Journalist Harrison Foreman's 1968 photograph of Rizal Avenue at its junction with Carriedo Street captures its significance according to its nickname in the public culture: "Crossroads of the Nation." Avenida, as it was commonly called, captivated the popular imagination as "Downtown," where both residents and migrants descended under the ambivalent radiance of its seemingly endless neon lights. In its vibrant print culture of newspapers and magazines, which numbered in the dozens,[1] the Philippines was described to be on the verge of a "pre-take-off" stage. Although this term highlighted the national economy's imminent boom based on norms of gradual linear development resulting from state protections of local industries, the same publications revealed seemingly entrenched conditions of poverty, violence, and crime. Writing in the *Philippines Free Press* under his nom de plume, Quijano de Manila,

FIGURE 9. Overlapping streams of pedestrians vigorously cross the busy junction of Rizal Avenue. (Photo from University of Wisconsin-Milwaukee Library)

eminent fictionist, dramatist, poet, and journalist Nick Joaquin christened the historical period the "Seething 60s" for being characterized by the restless energy and vigorous movement of youthful delinquents who refused the norms of the established order.

Featuring crowds of pedestrians strenuously crossing the thoroughfare from opposite directions with expressions of determination etched on their faces, Foreman's photograph of Rizal Avenue shows it stretching off into the promise of the horizon. In the picture, two streams of pedestrians are depicted with gestures of physical and spatial movement caught at the peak of their action. Through these visualizations of restless mobility, Foreman's photograph of Avenida's crossroads hints at the uncontainable youthful dynamism that could suddenly erupt from the mundaneness of urban spaces. Seizing an image of an everyday scene in the bustling, congested metropolis, the camera lifts the pedestrians' bodies from their immersion in the anonymity of the crowd and the banality of life.

Akin to 1950s and 1960s Singapore, the public culture of 1960s Manila was distinguished by youthful activism. The streets of the metropolis would resound with the collective chanting of slogans denouncing the established order of postcolonial Philippines: "*Diktador!*" (Dictator!), "*Tuta ng Kano!*" (America's Dog!), and "*Makibaka, Huwag Matakot!*" (Solidarity, Don't Be Afraid!). This chapter examines the fervor for resistance and transformation characteristic of the time, which led up to the explosion of the First Quarter Storm movement and the declaration of the Martial Law dictatorship in the early 1970s. Protesters in 1960s Manila defined themselves by the performance of their identity as youth,[2] which involved the propensity for vigorous mobility and the desire for immediate change. Nick Joaquin explained how this activism shifted away from delinquency and gangsterism in the early 1960s as it channeled its restless, immanent energy into formal political mobilization and organization with the *Kabataang Makabayan* (Nationalist Youth) and *Samahan ng Demokratikong Kabataan* (Association of Democratic Youth) in the mid- to late 1960s. Calling for an upheaval of the established order because of its failure to provide for the subsistence of the majority of the population, this delinquent, fugitive modernity contrasted with the sanitary, air-conditioned modernity of Ferdinand Edralin Marcos and Lee Kuan Yew, whose uncompromising authoritarian visions dictated an overarching linear trajectory of economic and material growth.

This chapter focuses on how visual infinitude and popular commonality in the metropolis defined everyday life in 1960s Manila through the commercial, architectural, and technological innovations of neon lights, movie theaters, and supermarkets, which facilitated and delimited the potential for dynamism of delinquent, fugitive modernity. I start by tracing the microhistory of the main street of Rizal Avenue as it developed into "Downtown," its nickname in the public culture. Among the recurrent words in the media ecology of newspapers, magazines, and advertisements associated with Avenida was "popularity," which I examine in this chapter as a vernacular concept for grasping what Benedict Anderson calls "unbound seriality" in the public spaces of the metropolis. Using Edgardo M. Reyes's award-winning novel *Sa Mga Kuko ng Liwanag* [In the Claws of Neon] serialized in the Tagalog-language *Liwayway* magazine in 1967–68, I analyze the spectatorial experience of neon as sensorial profusion in the urban environment. Less scholarly attention has been paid to the original novel, as opposed to Lino Brocka's seminal 1975 film adaptation. Referring to Nick Joaquin's journalistic writings, which eloquently document the urban and political cultures of the time, I uncover the configuration of modernity during this historical period as vigorous transformation, which was discernible in representations of the restless energy of Filipino youth in newspapers and advertisements. Last, I explore how the perception of widespread crime and violence at the corrupted heart of Manila drove middle-class families to relocate to the suburban outskirts of the congested metropolis, where new supermarkets afforded residents the freedom of consumerism while containing the dynamism of their movement.

The Logic of Downtown

By the 1960s, Rizal Avenue had attained significance in the public culture as "Downtown," the spatial and symbolic heart of the metropolis. Crowds regularly thronged the main commercial street, which had become the favored destination among the majority for affordable products and movies. The Avenida drew multitudes of young students because of the number of higher educational institutions, such as University of Santo Tomas, San Beda College, University of the East, and Far Eastern University, in the U-Belt or University Belt area.[3] Connoting a concentration of mass activity, the term "downtown" commonly referred to a popular public space where large multitudes of people from the different cities and municipalities of Greater Manila regularly descended and congregated. From serving as a prestigious enclosure for ascending the established hierarchy, as it had in prior historical periods, the main commercial street now functioned as a bustling hub for immersing in popular activity during a period of exponential growth in the urban population that overwhelmed its existing facilities and infrastructures.

Avenida Rizal was formed in 1911 from the merging of Calle Salcedo with Calle Dulumbayan, whose name is a Tagalog word meaning "town's end." Rizal Avenue had a more expansive area than Calle Escolta, whose compact, enclosed spatial configuration was suited to the main commercial street's earlier significance as a source of exclusive and inaccessible luxury goods. Through the decades, new physical structures for business and entertainment, such as the four-story Kneedler Building on the corner of Avenida and Carriedo, would be erected on different sections of its span. At the time of its completion in 1912, the Kneedler Building was the city's tallest edifice.

Prominent public buildings included the 1901 Manila Grand Opera House, which hosted important political and cultural events like the inaugural Philippine National Assembly, and the 1917 Olympic Stadium, which showcased popular sporting and entertainment events such as Saturday evening boxing matches.[4] These large-scale spectacles regularly drew crowds of people to the area, which contributed to its lingering popularity in the public culture as a destination for mass consumption and spectatorship.

In the years following the Pacific War, the heart of Manila shifted from Calle Escolta to Rizal Avenue as the anatomy of the population changed. The destruction of Manila from the competing U.S. and Japanese forces at the conclusion of the war forced the families who resided in its core to relocate to the suburbs while the city was being rebuilt.[5] The departure of these longtime residents coincided with an influx of migrants from across the archipelago. Tens of thousands of Filipinos began settling in Manila immediately after the Pacific War because it served as the center for the distribution of relief goods to war survivors and refugees. The devastation to farmland and livestock from the war deprived families of important agricultural resources that they had depended on for their livelihood. The mass internal migration of Filipinos to the city continued over the next decade with the escalation of the Hukbalahap rebellion in Central Luzon.[6] Driven by the scarcity of resources and opportunities in their locations, they were allured by the potent image of Manila as a Promised Land that was said to deliver its inhabitants from poverty.

By the 1960s, Avenida had become a synecdoche of Manila. In the print and audiovisual cultures of newspapers, films, and novels, it gained renown as the spatial and symbolic heart of the metropolis, where Filipinos who journeyed from different parts of the archipelago were first acquainted with the sobering realities of urban life.[7] With numerous bodies continuously alighting from trains in nearby Tutuban and buses in adjacent Quiapo, the area unfolded as a restless terrain of transit and arrival. Popularized as "Downtown," Avenida epitomized the collective imaginary of Manila as a city of ambulant workers and internal migrants that accommodated all Filipinos seeking better opportunities.

Manila's imaginary in the public culture as a destination for internal migrants was captured in Edgardo M. Reyes's novel *Sa Mga Kuko ng Liwanag* [In the Claws of Neon], which was serialized in the Tagalog-language *Liwayway* magazine in 1967–68. *Sa Mga Kuko ng Liwanag* narrates the alienated urban experience of Julio Madiaga, a transplant from a rural fishing village, who desperately searches for his lover in Manila in the wake of her disappearance, unaware that she has been forced into prostitution. Divided into short, fragmentary chapters, each prefaced by a poetic prologue, this work of social realism pictures 1960s Manila as a bustling, neon-lit metropolis marked by an immense, relentless swell of humanity. Contrasting it to the idyllic innocence of the remote countryside, the novel discloses the overwhelming corruption of the inner city, which had driven longtime residents to seek refuge in the suburban periphery. The narrative's various episodes illustrate how the protagonist, a construction worker, must survive by submitting and adjusting his body, which is accustomed to the languid pace of everyday life in his fishing village, to the dehumanizing labor of building infrastructure that would enable the 'take-off' of the national economy. Using the metaphor of neon to critique the blinding promise of the metropolis, *Sa Mga Kuko ng Liwanag* unveils the complex tension between fact and fantasy through its jarring juxtaposition of realism and poetry.

Unbound Seriality and Popularity

Although Rizal Avenue stretches five kilometers to Caloocan, it was the popular shopping district from Carriedo Street to Claro M. Recto Avenue that became synonymous with the name "Avenida." This section of Rizal Avenue formed a straightforward path across a labyrinth of shorter and narrower roads and alleyways dating to Spanish colonial rule. Between Carriedo and Recto, four winding streets—Bustos, Ronquillo, Raon, and Soler—intersected with Rizal Avenue, containing the surplus from the profusion of activity that spilled over from the main thoroughfare.

Avenida was renowned for its multiplicity of affordable goods that could be found in the shelves and bins of its stores at cheaper prices than in those of the Escolta. Even if Manila's center of commercial exchange and consumption had shifted to Rizal Avenue, Escolta Street continued to retain its prominence as an exclusive source for luxury items because of the banks and boutiques located there. On Rizal Avenue, many of the stores that carried affordable goods were called emporiums, which were less regimented and more informal versions of department stores. According to writer Sylvia Mayuga's personal recollections, the opposite sides of the boulevard were divided between emporiums for casual clothing, beauty products, costume jewelry, and leather shoes and those for home furniture, household appliances, sporting equipment, and electrical supplies.[8] A wider range of products and services was available in the different streets perpendicular to Rizal Avenue. If people could find metal tools and spare parts on Soler, they could have lighters repaired and stamps manufactured on Ronquillo. Although home to printing houses, dental clinics, and billiard halls, Raon permeated the popular imaginary as a site where phonograph records, record players, transistor radios, and musical instruments could be tested and purchased. In the public culture, Raon was called Manila's noisiest street because of the dissonance of radio and stereo speakers blaring at full volume that competed with the cacophony of cars, buses, and jeepneys rumbling, honking, and screeching at the same time to form the distinct ambient soundscape of the metropolis.[9]

Reyes's serial novel *Sa Mga Kuko ng Liwanag* describes the multiplicity of sites of commercial exchange and mass consumption in Avenida as a sensorial profusion that overwhelms the built environment and social life of the city: *"Tindahan ng libro, tindahan ng libro, restawran, tindahan ng libro, restawran, panaderya, patahian, restawran, restawran, restawran, sinehan, otel, restawran, restawran, tindahan ng sapatos, restawran. Nangingibabaw sa lungsod ang pangangailangan ng sikmura."*[10] Alternately repeating the words "store" and "restaurant" in a series within the same sentence, the reiteration and variation of common typologies of consumer space create a picture of abundance and endlessness. Writing about the modern formation of political communities in Southeast Asia, Benedict Anderson uses the concept of "unbound seriality" to refer to a pluralistic, seemingly endless series of bodies or objects in concurrent coexistence and activity.[11] According to Anderson, the imagination of simultaneously participating in the same series creates the impression of belonging to a shared commonality. Itself comprising fragmentary episodes within the frame of a serial novel, *Sa Mga Kuko ng Liwanag* depicts the simultaneity of bodies and objects in the metropolis as a seemingly virtual infinitude that immerses residents in their accumulative spectacular experience.

With its urban surroundings defined by this sensorial profusion, Avenida is visualized in *Sa Mga Kuko ng Liwanag* through the abundance and variety of bodies that constitute the anonymous crowds of the bustling metropolis: "*Sa magaspang na mukha ng mga bangketa, sumayad-umangat ang laksang sapatos. Butangero. Doktor. Kirida. Propesor. Barbero. Pilay. Magnanakaw. Pari. Tomboy. Burikak. Pulubi. Bugaw. Ditektib. Milyonaryo. Mangkukulam. Lahat, lahat sila'y narito sa bangketa. Sa bangketa'y umaagos ang lahat ng uri ng kaluluwa.*"[12] With staccato language pointing to a succession and accumulation of images of prototypical figures of urban residents akin to a cinematic montage, this extract captures the seemingly infinite, relentless flow of bodies of diverse crowds on the sidewalks, which struggle to contain its immensity. One of the characteristics of unbound seriality that Anderson highlights is the paradoxical duality of elements in a series in which each element is immersed in a series while being singular.[13] If the first set of lines enumerates and reiterates the city's various public spaces with commas to evoke their virtual infinitude, the second set of sentences designates and distinguishes its diverse social identities with periods to emphasize their autonomous exceptionality. Presented at the tragic conclusion of the novel, this rendering of the urban environment of 1960s Manila submerges the seemingly singular narrative of the protagonist in the anonymity and endlessness of the metropolis, whose rhythms continue to unfold after his death, indifferent to his experience of oppression and anguish.

Metaphors of Restless Mobility

Visualizing the unbound seriality of popular activity through an image of the simultaneity of restless, mobile, overflowing feet on the sidewalks of the metropolis, the same extract highlights how the collective imaginary of 1960s Manila was captivated by the proliferation of shoe stores and brands. In the 1960s, Rizal Avenue and Carriedo Street were both lined with shops and emporiums that carried an abundance of shoes with a variety of shapes, colors, and designs. On Rizal Avenue, the commercial spaces that specialized in the sale of shoes included Madison Shoe Craft, Shoeworld, Douglas Shoe Store, Cuylin Shoe Store, Sportman's Shoe Store, and Princeton Shoe Store, some of which were located near movie theaters. Previously renowned for its booksellers, the adjacent Carriedo Street was called the "the poor man's Escolta" in the print culture for its many shops and emporiums with affordable footwear—most notably Henry Sy's Shoe Mart, the precursor of SM Supermalls. Numerous names of shoe brands and styles, such as Gerwin, Gregg, Taylor, Edwardson, Marvel, McDowell, Orchids, Alex, Atlas, Bantex, Chancellor, Camara, Craftsman, Spartan, Playboy, Playmate, Plymouth, Jayson's, Jayson's custom-built Challenger, and Jayson's custom-built Viscount, suffused the media ecology of advertisements and billboards. Advertisements and billboards for shoes marketed their products as being comfortable, enjoyable, and durable. The relative success of the local shoe industry during this historical period was understood to be a triumph of Filipino economic nationalism, an idea with much currency as a governmental policy that regulated the influx of imported goods and nurtured the growth of local businesses.

The proliferation and popularity of shoes in 1960s Manila corresponded with the qualities of mobility and transcendence characteristic of the time. The popularity of shoes in the public culture derived from their being among the first new possessions that migrants to Manila would acquire on their arrival.[14] Writer Jose Lacaba highlights how the multitudes of migrants from other parts of the archipelago would purchase them as a replacement for their outworn *bakya*, the wooden sandals that they had worn as a fact of everyday life in the rural provinces they had been forced to abandon.[15] In contrast to the *bakya*, which were commonly deemed a shameful sign of poverty and underdevelopment, shoes were embraced as a modern means of perseverance and prosperity. Enhancing their users' physical, spatial, economic, and social movement through the metropolis, durable shoes signified their transcendence of the bare materiality of everyday life.

Transcending bare functionality, objects as ordinary as shoes were invested with values of mobility and modernity. Their availability and affordability reflected the democratic tendency of the period. Because anyone could acquire them for individual use, everyone could participate in the new form of modernity they represented. In contrast to 1930s Manila, modernity no longer implied the exclusivity of hygiene and comfort but the affordability of vitality and endurance, qualities that enabled bodies, structures, and objects to cope with the hectic, unrelenting character of 1960s Manila. Illustrated by the seemingly infinite number of advertisements and billboards that used modernity as a selling point to appeal to the mass of consumers, shoes could be seen as a metaphor for a time of restless energy and vigorous movement, which was exemplified by the transgression of outworn boundaries and the espousal of newfound rights.

As evident in this example, 1960s Manila was characterized by the growing currency of the word "popular," which referred to anything that a large majority was said to appreciate, favor, and consume. Visible in features and advertisements in the print and visual cultures of the time, the term "popularity" found its fullest significance in a period in which the reach of the media had spread across the archipelago while the majority of the population had concentrated in the city. From the standpoint of government and business, the epistemological category of "popular" allowed for groups of citizens and consumers within the larger, anonymous mass to be distinguished from each other. But the popular likewise suggested an accumulation of interest, usage, and approval that was not completely governable akin to unbound seriality.

According to Lacaba's 1970 *Philippines Free Press* essay "Notes on '*Bakya*,'" the crudely popular was called "*bakya*," a term that had metamorphosed from an ordinary noun into a pejorative adjective. *Bakya* originally denoted a plain physical object for everyday use. Through a shift in meaning, the word came to refer to any reality that was cheap, shoddy, uncouth, and provincial.[16] Cultural objects that were labeled "*bakya*" included local merchandise, ungrammatical English, and Tagalog cinema. Attracting a large market, they were believed to possess the capacity to generate exponential profit. Regardless of their social value, the quality of profitability now extended to products that a large majority would be capable of acquiring. Businesses attempted to tap into this unpredictable, uncountable force of popularity but without being able to fully domesticate or control it.

Instead of resting entirely on a predetermined business strategy, the proliferation of shoe stores, brands, and styles revealed the growing influence of mass consumer demand. Because the values of products were fashioned from common impressions, these values could easily and unpredictably change depending on public sentiment. Even supposedly stylish or sophisticated practices that had been embraced by the multitudes could suddenly acquire the label of "*bakya*."[17] In binding together the disparate individuals who participated in the collective activity of appreciating, favoring, or consuming the same object of interest, the force of popularity provided the basis for a more coherent form of affiliation. In the case of 1960s Manila, however, "popularity" rested on the threshold of community. It implied a tenuous commonality that could quickly dissipate without having left a more indelible or lasting solidarity.

Articulated in the public culture of 1960s Manila, popularity could be understood as a state of ordinariness that attained transcendence through its desirable commonality, the participation of a multitude in an achievable, shared activity. While based on the accessibility of what is popular, this shared practice should be seen as being more than a simple act of conformity. Anderson contrasts the popular commonality of "unbound seriality" with the regimented system of "bound seriality," which he associates with the governmentality of the state. According to Anderson, governmental institutions depend on the certainty of bound seriality through mechanisms such as national registers and censuses to enumerate, classify, and delineate in statistical terms the strict demographics of its population to manage it with greater efficacy.[18] Contrasted with the systematic order of bound seriality, the virtual infinitude of popular commonality could be seen to exceed the limits of established authority by being open to encompassing every possible reality.

Neon Spectacle and Virtual Infinitude

During this historical period, crowds of urban residents regularly descended on "downtown," drawn by the popularity of the Hollywood and Tagalog films that were exhibited at the stylish movie theaters in Avenida. The theaters were designed by prominent local architects like Juan Nakpil and Pablo Antonio, whose monumental architecture was characterized by striking rectangular shapes, angular corners, and rectilinear striations. Contributing to the spectatorial experience of the urban environment, the visual infinitude of neon red, blue, and yellow signs that extended from their façades and rooftops suffused the area with their radiance.

In 1964 alone, Manila's movie theaters accounted for 36.5 million admissions.[19] Among the theaters that drew the largest crowds of people was the Ideal, an Art Deco monument that had stood at the intersection of Rizal Avenue and Carriedo Street since 1933. During the 1960s, the distinctive polygonal structures of the State and Ever were situated across from the Life, Dalisay, and Avenue theaters in between Carriedo and Raon streets.

FIGURE 10. Neon from the signs of theaters, emporiums, and advertisements suffused Avenida with their spectatorial experience of virtual infinitude.

The Odeon sat at the northeast corner of the junction of Rizal Avenue with Claro M. Recto Avenue, the newly renamed Calle Azcárraga, where prominent structures such as Tutuban Station, Bilibid Prison, Far Eastern University, and the Roman Super Cinerama were arrayed. Occupying a few blocks north of the Manila Grand Opera, the Scala Theater could be found on the side of Avenida facing west. Located at the farthest end of Rizal Avenue, the Apolo and Noli, like the Life and Dalisay, were known for screening popular Tagalog movies.

The radiant lights from Avenida's polychromatic multiplicity of neon signs, advertising billboards, and theater marquees generated an exuberant atmosphere that was likened in newspapers and magazines to that of New York City's Broadway. Writing about early technological modernity in the metropolis, Nye explains how the allure of the electric cityscape of New York City derived from the profusion of such spectacles in the early twentieth century: "The vibrant landscape was the product of uncoordinated individual decisions, yet it had a collective effect—a kinetic impact—that no one had anticipated. Taken together, the myriad lights produced a lively landscape with strong popular appeal."[20] A 1960 newspaper feature in the *Singapore Free Press* explained that the "blaze" of neon lights in Singapore and Hong Kong distinguished their cityscapes by creating a "festive atmosphere" whose "eye-catching" "colour" and "brightness" attracted crowds.[21] Due to the abundance and variety of innovative spectacles arrayed in the commercial street, individual attractions combined to transform the entire commercial street into a spectacular experience. At the limits of cognitive absorption through visual apprehension, this reverberating radiance was first experienced as an enthralling sensory overload, a modern form of the sublime that surpassed the capacity of dominant modes of perception to comprehend.[22]

Driven by ideals of air-conditioned, sanitary modernity, the Singapore government under the People's Action Party considered these technological innovations to be unmanageable threats to public order and social life. Determining the terms of visibility of the urban environment, its Ministry of National Development prohibited neon lights from the walls of public structures, residential estates, and commercial buildings in 1972.[23] As the state failed to comment about the rationale behind the ban, gossip reported in newspapers and spread through coffee shops surmised that it regarded neon as disruptive to the mobility and safety of land and air transportation because of the dangers of distraction from cognitive absorption in its spectacle.

In *Sa Mga Kuko ng Liwanag*, neon is pictured as the expansive radiance of polychromatic lights in Avenida that engulfs all reality: "*Dilat na ang mga neon light. Pula, asul, dilaw at mga kulay sa pagitan. Maningning ang lunsod, makulay ang lunsod. Kung ang daigdig ay isang malaking lunsod, walang gubat at walang dagat at walang disyerto, ang buwan pati ng mga bituin ay maaari nang magpatiwakal.*"[24] Reyes's conception of neon in 1960s Manila in *Sa Mga Kuko ng Liwanag* highlights how the spectatorial experience of neon lights in the main commercial street transpires as a sensorial profusion that immerses the field of vision with its seemingly endless presence. Echoing Reyes's conception of neon, Debord's seminal 1967 text *The Society of the Spectacle* famously opens with a similar provocative assertion, "The whole life of those societies in which modern conditions of production prevail presents itself as an immense accumulation of spectacles."[25] Arranged haphazardly throughout the commercial street, the accumulation of spectacles from the lights, vehicles, signs, marquees, and billboards in the urban environment constituted a luminous yet nebular spectacular experience that suffused the entirety of their immediate surroundings. Their ubiquitous visibility enthralled the restless and hurried pedestrians, who were unable to devote their full attention to cognitive absorption in the bustling, congested metropolis. Through the visual apprehension of their abundance and variety, a small constellation of spectacles encountered in succession unfolded as a spectatorial experience of virtual infinitude.

Accommodating its growing population, the teeming movie theaters of 1960s Manila were inclusive public spaces of mass consumption akin to Singapore's amusement parks. Unlike the theaters of 1930s Manila, which had served as exclusive sites for enhancing social prestige, these popular venues allowed large crowds of urban residents to congregate and interact. Before the Pacific War, a majority of Manila's population would visit the cinema only twice or thrice a year. This leisure activity had been a luxury reserved for special occasions such as birthdays or anniversaries, in which people would dress in their best clothes as if they were attending a formal evening gala.[26] Once an exceptional event, it became an ordinary pastime for Filipinos, who routinely watched movies in the evenings or on the weekends during their time away from work.

No longer simply attracted by luxury goods to visit the commercial street, people were enticed by the popular spectacles of movie theaters, narratives, and stars, which resonated with the virtual infinitude of neon. Downtown's most popular cinemas were often packed with the bodies of spectators. Whenever all the seats inside the venue had been occupied, the box office that guarded its entrance would post the sign "S.R.O.," or "Standing Room Only."[27] Swathed in the anonymity of a darkened room, amid the swirls of thick cigarette smoke and the noises of restive chewing mouths, the people in the audience surrendered to the alluring images of an alternate world that flickered to life on the giant screen before them. Akin to the consumers of the commodities in Avenida Rizal, these spectators entered the movie house with the assumption that the film narrative was a mass product that adhered to a prescribed template. Part of their pleasure in being entertained came from the fulfillment of their expectations. Marked by participation in an amorphous mass, the anonymity of the darkened theater was a site where the imagined seriality of popularity could be conceived. Because it obscured the magnitude of the crowd gathered inside, it allowed spectators to envisage an infinite series of bodies simultaneously performing the same activity. Through this imagined seriality, individuals could attain the transcendence of having exceeded the given necessity of everyday life without renouncing the mundaneness of their membership in a crowd.

In its critique of 1960s modern consumer society, Debord's *Society of the Spectacle* perceives the spectacle as alienating individuals from their lived experiences, social relations, and productive capacities. Frequenting the teeming commercial street, the alienated urban inhabitants described in Reyes's *Sa Mga Kuko ng Liwanag* found themselves regularly immersed in the physical immediacy and sensorial profusion of the metropolis. Whereas Debord visualized a world of abstraction where no form of collectivity or community was possible, occupying Avenida Rizal meant participating in the shared experience of popular activity. Subsumed under the mundane rhythm of everyday life in 1960s Manila's city center, where the majority of the population concentrated, spectatorial experience was not exceptional but more ordinary in character. The tendency toward atomization was diminished because of the popularity of collective immersion in this milieu. If any degree of atomization occurred, it was more the result of the hectic character of the commercial street, which kept crowds amorphous as individuals pursued disparate trajectories and temporalities. These crowds tended not to cohere into a tight social body, having been brought together by the increased value of popularity, whose configuration lay on the threshold of community.

Delinquent Modernity and Restless Youth

The virtual infinitude of popularity as being open to every possible reality permeated the sense of restless energy and vigorous transformation of the historical period. In a provocative assessment of the "Seething '60s" in the *Philippines Free Press*, Nick Joaquin pictured the Philippines in the middle of the decade as a society in transition. With emphatic language, he described the revolution that was inexorably unfolding: "We cling to the static society, where today is just like yesterday and tomorrow will be just like today. And we are so fearful and furious today because that society has exploded from under our feet; we are up in the air; and nothing will ever be fixed again."[28] With growing skepticism about the capacity of dominant frameworks to deal with prevailing circumstances, Filipinos were learning how to approach reality with "fresh eyes," with new modes of perception braced by a forceful assurance that longstanding norms and routines no longer offered any certainty.

While local newspapers and magazines such as the *Manila Times*, *Manila Chronicle*, *Philippines Graphic*, and *Philippines Free Press* painted a macroscopic picture of the burgeoning air-conditioned modernity of the Philippines being in a "pre-take-off" stage, they portrayed the nation as being mired in the inescapable seriality of crime, violence, poverty, and congestion. Made visible through their articulation in the print culture, the epistemological delineation of impunity and exclusivity illustrated how the benefits of the Philippines' postwar economic growth were restricted to members of the elite in a seemingly "static" and insurmountable established order. News reportage disclosed the entrenched corruption, in the form of smuggling, bribery, swindling, racketeering, illegal logging, and influence peddling, that impeded the effective operation of political and social institutions. Based on the crime statistics of the National Bureau of Investigation, a sexual offense occurred every two hours, while a murder was committed every hour.[29] In a piece published on Philippine Independence Day at the halfway point of the decade, Joaquin lamented, "We glance at the state and say that, politically, we are a failed society. We study the prices and say that, economically, we are a bankrupt society. We peruse the crime figures and say that, spiritually, we are a violent society. We devour the latest scandals and say that, morally, we are a sick society."[30] Anthologized in *Reportage on Crime*, Joaquin's news features from the 1960s dramatized and spectacularized the narratives behind murders, confrontations, and criminals that resonated with the propensity for violence of the time.

The official report of the Presidential Peace and Order Council under the Marcos administration blamed the worsening crime rate on the leniency given to criminals belonging to the social and economic elite. According to sensationalist representations of their exclusive lifestyles in newspapers and magazines, members of the elite appeared to believe that they owned rights to possibilities that were withheld from the rest of the population. Because not every citizen was prosecuted and punished for violating the law, people acted as though they could disregard its norms with impunity.[31] Describing this delinquency, Joaquin's 1961 *Philippines Free Press* feature "The Boy Who Became Society" explores the impunity of members of the elite as the freedom to act without fearing the consequences of their deeds because one's wealth and standing protect one from penalty.[32] The article focuses on the rise to notoriety of a young criminal delinquent named Boy Nap who moved from poverty to exclusivity with the "apparent ability . . . to come and go as he pleases."[33] Joaquin referred to this "audacity" as "nerve": "the nerve to crash a party you were especially excluded from; the nerve to stand up in class and insult the teacher; the nerve to go into a swanky restaurant and do the one-two-three there, that is, walk out, one after the other, without paying the bill." Described as "living beyond all his means—financial, physical, and emotional,"[34] "nerve" involved the transcendence by their autonomous capacities of the "static" bounds of the supposedly "failed" established order.

Stuart Hall writes about how media representations of widespread crime and violence generated the impression that the established order was insurmountable by defining the limits of what people could expect from the government in the improvement of their living and working conditions.[35] In 1960s Manila, however, the prevailing atmosphere of restless energy in the public culture disclosed the potential for upheaval. For Ranajit Guha, the increased frequency of illegal activity evinces the burgeoning energy in the population to resist the established order.[36] This "nerve" or impunity, in which individuals were free to perform acts of violence without fear of penalty from the law, restrained the economic opportunities for national development while expanding the epistemological possibilities of personal action. Refusing the coherence of the official discourse of development, media representations of impunity heightened the consciousness among urban residents that they themselves could act spontaneously and purposefully without fearing the consequences.

In the print and visual cultures of the time, modern life signified youthful dynamism, restless activity, and vigorous transformation. Reverberating with the dominant tendency of the milieu, the trope of youthfulness permeated the collective imaginary. Two-thirds of the Philippine population during this period were aged twenty-four and below.[37] Half of Manila's residents were younger than seventeen.[38] Local newspapers, novels, advertisements, and movies consistently depicted the Filipino youth as being dynamic individuals who restlessly needed to expend their surplus energy.

In 1960s Manila, print advertisements suggested an ideal lifestyle that reflected the configuration of modernity in this milieu. Aiming to capitalize on the latest trends, advertisements tried to tap into its popularity by characterizing their products as modern. Instead of relying on striking descriptors to generate appeal, they emphasized the capacity of commercial products for immanent transformation. The advertisement for Life Buoy soap presented it as a daily necessity for "active, modern people" with its "new, vigorous" composition. Accompanied by a caption that described the product as having a "new perfume, new germicide, new shape, new color, [and] new pack," the picture in the advertisement was divided into three frames that showed young individuals engaged in different youthful activities like sports and dancing, with gestures and poses evoking tireless movement. The series of three different images highlighted the quality of dynamism, whose "vigorous" character needed to be captured through a succession of similar yet varied depictions.

This advertisement for Life Buoy from the 1960s contrasted with the advertisement for Ivory soap from the 1930s, which had depicted the product as a sacred object whose magical power bestowed cleanness and well-being on its consumer. Whereas happiness had been understood in the 1930s to be translatable into reality only through transcendent intervention, it was apprehended in the 1960s as something that people could generate with their own capacities if they engaged in dynamic activity. The series of 7-Up advertisements that appeared in local periodicals proclaimed the soda to be a vital prerequisite for engaging in any form of activity: "Whew! Jerking's real action and gets you all warmed up. Have 7-Up! It's got the sparkle that swings. . . . The taste that's fresh and frisky. . . . The all-out quenching power to make thirst quit. Dance time . . . anytime . . . get 7-Up!" With language that conveyed the speed and exuberance of the historical moment, individuals were characterized as being restless with constant motion, for which the drink supplied nourishment and vigor. Every space in the cityscape was pictured as bearing the transformative potential to become a site of activity, to be seized spontaneously at any instant for the purpose of releasing restive energy.

Joaquin defined youth as a disposition that blurred the boundaries between imagination and reality.[39] Enthusiastic about future possibilities, the youth fervidly produced countless ideas for transforming the established order. Whereas modernity in the 1930s became tentatively experienced as a sweeping, uncontrollable force embodied in the infrastructure, architecture, and technology of the time, modernity in the 1960s was something that people assuredly believed they themselves could actualize through their own rights, passions, and capacities. For Joaquin, young urban residents were endowed with the restless energy to give these ideas a material presence in the world. Being anxious and tentative, however, they helplessly and impatiently floundered without the necessary know-how to fulfill their aspirations over a long period. Diverging from the official trajectory and temporality of linear development, the delinquent, fugitive modernity of youth defined by "nerve" forced the established order to become unsettled.

The prevalence of the delinquent, fugitive modernity of youth corresponded with the proliferation of changing modes of sociality. No longer confined to the dominant sites of residence, work, commerce, and leisure, they represented the extension of the public sphere to the neon-lit streets of the metropolis. In local periodicals, the restless and energetic activity of ordinary young people was characterized as being necessarily social and collective. Participation in all types of groups, including gangs, bands, unions, parties, and crowds, defined their identity as youth.[40] Young people liked to spend their leisure time away from school or work by idling with their *barkada*, an exclusive coterie of bosom friends. Dissatisfied with the norms of the established order, the youth held their *barkada* in greater esteem than their family.[41] Their popularity intimated a nascent form of community that extended beyond family and friendship toward an amorphous yet inclusive commonality.

The proliferation of changing modes of sociality indicated a growing restiveness among the multitudes of Filipinos. An article from a local periodical about Manila's impoverished city center vividly described the characteristic disposition of the anxious youth in relation to the dominant hierarchy by performing seemingly petty illicit acts like drunkenness, pilferage, gambling, and vagrancy in defiance of social and legal norms. Its language underscored the inevitability of upheaval, which Nick Joaquin ardently anticipated. In a sequence of pieces published over the decade, Joaquin describes the shift

of Filipino youth over the 1960s from delinquency, based on "excess energy,"[42] to rock and roll, to activism. Young Filipinos who desired change
in the social landscape challenged the terms of the established order with a
recalcitrant stance that emulated that of the popular movie stars of the moment. Departing from the enclosures of their classrooms, homes, or offices,
they began to occupy public spaces such as streets and plazas that were situated beyond their normal routine, and that they now used not for transit or
leisure but for dissent and protest.[43] Instead of their fugitive quality being
devalued and banished to the outside of the domain, the inclusive commonality of this collective delinquency became constitutive of the transformative
potential of the metropolis for revolutionary upheaval, which threatened to
overturn the established order.

The anxiety and tentativeness of the moment was captured in representations of the youth, who highlighted the constant opposition and oscillation between normative states of idleness and vitality. One article about the
musicians of combos or bands who awaited employment on Raon Street
portrayed them as dawdling on the sidewalks while being "idle."[44] According
to the language of the public culture, to be idle was to be a nonproductive
member of society like the "*kanto boys*" and "*istambays*," shiftless, indigent
men who spent their time "standing by" the "corners" of neighborhood *sari-
sari* stores.[45] Refusing the model of the dynamic public figures that strived
to build the nation, idlers insouciantly waited for opportunities to arrive
instead of actively seeking them. Bereft of any sense of urgency to adhere
to prescribed norms, they embraced a discordant experience of time that
diverged from the routine trajectory of schoolwork and employment.

The tentative boundary that separates idleness from vitality is recurrently
associated in the public culture of the time with the ambivalence and tenuousness of popular commonality. In his scintillating, evocative account of the
civil unrest of 1960s Manila, Jose Lacaba describes a protest rally comprised
of the youth on the inaugural day of the legislative season: "And suddenly,
what had earlier seemed a most sluggish, spineless, easygoing, disorganized
assortment of oddniks was galvanized into a cohesive force, about a thousand strong, that rose as one."[46] Investing his language with a breathless
succession of adjectives so as to approximate the excitement of the moment,
Lacaba stages the historic event as a battle between government forces and
young citizens. He deploys the contrast between idleness and vitality to dem-

onstrate how the moral exigency for the upheaval of the established order can immanently refashion seemingly idle bodies into a dynamic collective.

The Ambivalent Democracy of Self-Service Consumerism

The explosion of youthful energy on the streets of the teeming metropolis coincided with the emergence of self-service commercial spaces in its out-skirts. In Manila's weekend lifestyle magazines *Philippine Panorama*, *Sunday Chronicle Magazine*, and *Sunday Times Magazine*, news about politics would be juxtaposed with features and advertisements about its newest supermar-kets. During the 1960s, segments of the population started relocating from the congested, crime-ridden city center to its exterior, where they settled in recently developed residential areas sprawled across the outskirts of Greater Manila. The first supermarkets in the post-war United States had grown in popularity as a result of a similar mass migration to the suburbs.[47] Flourish-ing suburban municipalities such as Makati and Mandaluyong were first to experience the opening of supermarkets, which were "modernized" versions of the local corner *sari-sari* stores that anticipated the future prosperity of the Philippine nation according to the promise of its "pre-take-off" stage.

Satisfying the primary function of grocery and corner stores to provide basic supplies, the supermarket adopted the sanitary order of the department store but without its elite comfort and prestige. Promoting the principle of self-service shopping among urban residents through the seriality of their merchandise, supermarkets were defined by both the standardization of their mass goods and the utilitarianism of their streamlined spaces.[48] Capsules in the *Singapore Free Press* highlighted the perception of supermarkets as being "orderly" and "efficient," as opposed to the "happy confusion" of groceries,[49] which evoked the exuberant atmosphere of the *pasar malam*. Discussing the "quiet revolution" in the "habits" of commercial exchange and mass con-sumption of younger generations, S. R. Parker, the general manager of the newly refurbished Cold Storage on Orchard Road in 1960s Singapore, ex-plained the "advantages" of the supermarket: its "convenience" of gathering a "variety" of international refrigerated goods at a reasonable "price" under the "comfort" of a single, air-conditioned enclosure.[50] As paradoxical sites of freedom and enclosure, supermarkets reconfigured the complex relationship between consumers and products in containing the tendencies toward dynamism and collectivity that typified the historical period.

Featured in the print culture of magazines and advertisements, the most notable supermarkets included Cherry Grocery Store and Tropical Hut Food Market, which were established in the emerging suburban outskirts of Mandaluyong and Quezon City. Amid the bustle and congestion of 1960s Manila, these streamlined commercial spaces supplied the pleasurable experience of a clean, orderly, and air-conditioned enclosure for a quick duration. They were described in magazine articles and advertisements as "sensational" because their commercial infrastructures and technologies of counters and freezers were "spotless" and "immaculate."[51] Opening at the Makati Commercial Center in December 1963, in time for the lucrative Christmas season, Makati Supermart drew shoppers from all over the metropolis who were enticed by its unique selection of imported food, which constituted the majority of its sales. Extending over 15,000 square feet of retail space, this supermarket was situated in the burgeoning business district of Makati, which was heralded as supplanting Escolta and Rosario streets as the financial hub of the Philippines. Approximately two-thirds of its sales came from food products such as sardines from Spain, pears from Japan, apples from Australia, red wine from Italy, and smoked herring from Sweden. For the brief duration they inhabited this rarified enclosure, residents were liberated from the mundane routine of everyday life and the relentless tumult of the urban environment. Furnishing an experience of comfortable luxury without social mobility, the air-conditioned modernity of 1960s Manila's supermarkets offered a glimpse of an alternate future of democratic, cosmopolitan prosperity.

Improving the visual order of products and eliminating the physical presence of salesclerks, the supermarket aimed for the minimal expenditure of time, labor, and money.[52] In contrast to the neon profusion of retail emporiums in Avenida Rizal, this confined enclosure emphasized pristine whiteness. Diverging from the baroque ornamentation that distinguished the exterior of the movie theater and the interior of the department store, the design of the supermarket was functional and streamlined in keeping with its purpose as a venue where customers did not casually linger for long hours but speedily obtained basic supplies. By organizing items on open shelves, the supermarket limited its mediation of the interactions between consumers and products, which could obstruct the process of shopping, by affording individuals the capacity to choose purchases without assistance or supervision.[53] Designed for high turnover through speed and efficiency, supermarkets emphasized independent choice[54] in which customers were encouraged to move freely but within the enclosure of the supermarket.[55] In refashioning commercial space, the self-service supermarket strove not only for a high turnover of products but also for a high turnover of bodies, which accommodated and facilitated the movement of restless shoppers, who were otherwise busy with the rhythms of everyday life in a busy, expanding metropolis.[56]

Supplanting the creativity of bargaining, the practice of self-service shopping in the modernized corner store afforded consumers the semblance of responsibility when the multitude during the current period were demanding the democratic right to express their autonomous desires. While reducing the operating costs for hiring salesclerks, this architectural typology compelled shoppers to supply their own labor for selecting and carrying goods to be purchased.[57] Simultaneously affirming and exploiting their newfound initiative, the spacious topography of supermarkets allowed the dynamic urban residents of the time to expend their restless energy while meandering throughout its domain. As two integral components of its commercial infrastructure, the supermarket's pristine whiteness and bright illumination enabled customers to scan the seemingly unbounded seriality of products being displayed on the gondolas with greater facility and speed. Without the intervention of salesclerks, supermarkets suggested possible purchases by strategically arranging their merchandise. Impulse products with higher profit yield were more prominently displayed.[58] According to local newspapers, because specific types of goods would be evocatively positioned next to each other, individuals bursting with restless vitality could be tempted into spontaneously buying items they had not originally been interested in.[59]

Away from the overwhelming congestion and neon of "Downtown," the sanitary, air-conditioned modernity of supermarkets presented for urban residents an alternate experience of necessity, derived from the indispensable value of basic goods but shorn of any trace of the arduous labor that originally produced them and the disordered space that traditionally distributed them. The incorporation of supermarkets into the routine of everyday life on the growing fringes of 1960s Manila coincided with changing conditions in the metropolis, such as the increase of the population, the expansion of the city, and the ascendancy of cinema. Self-service shopping became configured as a democratic and urbane activity that permitted the youthful, dynamic consumers of the milieu to exercise their rights to freedom and movement. By propagating the norms of personal self-determination while immersing them in the virtual infinitude of consumerism, these newly established domains of commercial exchange cleansed the popular commonality of public spaces of their potential for revolution.

CHAPTER 6

Public Spheres of Postcolonial Fantasy

Whereas capitalist modernity and mass consumption in 1960s Singapore were characterized by informal, itinerant markets sprawled across the urban periphery, their vernacular configurations and experiences in 1960s Manila were typified by retail emporiums and movie theaters concentrated in the city center. The spatial and social landscapes of Singapore and Manila during this historical period were perceived to be marked by the seeming entrenchment of poverty and congestion, which demanded ambitious master plans from their governments for urban renewal and national progress. If Singaporeans resigned themselves to the inevitability of the relentless trajectory of industrialization implemented by the ruling People's Action Party, Filipinos were faced with uncertainty about the failure of the discourse of development, in which the promise of economic nationalism was beset by endemic issues of corruption, inequality, and crime. Such affinities and disparities in the urban environments and media ecologies of 1960s Singapore and Manila reveal the contingency and anxiety surrounding the transitions and transformations in the regimes of production and sovereignty, which were articulated in the public culture of the time.

The commercial and leisure spaces that epitomized this historical moment were teeming streets and bazaars distinguished by their immense popularity. The residents of Singapore and Manila spent their leisure time outside the work regime in crowded movie theaters surrounded by hawker stalls and coffee shops, where they would congregate to socialize and gossip before and after screenings. Produced in the heyday of the Philippine and Malayan film industries, the most popular works of the period visualized its characteristic tendencies of restless mobility and imminent transformation. Through their hybrid structure and antagonistic stance, their audiovisual narratives negotiated the normative boundaries between fact and fiction by proposing alternate imaginaries of modernity, self-determination, and community, which were vibrantly discussed in the public spheres of coffee shops.

This chapter examines the understudied work of P. Ramlee and Joseph "Erap" Estrada set in 1960s Singapore and Manila. While enormously popular during their heyday, the films of Ramlee and Estrada have received less critical attention because they are commonly regarded as commercially oriented products designed to appeal to mass audiences. A mayor and senator known for his pro-poor, nationalist record, Joseph Estrada attained notoriety for being ousted from the democratically elected presidency in 2001 after allegations of corruption and incompetence. But he first gained prominence from his cinematic persona in urban noir films, where he starred as a coarse yet compassionate solitary delinquent from an impoverished community in the metropolis who rebels against the established order. On the other hand, the versatile actor, director, and musician P. Ramlee obtained success from his melodramas, comedies, and fantasies that, visualizing the languid timelessness of the rural village in the *kampong* where his characters originated, dwelt on the tension between tradition and modernity. In postcolonial Singapore and Malaysia, Ramlee became an ambivalent public figure as his multicultural, cosmopolitan background failed to conform to the discourses of development of the ruling People's Action Party, or PAP, and United Malays National Organization, or UMNO.[1]

The chapter opens by describing the spatial and social landscapes of 1960s Singapore and Manila, which, dominated by movie theaters, were permeated by cinematic imaginaries about metamorphosis and rebellion. Looking at P. Ramlee's early 1960s comedy fantasies, which playfully explored shifting identities, I analyze their visualization of the *kampong* or rural village, which was condemned by the ruling People's Action Party for its supposed languor, disorder, and backwardness. I contrastingly examine how fugitive delinquency in the urban noir films of star Joseph Estrada during the mid-1960s negotiated the paradoxical duality of mundaneness and exceptionality, which offered models of mimicry for youthful politicians such as Manila Mayor Antonio Villegas striving to transcend the established order of squalor and underdevelopment for the sake of national progress. The chapter concludes by exploring the subversiveness of gossip in the public spheres of coffee shops, where urban residents exchanged and debated speculative visions and blueprints for self-determination and democracy from political speeches and commercial movies while waiting for imminent change to arrive.

Cinematic Landscapes

The spatial and social landscapes of Southeast Asian cities during this historical period were permeated by cinematic fantasies that shaped how urban residents visualized the entrenchment of present conditions and the prospect of future realities. Because film spectatorship was a popular activity for mass entertainment in 1960s Singapore and Manila, the immediate surroundings of movie theaters became defined by their sensorial profusion and inclusive commonality. The busy commercial areas of Rizal Avenue and Orchard Road, where most theaters were located, were illuminated by the virtual infinitude of neon from shop signs and advertising billboards. Contrary to the dominant conception of docile, solitary spectatorship, the bustle and exuberance of moviegoing crowds spilled over to the nearby sites of mass consumption and leisure where diverse people would gather before and after screenings.

Despite their immense popularity, the 1960s were marked by the abrupt decline of the Philippine and Malayan movie industries, which had flourished in the preceding decade. Established by wealthy families in 1937 and 1938, the two major Philippine studios Sampaguita and LVN flourished under matriarchs Azucena "Mama Nene" Vera-Perez and Narcisa "Doña Sisang" de Leon. Whereas their rival Premiere Productions focused on award-winning action movies starring Efren Reyes (*Ifugao* [1954], *Paltik* [1955], and *Kalibre .45* [1957]) and Fernando Poe Jr. (*Pepeng Kaliwete* [1958], *Laban sa Lahat* [1958], and *Pitong Gatang* [1959]), LVN and Sampaguita Pictures specialized in popular melodramas and comedies with mestizo "love teams" such as Rogelio de la Rosa and Carmen Rosales (*Camelia* [1949], *Maalala Mo Kaya?* [1954]), and *Ang Tangi kong Pag-Ibig* [1955]), Gloria Romero and Luis Gonzales (*Despatsadora* [1955], *Vacacionista* [1956], and *Lupa sa Lupa* [1960), Nestor de Villa and Nida Blanca (*Waray-Waray* [1954], *Talusaling* [1955], and *Tingnan Natin* [1957]). Run by diasporic Chinese businessmen, the Shaw Brothers and Cathay Organization had respectively opened studios in Singapore and Hong Kong right before and after the Pacific War to cater to Southeast Asian markets speaking Cantonese, Mandarin, and Malay.[2] Their local subsidiaries Malay Film Productions and Cathay-Keris Studios, formed in 1947 and 1953, found success from period fantasies adapted from Malay, Persian, and Arab classical epics such as *Hang Tuah* (1956), *Musang Berjanggut* (1959), *Ali Baba Bujang Lapok* (1960), and *Hang Jebat* (1961) and monster series drawn from Southeast Asian folklore including *Pontianak* (1957), *Orang Minyak* (1958), and their many sequels. Not only did they produce their own films, they dubbed and distributed imports from the Philippines, Egypt, and India,[3] which all had thriving movie industries at the time.

Because of fierce competition, these studios capitalized on each other's successful stylistic and promotional innovations. Critically and commercially more successful than Cathay-Keris because of its star P. Ramlee, Malay Film Productions released nearly one hundred pictures from 1952 to 1967. By the middle of the 1960s, two hundred Tagalog movies would be produced locally each year, which, amounting to 40 percent of all theater screenings, made it the fourth-largest such industry in the world.[4] By the end of the 1960s, however, the revenue of these studios had declined, with LVN, Malay Film Productions, and Cathay-Keris closing down in 1961, 1969, and 1973 due to a confluence of factors including the emerging media technology of television and intensifying geopolitical tension in the subregion, but supposedly also because of operational disruptions caused by labor strikes.[5] The waning of their dominance had freed the market for smaller independent companies driven by actor-producers such as Fernando Poe Jr.'s FPJ Productions and Joseph Estrada's JE/Emar Productions,[6] which increased the number of local productions while impacting their scale and inventiveness.

Singapore's biggest movie theaters were part of larger complexes that, reminiscent of the nine amusement parks owned across Southeast Asia by the

Shaw Brothers,[7] included restaurants and boutiques. Shaw Brothers and Cathay Organization derived a significant portion of their earnings from their regional distribution circuits, which included the Capitol Theatre, Cathay Cinema, and Lido Theatre, located on different segments of Orchard Road, a burgeoning commercial street in Singapore at the time. As these grand theaters were reserved for English-language Hollywood movies, their local Malay-language productions would usually be presented at the Rex in Little India and the Ocean, Garrick/Galaxy, and Odeon in Katong, on the outskirts of the city. During the 1950s and 1960s, Sampaguita, LVN, and Premiere would showcase their Tagalog films in the more central Life and Dalisay theaters on Rizal Avenue. Avenida's Ideal, Ever, Avenue, Odeon, and State Theaters respectively screened Hollywood movies by MGM, 20th Century Fox, Warner Bros., United Artists, and Columbia Pictures. Film exhibition during this period was based on the block-booking system in which studios would consign theaters to their productions, regardless of whether they drew an audience or turned a profit.[8] It was Manila mayor Antonio Villegas's inaugural Manila Film Festival in 1966 that undid Hollywood's monopoly over distribution by featuring Tagalog movies in the metropolis's premier theaters.[9]

Memoirs from urban residents describe how they would gather in coffee shops to gossip about the private affairs of movie stars and other public figures. Manila's vibrant coffee shops were located within a short walk and commute of its theaters in Avenida. Situated behind the Capitol Theatre, on the side facing away from Stamford Road, Saint Gregory's Lane was described to be an exuberant public space where spectators consumed food from the assortment of hawker stalls before and after screenings.[10] As visualized in representations of coffee shops in the print and audiovisual cultures of the period, they would speculate about the feasibility or futility of visions and blueprints for personal and national development, which were permeated by fantasies about metamorphosis and transcendence from popular cinema.

Fantasies of Self-Determination and Metamorphosis

As the landscapes of 1960s Manila and Singapore were marked by bustling streets and crowds, film studios produced and circulated audiovisual representations that pictured their restless energy and mobility. Whereas their urban environments were dominated by the presence of movie theaters, such cinematographic iconographies shaped the perception and practice of occupying them. Undoing the seeming entrenchment of the established order, their fantasies negotiated the sense of imminent change characteristic of the historical moment by exploring the boundaries between fact and fiction and imagination and possibility.

With the lines "*Singapura maju jaya . . . Zaman pun berabah sudah . . . ,*" the concluding song of *Labu dan Labi* (1962), "*Singapura Waktu Malam*" [Singapore at Night], encapsulates the pervading sense of imminent change in early 1960s Singapore.[11] Aspiring for a more affluent life beyond their financial scarcity, the protagonists of P. Ramlee's films set in Singapore aim to harness for themselves this transformative potential. Shot on location at the Shaw Brothers' Jalan Ampas studios off Balestier Road in Singapore, *Labu dan Labi* and *Seniman Bujang Lapok* (1961) both open with a panoramic establishing shot of Singapore's dynamic spatial environment in which the restless movement of vehicular transportation across the city visualizes the inevitability of rapid progress during the transitory *merdeka* period of national independence. Looking at unemployed men aspiring for a better livelihood as amateur movie actors, *Seniman Bujang Lapok* depicts a mobile film production crew truck navigating the streets of Singapore with images of significant monuments to colonial history and cultural entertainment like the Raffles Statue, Victoria Hall, and Lido Theatre before arriving at their remote *kampong* or rural village. Exploring the fantasies of social mobility of two household workers for a wealthy man, *Labu dan Labi* juxtaposes Singapore's bustling streets with popular sites of mass consumption and religious worship, such as the Capitol Theatre on Orchard Road, the Golden Mosque in Kampong Glam, and a coffee shop on Middle Road. Defined by the oscillation between traditional and modern public spaces, these representations of the urban setting, in their legibility, provide a backdrop to the gradual metamorphoses in identity that its protagonists undergo through the course of the narrative as they aspire for their own personal development and transcendence to resonate with the economic and material progress occurring around them.

Distinguished by his multiethnic background, P. Ramlee worked in a multicultural environment for creative labor. A descendant of Acehnese migrants from the Netherlands East Indies, Ramlee was born in the Straits Set-tlement of Penang, where he performed as a composer and musician in local club bands, influenced by the samba, rhumba, and Latin music popular in British Malaya, before being discovered in a talent contest by Shaw Broth-ers studios.[12] His commercial hits were shot in Singapore, which, during this historical period, was the intellectual, political, religious, and cultural hub of the Malay world.[13] Financed by the ethnically Chinese Shaw Broth-ers' Malay Film Productions and directed by filmmakers from India and the Philippines, these works featured adaptations of Arabic, Malay, and Persian folktales, which were influenced by Japanese and Indian cinema.[14] While under pressure from Malay nationalists to address economic and social is-sues concerning the Malay population, Ramlee's films adroitly negotiated the expectations of its diverse Chinese, Indian, and Indonesian audiences.[15] Exhibiting the cosmopolitan multiplicity of mass entertainment in a diverse port city, they bore the democratic, malleable quality of the *bangsawan*, whose pluralistic integration of different national languages, theater styles, and musical instruments offered a venue to experiment with new modes of identity and community.[16]

Ramlee's films were praised by local newspapers for their award-winning, innovative "versatility."[17] Many of the actors in those films began as *bang-sawan* performers. In her seminal study, Tan Sooi Beng describes the *bang-sawan* as a hybrid genre that diverged from the conventionality and ritu-alism of traditional Malay theater by flexibly combining the diverse styles and influences in the cosmopolitan port cities where it was staged.[18] Touring British Malaya, Siam, Burma, and the Netherlands East Indies, *bangsawan* troupes were skilled and versatile in alternately performing Hindustani or Arabic fairy tales, Shakespearean tragedies, and Chinese romances,[19] into which they incorporated clowns, pantomimes, acrobats, jugglers, and even boxers, depending on the location and audience.[20] Its Chinese, Malay, Euro-pean, and Eurasian performers represented the multiracial and multilinguis-tic character of the Straits Settlements.[21] Its spectators belonged not only to different ethnicities, but to different classes and professions with royals, offi-cials, traders, clerks, teachers, laborers, and dockworkers seated next to each other in the audience.[22] The versatility of *bangsawan* actors was epitomized by their adroitness at making adjustments to their identity and body that would be attuned to the varied, pluralistic conditions of their performance.

The sense of imminent change in 1960s Singapore is inscribed in the malleable, hybrid structure of P. Ramlee's works, which trace the pluralistic aspirations of their diverse spectators. During this period, the biggest hits were from Cathay-Keris Studio's Malay-language monster series, which, targeted to audiences from Singapore, Malaysia, and Indonesia, featured the metamorphoses of supernatural creatures from Southeast Asian folklore such as the *pontianak* and *orang minyak*. With multiple productions and sequels, these fantastical narratives could be seen to encapsulate the tendency of the period toward transformation. Looking at the prevalence of tropes of metamorphosis in anime during Japan's period of industrialization, Susan Napier explains how they could be understood to signify anxieties about shifting identities amid rapid development.[23]

Produced during a historical moment of transition, *Seniman Bujang Lapok* and *Labu dan Labi* likewise explore the capacities of the body to undergo self-fashioning and modification in response to imminent change.[24] These comedic fantasies focus on characters belonging to the working class who, finding intermittent jobs as chauffeurs and entertainers, aspire for improved living conditions. Hired for contractual creative labor as movie actors, the three unemployed protagonists of *Seniman Bujang Lapok* must learn the unfamiliar language of cinema as a burgeoning form of mass entertainment in adjusting their anatomy and speech to its modern norms. Episodic and hybrid in structure, *Labu dan Labi* features multiple metamorphoses that its destitute characters undergo through a succession of humorous dream sequences patterned after different popular movie genres[25] and culminates in one protagonist's transformation into a wealthy businessperson. Like the comic book character Kenkoy, the exaggerated physicality of the actors' performances could be seen to enable them to accommodate the abrupt, dynamic forces of material progress acting on their bodies and surroundings.

Each transition to a new dream sequence in *Labu dan Labi* is punctuated by the reverberating bell of the Victoria Memorial Hall's clocktower, which signals the metamorphosis of the characters in a different narrative and setting. Accommodating the pluralistic, alternate identities the characters assume across the film's multiple dream sequences, this episodic, hybrid structure reverses the established hierarchy. The first dream sequence transpires in a nightclub, where the protagonists Labi and Labu adopt the guise of wealthy professionals with affected British accents, while their abusive, real-life employer Haji Bakhil is reinvented as a service worker. Referencing popular Hollywood genres, the subsequent episodes reimagine the characters as cowboys and adventurers, with their employer denigrated to the role of a comic foil whom they maltreat and ridicule in a form of moral justice. Built on a series of episodes, its *Labu dan Labi* suggests how personal and collective development may occur over incremental stages before reaching an apex of affluence and prestige. Unlike Kenkoy, who struggles to harness the possibilities of modernity with awkwardness and embarrassment, Labi and Labu submit themselves to an effortless succession of changes to their physical bodies and social relations. Visualizing an insurmountable, entrenched hierarchy against which its protagonists are counterposed by their ambivalent stance, these individuals are depicted as successfully acquiring material wealth and social standing less by striving for their vigorous self-determination than by waiting for an accidental miracle.

Sanitary Modernity and Urban Informality

P. Ramlee's works *Seniman Bujang Lapok* and *Labu dan Labi*, set in 1960s Singapore, contrast its busy public spaces in the center with its sprawling rural villages on the outskirts. Writing about literary representations of urban renewal in *Tiger Economies*, Jini Kim Watson explains how official discourses of development in postcolonial Asian cities are typically visualized through fantasies of cleared informal settlements and rising building complexes.[26] This spatial iconography evident in P. Ramlee's urban settings appears to echo the People's Action Party's blueprint of sanitary, air-conditioned modernity during this historical period, which required transcending the tradition and squalor of the *kampong* or rural village for the sake of rapid linear progress.

During the *merdeka* period of transition to independence from Britain and Malaysia in 1959 and 1965, the ruling People's Action Party sought to refashion and subordinate all the realities within its new national territory to the temporality of industrial productivity and national development. Striving to realize its vision of economic growth and urban renewal, the Singapore government implemented a succession of short-term master plans that subjected the spatial and social landscape to incremental interventions and adjustments. Assuming the form of protest bans, housing schemes, and health codes, each pragmatic intervention aimed to further the linear, upward advancement of progress by adjusting the bodies within its territory to its relentless trajectory.

In public speeches by its ministers, the People's Action Party blamed the British colonial regime for its failure to address the problem of congestion, in which hundreds of residents continued to dwell in dim, airless shophouses and sprawling rural villages. The Straits Settlement's housing shortage had worsened after the Pacific War because of increasing birth and migration rates.[27] Upon being granted autonomy, the government under the People's Action Party established the Housing Development Board in 1960 to address the one-third of a million of the population residing in informal settlements with the goal of introducing sanitary, air-conditioned modernity to the spatial and social landscape.[28] Writing about urban informality in Southeast Asian cities during the 1960s, Aprodicio Laquian observed that Singapore resembled Manila, which was similarly plagued by inadequate infrastructure for habitation, as its national government was without a sustained program of mass housing. By the early 1960s, one-fifth of Manila's population resided in what were called *barong-barong*,[29] comprised of improvised shanties that their residents had resourcefully cobbled together from discarded cardboard, wood, and metal salvaged from old automobiles and construction sites. Built next to seas and rivers with packed structures, makeshift weights, and deficient drains, these informal settlements were highly vulnerable to fire and flood. In his social history about the clearing of informal settlements in 1960s Singapore, Loh Kah Seng suggests that the implementation of sanitary, air-conditioned modernity was driven by fears of fire and catastrophe,[30] which demanded the refashioning of the local milieu based on the anticipation of its inevitable destruction.

The official report of the United Nations on informal housing from this period concluded that their conditions of overcrowding, poverty, squalor, and degeneration were detrimental to the well-being and morality of their residents,[31] resulting in delinquency and crime. To transform its disorderly, congested cityscape for the sake of national development, the Singapore government enacted the Land Acquisition Act of 1966, which permitted it to repossess private land for the purpose of public utility in exchange for monetary compensation.[32] The law granted the state the authority to suspend property rights by designating spaces it deemed filthy, unruly, or backward for refurbishment or demolition in the building of vital infrastructures for transportation and habitation.

In Ramlee's movies set in 1960s Singapore, the panorama of the city-states' dynamic urban environment is contrasted with the backdrop of its remote rural outskirts, which the Singapore government designated as requiring refurbishment or demolition. Intermittently employed with enough material wealth for their daily subsistence, the protagonists of *Seniman Bujang Lapok* and *Ibu Mertua Ku* (1962) reside in *kampongs* or rural villages, whose audiovisual representations are characterized by their languor and scarcity. Echoing the spatial iconography of these films, archival photos from the period visualize how village houses were organically sprawling across rugged dirt paths that diverged from the paved main avenue while shaded by the tangled branches of unpruned trees. Fostering social interaction among its residents, the seemingly haphazard configuration and slower temporality of the *kampong* was said to allow for the formation of emotional attachments and communal bonds among its neighbors. In *Seniman Bujang Lapok*, the characters dwell in a dormitory-like longhouse without adequate facilities for sanitation where the three companions share the same small room with thin, wooden walls that allow them to overhear disruptive music and noise from their neighbor. Illustrating the languid rhythms of everyday life in the *kampong*, the film comically depicts the communal activity of residents queuing for a prolonged duration while waiting to wash and bathe at outdoor toilets and public standpipes, which supplied water and sanitation to the village, before undertaking their long commute to work. In contrast to the brisk pace of the scenes set in the studio, where its protagonists are contracted as fledgling actors, those that transpire in the *kampong* feature stretches of cinematic time in which the three companions experience collective idleness. Contrasting it with the amorality and alienation from commercial capitalism in the modern city, Ramlee's narratives reveal how the rural village ordinarily featured multiple opportunities for conversation, gossip, and conviviality.

Joel Kahn highlights how the *kampong* was celebrated by Malay nationalists such as Mohamed Eunos bin Abdullah as a source of tradition and identity for self-determination.[33] Regarding it as a source of disorder and unrest, however, the People's Action Party put forth its official discourse aimed to reorient the population away from ethnic and religious identification as a

FIGURE 11. The iconography of the *kampong* in P. Ramlee's films resonated in public images of its languor, conviviality, and timelessness. (Photo from National Archives of Singapore)

basis for agency and community by portraying the *kampong* as a threat. This vocabulary echoed how popular *pontianak* monster movies, according to Rosalind Galt, would typically be situated in a *kampong*, whose setting was characterized by its timelessness.[34] The Singapore government disseminated public images of the *kampong* that equated its rural squalor with the languor of collective idleness and economic stagnation. In the speeches of PAP ministers, the *kampong* was recurrently characterized with a cluster of negative meanings, which included connotative words such as "traditional," "primeval," "obscurantist," "backward," and "irrational."

In a 1960s speech underscoring the urgency of industrialization and modernization, Minister of Finance Goh Keng Swee asserted that the local population must learn to transcend its outworn customs, which failed to adhere to the temporality of development: "In the traditional villages, people live very much as they did over the past thousands of years. They grow food for themselves, and the little extra they have, they sell or barter for the things that they need. They believe in the ancient gods, in evil spirits and practice the most benighted superstitions which had been handed down to them over the ages."[35] According to the speech, the "benighted" norms of the *kampong* frustrated the linear trajectory of economic growth and urban renewal when they caused its residents to become caught in the uncertainty of cyclical time. Rural villagers were criticized for clinging closely to the languid comfort of traditional culture such that they were less open to changes associated with air-conditioned, sanitary modernity, which would supposedly lead to progress in the form of centralized government, scientific advancement, industrial progress, and social order.

While the representation of the *kampong* in P. Ramlee's films emphasized values of tradition and conviviality, it ambivalently appeared to echo how the People's Action Party regarded it as a threat because it signified a rural, communal space of idleness and waiting, which deviated from its linear trajectory of sanitary modernity and industrial productivity. With flexible work arrangements, Ramlee's characters are depicted as taking on jobs only for the purposes of their immediate, daily subsistence. In *Seniman Bujang Lapok*, for example, the three protagonists spend their leisure time in a *kopitiam* or coffee shop, where they fantasize about transcending the established order by becoming movie stars, which could possibly deliver to them material wealth. *Seniman Bujang Lapok*'s opening song "Menceceh Bujang Lapok" satirically mocks the stingy, listless companions who commute to work by riding a single bike together for being *"semacam beruk taka da kerja tolak habuk."*[36] Dispossessed of the stability and certainty of regular employment, rural villagers are comically portrayed with an image of unproductiveness and inertia.

Popular movies in 1960s Manila such as those of Fernando Poe Jr.'s Westerns pictured rural spaces as an idyllic remote landscape that remains inert and stagnant because of an established order of crime and oppression. In this provincial countryside, the everyday life of rural villagers is subjected to the arbitrary violence of landlords and their bandits. While such audiovisual narratives characterized the established order of 1960s Manila as being insurmountable, the public culture of 1960s Singapore emphasized how the People's Action Party possessed the political will to overcome seemingly entrenched conditions of congestion, poverty, and squalor.

Eulogizing the People's Action Party's trajectory of national development after it had successfully implemented many changes to the spatial and social landscape in 1977, Eurasian Singaporean writer and teacher Edwin Thumboo, in his poem "Catering to the People," described the past historical period as "delinquent days."[37] The persona in the poem appears to associate delinquency with the "anger" and violence of 1950s and 1960s youthful activism, which needed to be "level[ed]" and conquered with "little choice" for the sake of the economy and nation. From the standpoint of the Singapore government, the languor of the rural village equated to a mode of delinquency, which, considered to be unproductive and illicit, deviated from its robust trajectory of rapid, linear progress. Encapsulated by the collective imaginary of the *kampong*, the delinquent form of modernity in 1960s Singapore, in fact, meant waiting for the contingency of employment while relying on conviviality for solace. Refusing the terms of sanitary, air-conditioned modernity of pragmatic governmentality, which state discourse extolled as crucial for transcending the established order of tradition and poverty, delinquent modernity was marked by the embrace of a slower, more languid, more ambivalent pace amid the uncertainty of the future.

The Paradoxical Duality of Movie Stardom

Incarnating the restless transformative potential of the historical moment, the most popular movie stars of 1960s Singapore and Manila offered models of mimicry for urban residents to exceed the necessity of everyday life in a bustling, congested metropolis by assuming an ambivalent stance toward the established order. Negotiating the boundaries between imagination and possibility, their cinematic personas were defined by impoverished protagonists with intermittent employment who challenged the dominant norms of self-fashioning and transcendence in their fictional narratives and public activities. Whereas the convivial protagonists of P. Ramlee awkwardly straddled tradition and modernity with their pluralistic identities, the solitary antiheroes of Joseph Estrada assertively embodied the anomie and disquiet of youth.

While criticized by writers like Nick Joaquin for being commercially oriented, most of the hits of stars Fernando Poe Jr. and Joseph Estrada were rural Western and urban noir narratives that could be said to negotiate the conventions of their genres and settings. Their cinematic personas assumed the form of enigmatic outsiders who, newly arrived in a town, transcended their solitude to confront gangs that terrorized impoverished, ordinary people who were helpless to protect themselves. Issuing from the failure of national development and entrenchment of the established order, the prevailing tensions between marginalized and elite were disclosed through their contrasting backdrops of the teeming city and remote countryside during this historical period. Marked by the recurrent victimization and persecution of the poor, these social conflicts were depicted as potentially erupting into violence.

From 1961 to 1969, Joseph Estrada appeared in nearly a hundred films, many of which he produced. Born the eighth of ten children to a middle-class family in Tondo, Estrada was expelled for disorderly conduct from the exclusive Jesuit-run Ateneo de Manila University, the alma mater of Philippine national hero José Rizal. Forbidden by his mother from using their surname in show business, Estrada built his career around a cinematic persona of being uneducated, coarse, and destitute. Acclaimed for his dramatic performances, Joseph Estrada earned one of his four Best Actor awards from the Filipino Academy of Movie Arts and Sciences, or FAMAS, during the 1960s for his iconic work *Geron Busabos, Ang Batang Quiapo* (1964). Leveraging his movie stardom, he unsuccessfully ran for mayor of his hometown, the suburb of San Juan, in 1967, before finally winning an electoral protest two years later. Starting out in villain roles, his real-life exploits would frequently appear in newspapers and magazines because of his propensity for carousing and violence.

In his most iconic works *Geron Busabos* and *Asiong Salonga* (1961), Joseph Estrada played young social misfits whose outlook and behavior were roughened by their experience of urban poverty. Marketed as "true-to-life" stories, Estrada's 1960s noirish films were usually set in a busy, crime-ridden metropolis that evoked the Manila of the period. *Gerun Busabos* visualizes the sensorial profusion of Manila's spatial environment by opening with establishing shots of crowds spilling over the sidewalks while an omniscient voiceover emphasizes its economic and material progress. With transient employment as a *kargador*, or stevedore, who transports goods for a local market, his cinematic persona is described by the voiceover as epitomizing the harshness and complexity of the prosaic conditions of marginalization and squalor.

As exemplified by Estrada's cinematic persona, the popularity of movie stardom in 1960s Manila rested on a stance of defiance against the entrenched norms of hierarchy and advancement. *Asiong Salonga* and *Geron Busabos*, for instance, highlight the antagonistic confrontation with the established order that straddles its dominant dichotomies of legality and morality. Characterized in the film as being uneducated and illiterate because of his uncouth and impetuous actions, Estrada's persona, Gerun Busabos, is motivated by a strong, instinctive sense of justice to protect the underprivileged and helpless even if it may conflict with the arbitrary enforcement of the law by the police. Opening with Estrada's eponymous protagonist embroiled in a violent fistfight before barreling through the crowds to run away from the police, *Gerun Busabos* highlights the tenuous relationship with the law that defines his fugitive delinquency. Featuring rumors about its eponymous protagonist clandestinely traveling from town to town while eluding the law, *Asiong Salonga* dwells on the subversive mobility of his mythic persona, which is constructed by gossip about his delinquency and criminality.

The default assumption is that movie stars, being mass commodities of the culture industry, validate the established order, yet the movie stars of 1960s Manila both reproduced and contravened its terms.[38] Rick Altman explains how the commercially oriented conventions of popular films unsettle established values when they feature protagonists who transgress dominant norms.[39] As their narratives unfold, according to Altman, the collective pleasure that audiences derive from their spectorial experience of these cultural transgressions intensifies.[40] As inscribed in the print and audiovisual cultures of 1960s Manila, the cinematic persona of Estrada refused the terms of the established order, which had perpetuated the marginalization and oppression of the poor. If Ramlee's protagonists aspire for a trajectory of personal achievement and affluence in which they would overcome their poverty, Estrada's antiheroes define their sense of dignity and morality according to their antagonistic stance against the dominant hierarchy but without effacing their quotidian roots. Transgressing the normative expectation that the youth defer to authority, these solitary outsiders withdraw from the everyday routine of idleness and delinquency to obtain a subversive form of justice, which, having no place under prevailing conditions, their mass of spectators likewise desired.

In the 1960s, Nick Joaquin would write portraits of public figures of common interest such as Joseph Estrada, Ferdinand Marcos, and Antonio Villegas. Published in the *Philippines Free Press* under his pseudonym "Quijano de Manila," Joaquin's news features "The Boy Who Became Society" and "Gun Duel at LVN" describe impoverished youth who encounter a miraculous opportunity that allows them to transcend the entrenchment of the dominant hierarchy for a sudden attainment of popularity akin to these mythic personas. In these writings, delinquency is defined as a "striving . . . for an upper place in the sun."[41] Constrained from improving on their living and work conditions through the agency of vigorous self-determination, poor individuals must rely on their visible association with movie stardom. Equating it with the fugitive mode of modernity characteristic of the historical moment, these texts explore the striving of marginalized individuals with impoverished, everyday origins to realize a trajectory of personal development beyond their given conditions of scarcity and squalor.

Narrating the tragedy of an aspiring actor who stumbles into a dangerous relationship with Joseph Erap Estrada while striving to emulate him, Joaquin's "Gun Duel at LVN" explores the fragile boundary between fact and fiction. In this extract, Joaquin explores how, for the movie star, "there may have been no clear distinction . . . between his violent screen image and his actual self, or between the world where one shot it out with fake fire and the world where bullets burn."[42] Equally relying on both fact and gossip, these journalistic portraits reveal how the mythic personas of movie stars in 1960s Manila rested on the admixture of their onscreen adventures with their real-life experiences. Whereas their cinematic narratives focused on their quotidian poverty as outsiders, news features elaborated on the violent spectacle of their everyday life.

In contrast to the value of social prestige, which rests on the suppression or banishment of the undesirable appearance of mundaneness for ascending the established hierarchy, the popular allure of Estrada derived from the public image of their impoverished, quotidian roots. Notable for his roughened, pugilistic look, Estrada differed from the most prominent movie stars of Sampaguita and LVN Pictures during the 1950s—actors such as Rogelio de la Rosa, Gloria Romero, and Nida Blanca—who, with their light-skinned, Spanish and American mestizo/a features, were distinguished by their transcendent glamor. Exemplifying archetypical characters who were poor and simple but fought to protect the marginalized according to their own intractable sense of justice, their cinematic personas bore a mythic, transcendent quality that manifested their quotidian roots in their appearance, behavior, and identity. While ultimately beyond reach, this paradoxical duality of mundaneness and exceptionality inspired among their avid spectators and fans an emotional affinity for them.

Public Figures of Youthful Dynamism

Defined by the imminence of change, contrasting fantasies of development were articulated through public figures such as actors and politicians. Distinguished by the possibilities for transformation that they incarnated in their public personas, nationalist politicians were depicted in the print and audiovisual cultures of 1960s Manila as movie stars whose spectacles captivated the multitudes of Filipinos. Embodying the dominant tendencies of the historical period, the most prominent politicians were youthful, spontaneous, and energetic. Photos in local periodicals recurrently captured them in an array of vigorous poses, chatting, gesticulating, and orating with different lively expressions etched on their faces. Presented as models for mimicry, these public figures fashioned themselves as active builders of the infrastructure of the nation who appeared to be able to translate political vision into the spatial and social landscape. Informed by the aesthetics of cinema, the montage of varied stances and movements visible in news magazines and print advertisements highlighted how photography strove to exceed the limits of its medium in documenting the restless mobility characteristic of the historical moment. In these media representations, they were recognized as being restlessly dynamic, a quality that had become equated with the capacity for imminent transformation.

According to Joaquin, nationalist leaders during Philippine Commonwealth president Manuel Quezon's time before the Pacific War had been considered demigods whose unique talent and upbringing bestowed on them the quality and right to govern.[43] This impression had corresponded to the perception of modern forces during the 1930s as being governable only by transcendent figures. Filipino politicians during the 1960s vied to be identified with the youth, an important segment of the electorate such as

governor and senator Benigno Aquino Jr., Ferdinand Marcos's main political rival who, later imprisoned and assassinated in the wake of martial law,
enthralled the public with the movie stardom of his youthful dynamism.

This characteristic of youthful dynamism was evident in the young politicians who ran postcolonial Singapore in the 1960s. When the People's Action Party assumed control of the government in 1959, Minister of Finance
Goh Keng Swee was forty, Minister of Culture S. Rajaratnam was forty-
three, Deputy Prime Minister Toh Chin Chye was thirty-seven, and Prime
Minister Lee Kuan Yew was thirty-five. But they disavowed the charisma of
movie stardom for a tenacious emphasis on a political platform of visionary
ideas and concrete actions that would deliver rapid development to a fledgling nation.

In 1960s Manila, the public personas of nationalist politicians differed
from those of movie stars in that their policies and actions reinforced the
established order by proposing adjustments, but without overturning its hierarchies. Belonging to the two rival parties that dominated at the time, the
two Philippine presidents during the 1960s incorporated aspects of political reform and social transformation, for which pundits and activists were
clamoring, into their government programs. Appropriating connotative
terms like "democratic revolution," the Liberal Party's Diosdado Macapagal
planned to remake Philippine society through his New Era programs, which
would implement his reformist policies on neoliberal capitalism by shifting
away from economic nationalism. Presenting a narrative of himself as an
individual who had broken from the cycle of poverty and underdevelopment, he envisioned the nation as reproducing his own personal trajectory of
development from destitution to success. His successor, Ferdinand Marcos
of the Nacionalista Party, campaigned for the presidency on the promise
of restoring to the nation an image of greatness even while allegations of
corruption in local newspapers hounded him. With the goal of realizing his
slogan for national progress, "Fast-forward the Filipino," Marcos focused
during his first administration on the monumental tasks of providing R & R,
or Roads and Rice, to alleviate poverty and modernize infrastructure. He
fashioned for the public a persona of himself as a vigorous, youthful, and
dynamic leader, with hundreds of pushups that Marcos claimed to perform
regularly for fitness meant to project an ability to harness the productive
energies of the nation. His redeployment of resources and insistence on

decisiveness enabled the state to enlarge its dominion over the archipelago such that the brutal machinery of Martial Law could easily be implemented to advance his own blueprint for development by suppressing dissent. As Filipinos were unable to hold Marcos accountable for his illicit abuse of power, gossip about his adultery, corruption, and violence surfaced and circulated anonymously in the print culture, enabling his position of authority to be questioned and subverted.

Embodying the tenacious dynamism of 1960s Manila, Manila mayor Antonio J. Villegas was a physically imposing figure who was heralded as a future president. Standing six feet tall, he wore a broad, boyish face with the tough jaw of a brawling boxer.[44] Another one of President Magsaysay's youthful, idealistic protégés and adherents, Villegas liked to style himself as a movie star whose valiant feats would bring salvation to a once glorious city now mired in poverty, underdevelopment, and squalor. As he explained, the symbol of his office was a sunburst because "the sun is the source of life, light, and energy."[45] Garbed in his trademark plain red shirt, he would mouth his catchphrase of salutation and triumph: "Yeba!"[46] Articulating his vision of modern Manila, the mayor asserted, "A city progresses on motion, not on stagnation."[47] Echoing the cleanup campaign of the People's Action Party in 1960s Singapore, this program of urban renewal invoked the logic of sanitary, air-conditioned modernity with its ideals of order, health, beauty, and morality by purging the urban environment of its undesirable elements of filth, noise, disease, illegality, and disorder.

Painted by modernist artist Carlos "Botong" Francisco from 1964 to 1968, one of the sections of the mural Mayor Villegas commissioned for the Bulwagang Katipunan in Manila City Hall, *Filipino Struggles through History*, is centered around the insignia of a sunburst with the proud slogan "*Timbulan ng Laya/Diwa ng Dakila*" [Sanctuary of Freedom/Spirit of Greatness] juxtaposed with Villegas's proud, joyous visage. Drawing from folk motifs and nationalist myths, Francisco gained prominence for polychromatic murals that chronicled the profusion of important events and achievements in Philippine culture with sinewy, muscular characters marked by gestures and actions of energy and movement, whose rendering suggested an organic continuity of collective struggle for self-determination. Visualizing momentous triumphs in the *History of Manila*, its alternate title, light from the sunburst suffuses every element in the painting, which envisions material

FIGURE 12. Carlos Francisco's mural for Manila City Hall visualizes material and social progress centered on the youthful dynamism of Mayor Antonio Villegas. (Photo by author)

and social progress through the city government's provision of labor and infrastructure for sanitation, healthcare, and transportation. As the radiance of this sunburst engulfs all activity akin to the virtual infinitude and inclusive commonality of neon in 1960s Avenida, this section of Francisco's sprawling mural subsumes transformative potential under the youthful dynamism of state authority.

As the main proponent of the inaugural Manila Film Festival in 1966, which exhibited local productions in the Escolta and Avenida's exclusive theaters, Villegas tapped into the popular significance of cinematic fantasies as public spectacles of transcendence. Exemplifying movie stardom's paradoxical duality of mundaneness and transcendence, Villegas's public persona celebrated his impoverished, quotidian roots. Having risen from the blighted communities of Tondo at the heart of Manila, Villegas was described in news features as such: "He has daring and determination—afire with ambition, impatient with the humdrum, in a hurry to grow up, always on the lookout for the quickest way to get where he wants to go, never letting any opportunity pass unexploited, always competing with his elders and cashing in on his youth."[48] Impelled by restless passion, his relentless pursuit of activity was propelled by the belief that the trajectory of development could easily become undone. Although Villegas's pursuit of activity echoed the normative trajectory of development in striving to transcend undesirable conditions deemed primitive and retrogressive, several of his public housing projects ended up being left unrealized because of administrative neglect.

Despite his visible achievements as mayor, Villegas's restless drive for development resulted in an array of ineptly designed or executed blueprints to confront the issues of urban poverty and informality, which were reported as gossip about his failures and infelicities in newspapers. Aside from rehabilitating Intramuros as a cultural center, Villegas planned to construct, for P15 million, a five-story residential building in North Harbor with a rooftop garden and a ground-floor supermarket.[49] When his government relocated eighty thousand squatters from Tondo, Intramuros, and North Harbor in 1963, their new residence of Sapang Palay, thirty-seven kilometers from Manila,[50] was discovered to lack adequate facilities for housing, food, water, electricity, medicine, transportation, and employment.[51] Moreover, administrative incompetence caused Manila to suffer from a garbage disposal problem by the middle of the decade, which likewise emphasized the tenuous relationship between imagination and possibility.

The personification of nationalist politicians as figures of revolutionary change dispossessed the multitudes of Filipinos of their own transformative potential. Concentrated in the image of these public figures, political possibilities became restrictive and hierarchical instead of deriving from an inclusive popular commonality. Visionary projects for development initiated to improve the prevailing conditions of poverty and squalor ended up requiring the approval or intervention of larger, hierarchical political structures, which withdrew the responsibility for agency from ordinary people. Wrested from the majority of the population, the capacity for transforming the established order became entrenched in state authority.

Infelicities of Gossip in Coffee Shops

Ambivalent fantasies of development produced and circulated by popular films were consumed in movie theaters and discussed in coffee shops. Projecting alternate imaginaries of transcendence, these narratives intermingled with gossip about public figures such as actors and politicians, creating a symbolic space for the established order to be transformed and overturned. The print and audiovisual cultures of 1960s Singapore and Philippines depicted the coffee shop as a vibrant public space for social life and democratic exchange. While seated around tables drinking coffee and listening to the news, urban residents would congregate to debate their own visions and blueprints for political and societal change, in contradistinction to the government's plans for national development.

The precursors of coffee shops as sites of conversation, gossip, and conviviality emerged under U.S. occupation as the lunch counters and soda fountains of Calle Escolta and Plaza Goiti's Botica Boie, Plaza Lunch, and Tom's Dixie Kitchen, which supplanted the Luneta as a public space where members of the elite gathered to be seen. In 1960s Manila's newspapers and magazines, the coffee shops found on U.N. Avenue and M.H. del Pilar, particularly Taza de Oro, Rolling Pin, and Country Bakeshop, were pictured as sites for the production and circulation of ideas about current political events, economic conditions, and social issues. Photos from news features would highlight the "contagious[ness]" of "coffee shop talk," which would trigger customers and waiters into "animated" conversation.[52]

"Coffee shop talk" in 1960s Manila primarily consisted of *bulung-bulungan*, literally whispers and murmurs in the form of gossip about the truth of prevailing affairs.[53] The assumption was that news media failed to comprehensively represent important details about the practices and interactions of state institutions and public figures, which remained concealed from popular knowledge.[54] In addition to gossip, coffee shop talk consisted of critical and innovative ideas for addressing the urgent problems of the nation. Through the verbal communication and discussion of these ideas, new visions and blueprints were introduced to the public sphere, even if they were not necessarily pursued and implemented. Because periodicals repeatedly described coffee shops in 1960s Manila as sites for the exchange of rumors and ideas, these two collective activities of coffee shop talk could be understood to be complementary in their operation. Both raised to public awareness thoughts and sentiments that were normally kept discreet and private. Reported with the objectivity of news publications, they became invested with greater legitimacy and significance.

Writing about political affairs in the *Philippines Free Press*, Nick Joaquin would cite gossip to construct comprehensive representations of news events and public figures beyond the limits of objective knowledge. Instead of simply describing the exclusive lifestyles of celebrities, gossip centered on the corrupt activities and illicit relations of politicians and actors as well as the incompetent failures of government projects. According to James C. Scott, gossip undermines the dominance of public figures in the established order by affirming unspoken notions about how they fail to comply with accepted norms of propriety and legality.[55] In 1960s Manila's coffee shops, gossip's primary function was to defuse impunity. Fantasizing about the failures and infelicities of prominent members of the elite, gossip divested them of their seemingly unrestricted scope of action. By impugning their position atop the social hierarchy, it permitted the aspirations of ordinary people to become more realizable.

Instead of simply acting as a moralizing instrument in line with Scott's understanding, gossip unfolds as a shared knowledge about the transgression of norms. Contrasted with the facts about public affairs and events conventionally published in newspapers, gossip could be defined as the anonymous circulation of verbalized ideas about private realities whose veracity stays unconfirmed. Bound neither by authorship nor evidence, gossip in 1960s Manila's coffee shop talk hovered in the ambivalent frontier between fact and fiction, in which the imagination of alternate possibilities intervened in the seemingly entrenched conditions of everyday life. Such incorporeality and malleability could be understood to form the source of gossip's subversive, fugitive potency.[56]

Gossip is characterized by its democratic transmissibility, which enables it to spread and thrive beyond the moment of its utterance. Its subversive potency derives from the interest that people have in the truth it propagates.[57] Regardless of financial wealth or social status, any individual has the freedom to participate in the creation and dissemination of these narratives, which often reproduce the sensationalist plotlines of movie spectacles. For instance, narrating the real-life tragedy of a youthful delinquent who becomes embroiled in crime, Joaquin's feature "The Boy Who Became Society" highlights how rumors published, affirmed, and circulated in newspapers can lead to the building and enlargement of a mythic persona. Dramatizing how its protagonist mimicked the impunity of the elite, the article reveals how gossip enabled him to exceed his fixed standing in the social hierarchy. Constituting less as a rational critique that imposed an objective morality, gossip constituted an implicit refusal that envisaged and delineated the fantasy of an alternate trajectory of transcendence.

In addition to serving as venues where gossip spread, coffee shops in 1960s Manila were workshops for fantasies of self-determination, where the seeds of possibilities for upheaval gestated. According to news articles about them, coffee shops furnished a public space for intellectual exchange where alternate democratic futures could be envisaged and legitimated. Amid the discussions and debates about reform and revolution that occurred in these workshops, innovative visions and blueprints were given form and value while being tested against the opinions of peers. Educator Paulo Freire argues in his seminal 1968 book *Pedagogy of the Oppressed* that the potential for change rests on the capacity to reflect on the circumstances and incongruities of the established order.[58] When prevailing conditions are rendered intelligible and communicable as facts, they become objects of knowledge and inquiry that could be acted on.[59] Unconstrained by the necessity of truth yet inclusive in the production of its content, gossip becomes fugitive and dangerous for extending the limits of what can be said and therefore what can be made possible. Seen as a fugitive mode of modernity in 1960s Manila, gossip could be understood to abruptly and uncontrollably emerge from the margins of the public sphere to disrupt the established order's fixity.

In contrast to Habermas's conception of the public sphere that historically thrived in the coffee houses of Western Europe as being founded on the intentionality of reason,[60] the coffee shop served as an alternative institution outside the enclosures of the office and the school, where new identities and networks were imagined and cultivated. In the coffee shops of 1960s Manila, the principal sources of gossip were journalists, businessmen, and politicians, who constituted an elite circle of prestige and influence that regarded itself as the vanguard of the nation.[61] Although networks were formed from shifting connections and combinations of individuals, the regular customers of coffee shops developed close relationships, which, however, excluded other sectors such as students, workers, and employees from their debates and decisions. Curtailing its democratic potential, this exclusivity divested coffee shop talk of its subversive force.

Waiting as Modernity

Akin to 1960s Manila, many urban residents in 1960s Singapore spent their leisure time in a *kopitiam* or coffee shop, one of the centers of social life during this period alongside movie theaters and night markets. Historian

Khairudin Aljunied characterizes the coffee shop as a site of contestation that served as a staging ground for the articulation of economic rights and the exchange of subversive rumors.[62] In contrast to representations of coffee shops as vibrant sites in the print culture of 1960s Manila, however, P. Ramlee's films set in Singapore visualize how the *kopitiam* served less as a workshop of debate and development than as a sanctuary of conviviality and comfort. Instead of exploring alternate fantasies of self-determination based on the incapacity and failure of seemingly transcendent public figures, individuals could seek momentary reprieve in the coffee shop from the People's Action Party's relentless pace of economic and material progress while awaiting its inevitability.

In 1960s Singapore, coffee shops were busy, inclusive public spaces where people could sit around, meet friends, eat a quick meal, listen to the news on the radio, or catch up on the latest gossip.[63] Rooted in the entrepreneurship of migrants, the first *kopitiam*s were opened by Chinese from Hainan who worked as cooks and servants in the households of British expatriates. Left jobless when their employers repatriated, they established eateries and bakeries with the culinary skills they had cultivated.[64] In Malaysia and Singapore, according to Gaik Cheng Khoo, the *kopitiam* has served as a democratic, multicultural site for diverse ethnicities to *lepak* or unwind.[65] Echoing Khoo, Chua Beng Huat defines the coffee shop as a site of "collective idling."[66] According to Chua's account, each day at the coffee shop started early in the morning and ended late in the evening. Predominantly male, the stereotypical breadwinner of a heteronormative family, the regular customers of the coffee shop usually enjoyed languidly lounging on a bentwood chair at one of the marble-topped tables while sipping a hot beverage. As part of their predictable daily routine, they would read the newspaper and gossip about the news.[67] Although this scene could be understood as a picture of everyday life untouched by industrial capitalism, the reality was that Singapore's entrepôt economy could only supply these men with intermittent employment.[68]

The dissonance between the languid waiting of intermittent employment and the relentless bustle of rapid development in the 1960s is negotiated by the representations of coffee shops in P. Ramlee's films. Illustrating conversation, gossip, and conviviality among jobless residents of the *kampong*, *Seniman Bujang Lapok* presents the coffee shop as an important public space of social life and collective idling, where the three protagonists can together unwind and revitalize while awaiting their next adventure. With a cinematographic gaze that is level with their bodies, the opening of the film pictures them seated around a makeshift wooden table drinking coffee while exchanging speculative ideas about their options for livelihood, which have materialized with the sudden arrival of a movie production crew in their remote village. Lingering in place until they realize that their companion has left the coffee shop to seize a new job opportunity, the characters embrace a prolonged duration of languid comfort while their linear trajectory of personal development is suspended.

Writing about the temporal experience of eviction on the periphery of Ho Chi Minh City, where construction projects are delayed due to incompetent bureaucracy or insufficient funding, Erik Harms explains how its residents must either surrender to the oppression of their expectancy or assume control over its duration.[69] Refusing to lapse into complacency and despair over the uncertainty of the future, they exploit the flexibility that this condition of uncertainty permits by improvising on their situation. Shaped by the ease and stability of their leisure, this temporality does not incrementally work toward the arrival of the future and does not impulsively react to the urgency of the present but ambivalently lingers in the moment.

Instead of providing workshops for fantasies of self-determination, coffee shops in 1960s Singapore offered a sanctuary from the uncertainty of imminent change that unfolded as a momentary reprieve. Like the evictees of urban renewal in rapidly industrializing Saigon, the protagonists of Ramlee's *Seniman Bujang Lapok* wait to seize the succession of opportunities that present themselves to them, as they are not contracted to a steady occupation and income.[70] Instilling rhythms of slowness, languor, and expectancy, the coffee shop affords them momentary refuge where they can unwind and revitalize before proceeding to search for new sources of livelihood, identity, and self-determination.

Departing from the People's Action Party's public image of the *kampong* and its villagers as characterized by unproductiveness and inertia, 1960s Singapore's *kopitiam* was marked by its defiant slowness, which straddled the time of work and the time of repose with its postponement of vigorous action. While the coffee shop could be seen as a venue for agency, it did not necessarily induce any of the normative stances of identity or behavior, which would entail personal transcendence, resistance, or self-denial. Instead of encouraging urban residents to fantasize about transforming or overturning the established order, it produced an act of waiting that was not resigned to the fate of cyclical time but continued to be oriented toward the future.

Instead of being forced to accommodate the abrupt, dynamic forces of progress acting on their surroundings, the coffee shops of 1960s Singapore provided the idle stability of refuge and rehearsal for its citizens to grapple with them. Without letting it discourage and devitalize them, residents ambivalently welcomed the consciousness that their present landscape would eventually be demolished and superseded through rapid economic growth and urban renewal. Bereft of any anxiety or restlessness over an uncertain future, which Harms describes in his essay, they refused the terms of their given conditions by embracing the unavoidability of change on their own autonomous terms. By transgressing the normative expectation from the government that its citizens immediately submit to its overarching vision of national development, languor transformed into a form of tentative waiting for the inevitable arrival of the possibility to participate in its trajectory.

Oscillating constantly between the work regime and consumer space due to their intermittent employment, their experience of time was not so much cyclical as elliptical. Instead of pursuing a disruptive trajectory of personal transcendence, they suspended their participation in the relentless linearity of development as they occupied an interim node along its incremental stages. Amid the inescapable dynamism of the period, it was the temporal enclosure of the coffee shop that cultivated a proper mode of waiting, an unhurried stance that espoused openness and expectancy toward the imminence of change.

The "seething" 1960s were characterized by the vibrant public life of mass protests and labor strikes as the residents of Manila and Singapore, who frequently gathered in crowds in movie theaters, coffee shops, and night markets under the spectatorial experience of neon, constituted delinquent modes of transcendence and community through their seemingly infinite commonality. Popular commercial and leisure spaces such as supermarkets and cinemas facilitated the sensorial profusion of their bustling, congested urban environments teeming with the restless energy of youthful dynamism, which demanded the upheaval of the established order. Driven by fantasies of rapid, linear development, the efforts by the postcolonial governments of these Southeast Asian capitals to implement programs of sanitary, air-conditioned modernity during this historical period strove to accommodate and revalue all the realities within their territories for the sake of industrial productivity, collective discipline, and social order. The recalcitrant creativity and mobility of hawkers and activists on the streets of the metropolis offered an alternative temporality, which ended up being constrained by the public enclosures of an emergent consumer capitalist culture into an innovative neoliberal mode of civic responsibility.

PART III

Millennial Southeast Asia

CHAPTER 7

Neoliberal Cosmopolitanism in the Tropical World City

Toward the end of the first decade of the new millennium, monumental shopping malls in Manila and Singapore's urban centers were erected, refurbished, and expanded, exemplifying the degree of air-conditioned modernity attained through the growth in their national economies. Located on different sections of Epifanio de los Santos Avenue or EDSA, the main thoroughfare that connects Metropolitan Manila's various cities and municipalities, the utopian brutalism of privately owned supermalls SM Megamall, SM City North EDSA, and SM Mall of Asia represented the imagined, aspirational stability and normalcy of a bustling, emerging metropolis. The centerpiece of Orchard Road, Singapore's main commercial street, was the futuristic, deconstructivist architecture of the Ion Orchard, which, owned by its sovereign wealth fund, contributed to the government's vision to establish its thriving global reputation alongside leading world cities like London, New York, and Hong Kong as an ideal model of progress. Featuring the rise of Singapore and the Philippines as economic powerhouses and consumer societies amid the shift of the world market toward the Asian region, the first decade of the new millennium was defined by intensifying neoliberalism and consumerism together with increased global mobility from tourism and migration, a period of relative peace before the ascendancy of authoritarian state capitalism and digital populism in the mid-2010s.

From the early 1990s, shopping malls grew to become the principal hubs of public and social life in the bustling metropolises of Southeast Asia, where urban residents with increased purchasing power could gather, relax, and mingle in refuge from the heat and humidity of the tropical climate. First erected in the wintry Midwest of the United States in the 1950s, the typology of the shopping mall bore traces of Istanbul's covered bazaars and Shanghai's amusement halls. Through the neoliberal, axiomatic logic of market capitalism, Manila and Singapore's malls incorporated previously separate and autonomous consumer spaces such as amusement parks, commercial streets, department stores, bazaars, supermarkets, coffee shops, and movie theaters. Flourishing until the 1970s, the New World and Great World amusement parks were replaced by shopping centers City Square Mall and Great World City. Losing spectators to videotapes and computers, movie theaters in Avenida would turn to exhibiting soft porn and low-budget B movies as cinemas were reconfigured into twelve-theater mall multiplexes.

News features and online videos proclaiming the death of the shopping mall tend to focus on North America and Western Europe, where they are typically located in the urban periphery. In contrast, the emergence of Southeast Asian cities as consumer societies and cosmopolitan hubs correlates with the predominance of the shopping mall in their urban centers, where mass activity and public life are concentrated. Outside of office hours on weeknights and weekends, the multitudes of residents in Bangkok, Jakarta, and Kuala Lumpur frequent the atriums and corridors of malls like Siam Paragon, CentralWorld, Plaza Indonesia, Grand Indonesia Shopping Town, Mid Valley City, and Pavilion. In their bustling milieus, such monumental structures, with their polished interiors and fashionable products, epitomize the promise of global capitalism while being vital to their quotidian rhythms. Contrary to many critical theories of mass consumption, the consumer space of the mall is not a domain for exceptional processes of docility, alienation, atomization, and fantasy but a venue for more complex experiences of routine, self-fashioning, collectivity, and transcendence.

Studying their reconfiguration of capitalism, modernity, consumerism, and spectatorship in prior commercial and leisure spaces, which I discussed in the preceding chapters, I comparatively analyze how the built environments and media ecologies of shopping malls in Manila and Singapore during the late 2000s and early 2010s shaped the parameters of agency and collectivity by concealing economic inequality and facilitating market competition. Alternating between commercial and leisure spaces in Singapore and Manila during the late 2000s and early 2010s, the chapter opens by dissecting former Singaporean prime minister Goh Chok Tong's definition of cosmopolitanism, which, according to him, characterizes social identity in a world city with its hospitality toward transnational flows. Focusing on the main commercial street of Orchard Road, I uncover how the Singapore government deployed the spectacular branding of buzz to attract tourists with sophistication who might become professionals and investors who would stimulate its innovation economy. Looking at the global outsourcing of service labor through its representation in Glenn Diaz's multi-award-winning novel *The Quiet Ones* (2017), I explore how call center agents with increased purchasing power in Metro Manila negotiated the twenty-four-hour cyclical time of neoliberal capitalism with their demand for their right to a spatial landscape of air-conditioned, sanitary modernity no different from that of world cities like Singapore. Amid the insufficiency of existing urban infrastructure, the axiomatic typology of Metro Manila's supermalls reproduced and transformed the conditions of the tropical megalopolis with the aspirational normalcy of utopia. The chapter concludes with Kevin Kwan's bestselling *Crazy Rich Asians* (2013), a novel about the super-rich that discloses how their financial excess transpires beyond the bounds of public knowledge and consequence.

Model World City of Cosmopolitan Modernity

At the turn of the millennium, Singapore was of one of the most prosperous nations in the world, standing atop rankings of per-capita income and standard of living. Driven by its programs of national development and air-conditioned modernity, the People's Action Party, which had run the government since independence in the 1960s, constantly refashioned and rezoned the spatial and social landscape of Singapore for the sake of economic growth. The state maintained extensive influence over various areas of society, including racial identity, language use, residential housing, family size, personal income, creative expression, and public space.[1] With its stance of pragmatic governmentality, whose flexible ideology and policy enabled it to achieve long-term goals, Singapore adjusted to changing global economic and geopolitical conditions beyond its immediate control by altering its territory and population in response to this contingency. As it was confronted by the threats of stagnant growth and low fertility, one-third of its population became composed of foreign professionals and migrant workers. To accommodate the outside of transnational forces, which would allow Singapore to maintain its prosperity and competitiveness, it was urgent that its norms of spatial configuration and social behavior be made pliable to constant restructuring, regardless of the degree of shift in political or economic direction.[2]

David Harvey explains how the shift in the global economy toward a dominant regime of neoliberal capitalism began in the United States, United Kingdom, and the People's Republic of China in the 1970s and 1980s.[3] Defined by neoliberalism, national sovereignty withholds state intervention in the free market by affirming the right to freedom of private businesses. Unlike colonial occupation, in which local industries were developed for the benefit of the economy of metropole, the government now relied on its rezoning of spatial environments to permit overseas companies to invest and operate in its territory with legal exemptions on foreign ownership and labor compensation.

To maintain its global competitiveness, Singapore, beginning with the administration of Prime Minister Lee Hsien Loong, Lee Kuan Yew's son, strove to transform itself into a model world-class city, which would serve as a regional center for financial capital, scientific research, and corporate management. According to its definition in *Foreign Policy*, which published a Global Cities Index based on Saskia Sassen's seminal theory, globally interconnected cities had developed into the key engines of the world market. Containing an array of international ports, corporate headquarters, consultancy firms, art museums, and research institutes, they functioned as influential hubs where transnational flows of money, culture, talent, and innovation concentrated, interacted, and flourished.[4] A 2011 economic subcommittee

report on "Making Singapore a Leading Global City" advised that intensified competition among leading global cities in Asia, such as Shanghai,
Seoul, Dubai, Doha, and Hong Kong, impelled Singapore to project the
attractive, spectacular image of a livable environment, which would simultaneously provide a laboratory for innovation and a home for talent.[5] Representing its new national crisis, Singapore purportedly needed to draw on
transnational flows; otherwise, its economy and reputation would decline.

In Prime Minister Goh Chok Tong's 1999 National Day Rally Speech,
he stressed the importance of cosmopolitanism to adapt to the demands of
shifting global economic and geopolitical conditions in the period of neoliberal capitalism.[6] Based on his understanding, cosmopolitanism could be seen
as a neoliberal stance of openness toward the contingency, diversity, and
complexity that accompanied the dynamic flows, porous borders, and deep
interconnections of an important hub in the world market. From the standpoint of the ruling People's Action Party, Singaporeans were expected to
become amenable to the policies of neoliberal capitalism by being hospitable
to migrants whose outsourced labor would be able to address manpower
shortages and boost consumer profits. Cosmopolitanism was the appropriate modern stance that Singaporeans needed to adopt as responsible citizens
of a model world-class city to enable Singapore's economy to negotiate external flows with greater efficacy.

Writing about cosmopolitanism, Pheng Cheah explains that its practice
has historically been entangled with personal and collective endeavors of
transcendence, self-actualization, and development.[7] According to Cheah,
cosmopolitanism could be understood as a response to the particularity of
nationalism, which had relied on existing local attachments to form a larger,
more transcendent collectivity. The potency of cosmopolitanism as a discourse and a stance reveals the limit of national sovereignty and culture,
whose inclination toward particularity becomes perceived as "oppressive,"
even recalcitrant and retrogressive.[8] Reexamining Kant's writings, Derrida
explains how cosmopolitanism might be reconciled with nationalism.[9] For
Derrida, cosmopolitanism is founded on hospitality as an openness to strang-
ers, who are seen to possess the right not to be treated with hostility. This
openness does not issue from the sentimental emotion to be magnanimous
but from the ethical obligation to be hospitable to what arrives from the outside. Hospitality becomes universal when it is unconditional, meaning that

the host accepts the stranger as a guest without fixing the particularity of the stranger's identity as a stranger. A host can only be hospitable to the stranger who becomes his guest if he maintains his authority over the identity of his domain without foreclosing the inclusion of the guest in that domain.

Marked by mobility and flexibility, hospitality was an important element of modernity and agency in millennial Southeast Asia. Under conditions of global capitalism, the neoliberal cosmopolitanism of hospitality toward the foreignness of the outside translated to the capacity of a government and its citizens to administer transnational flows. If the modernity of evangelical sanitation in the 1930s imposed a strict enclosure and delineation of the inside while exiling undesirable realities to the outside, the modernity of postcolonial development in the 1960s accommodated and reconfigured all the contents of the national territory to achieve sustained, incremental growth. In the modernity of neoliberal cosmopolitanism after the turn of the millennium, the capitalist axiomatic rested on spatial zoning and business outsourcing to manage the contingency and multiplicity of external flows beyond the authority and scope of national sovereignty. Shaped by their negotiation of vernacular norms and global imaginaries, Aihwa Ong describes how spatial environments and migrant professionals who interacted with transnational flows modulated their identities based on the calculations of economic instrumentality without reducing them to the overarching framework of the larger territory.[10] Defined by their dislocation, flexible and mobile subject-making were no longer sought for their long-term stability but for their capacity to adjust to continuous processes of capital accumulation amid the volatility of the world market.[11] Whereas the Philippine government's ad-hoc, laissez-faire approach to macroeconomic planning allowed an oligarchy to monopolize the free market, the Singapore government crafted market conditions where competition between local and foreign businesses would boost key industries.

The Buzz of the Commercial Street

Ong is interested in how zoning could be applied as an exceptional administrative and legal mechanism for experimenting with external flows that would deliver increased profit.[12] The refashioning and rezoning of Singapore into a spatial environment that attracted, welcomed, and managed the outside was tied to the development of its tourism industry. To stay globally competitive, its "Tourism 21" report from the late 1990s proposed that if New York and London were the capitals of finance, Milan and Paris the capitals of fashion, and Rome and Mecca the capitals of religion, then Singapore could present itself as the capital of tourism of the twenty-first century. Having rapidly grown since the late 1990s, the Singapore tourism industry experienced a record year in 2010 with 11.6 million tourist arrivals and $18.9 billion in tourism receipts constituting a 20 percent overall increase.[13] Applying an expanded definition of tourism, the "Tourism 21" report conceived of a tourism capital as a destination not only for tourists but also for investors and professionals. Although not conventionally associated with tourism, these external flows of migration and money were favored by the government because their presence would supposedly contribute to the dynamism of Singapore's economic and material growth.

According to the "Tourism 21" report, it was imperative for Singapore to compete with other global cities to outsource and attract creative talent, which would infuse its corporate culture with innovative ideas and methods for increased efficiency and profitability in a volatile world market.[14] As Richard Florida argues, the neoliberal and cosmopolitan values of risk-taking and independence that fuel the immaterial production vital to an knowledge-based economy are contradictory to the rigidity and regimentation of the established work regime.[15] From the standpoint of the government, creativity should issue from educated and skilled professionals with the sophistication of cosmopolitanism who would introduce a unique approach to corporate culture without overturning their norms.

In line with its blueprint to transform Singapore as a world-class city, the "Tourism 21" report envisaged Orchard Road as its "Great Street." It proposed rezoning the boulevard into a premier commercial street on the same level as Fifth Avenue in New York, the Champs Elysées in Paris, and Nanjing Road in Shanghai. In contrast to the commercial streets of previous historical periods, which acquired prestige from their elegant retail shops, Singapore's foremost boulevard was famous for its spectacular shopping malls, which served as its main tourist attractions. In the mid-nineteenth century, Orchard Road was known as a forested thoroughfare that passed through the nutmeg, fruit, and pepper plantations sprawled across the surrounding hills to the cloistered expatriate enclave, where European colonial officials and company employees resided in tropical bungalows. During the first decade of the new century, commercial spaces started to be established on sections of the thoroughfare, which serviced residents of the nearby Tanglin district. By the 1960s, Raffles Place, the most prominent commercial space over the first half of the twentieth century, was struggling to accommodate the growing mass of consumers. The shift in Singapore's commercial center from the enclosed square of Raffles Place to the expansive boulevard of Orchard Road commenced when the landmark Robinson's Department Store was destroyed by fire in November 1972. Erected on the site of the Pavilion Theatre in time for the 1973 Lunar New Year, the Specialists' Shopping Centre was Orchard Road's first major shopping mall, which featured branches of Robinson's, B. P. de Silva, and John Little's.[16] The subsequent construction of Wisma Atria in 1986 and Ngee Ann City in 1993 adjacent to the Orchard MRT station represented pivotal stages in the transformation of Orchard Road into a premiere commercial street of world-class shopping malls.

From the standpoint of the "Tourism 21" report, a vibrant tourism capital must provide consumers with the immersive spectacles of "delightful" and "memorable" experiences. The report recognizes that global tourists now have greater cosmopolitan sophistication with higher standards and expectations because of their broader exposure to diverse realities around the world, with easier and more affordable internet access and air travel. To be successful as tourist attractions, urban spaces must be upgraded into consumable experiences endowed with a greater "pulling power."[17] Akin to the sensorial immersion of amusement parks in 1930s Singapore and the virtual infinitude of the commercial street in 1960s Manila, the spectatorial experience they supply must be vivid and potent enough to become inscribed in the memory of visitors. The marketing strategy for Singapore's tourism industry aspired to overturn the general impression in the global public sphere formed by writers and architects like William Gibson and Rem Koolhaas and surveys in *Time Out* magazine that Singapore was sterile and artificial.[18] These spectacles aimed to produce not only sources for consumerism and entertainment but also flows of migration and investment by creating the legible image that Singapore furnished a sanctuary characterized by livability and play.

Coherence in the legible characteristics of different tourist attractions and immersive spectacles helps constitute a city's brand identity, which, according to public policy consultant Simon Anholt, has a significant impact on its global reputation. The spectacular image that a geographic location projects in the world market determines the general impression about the quality of its products and the aptitude of its residents. Anholt argues that tourism is the principal means by which a city or a nation can enhance its branding,[19] which would shape its monetary value in terms of market capitalization.[20] In the period of neoliberal capitalism, not only companies listed in the stock exchange but also nations competing in the world market rely on the public perception of their economic potential to generate investments.

Exploring innovative methods to upgrade the buzz of public life in Orchard Road, a 2003 government document entitled *Street of Singapore* proposed important refurbishments to its built environment.[21] Throughout the document, the urgency of generating vibrancy or "buzz" is reiterated. Anholt emphasizes that buzz is crucial to the branding of a geographic location.[22] Based on its definition in the Oxford English Dictionary, buzz refers to a state of excitement that is often accompanied by "busy talk" about its source.[23] In marketing parlance, buzz denotes the "explosive self-generating demand" for a product.[24] Unlike the vibrancy of the bazaar, buzz is not restricted to the immediate confines of a physical enclosure but is expected to spread across networks of interpersonal communication through social contagion. Buzz resembles Malcolm Gladwell's idea of stickiness from his 2000 bestseller *The Tipping Point* as an attractive reality whose spectacular design would cause an idea or product to gain exponentially in popularity.[25] In the "Tourism 21" report, it assumes the form of a manufactured atmosphere of vibrancy that is intended to generate crowds and profits. Victor Gruen argues that a psychological climate conducive to shopping must be created in commercial spaces. This climate must offer an immersive pedestrian experience with buzz to entice consumers to linger and return, which would lead to greater revenue.[26] According to Gruen's theory, a commercial space would acquire buzz if it offered a comprehensive abundance and variety of activities whose attraction would spread spontaneously and exponentially with limited expenditure of resources among a large participatory community of consumers.[27]

Gruen's theory differs from Frederic Thompson's conception of the carnival spirit, which requires bodies to be in constant states of movement and pleasure without ever lapsing into the stillness of repose.[28] For its efficacy, buzz does not require a strict physical enclosure, where it could bombard a captive market of consumers with an abundance and variety of dynamic spectacles. Buzz relies less on virtual infinitude than on irresistible uniqueness.[29] It can originate from a singular object whose allure is potent enough, regardless of its size, to generate excitement. Instead of issuing from the contingency of simultaneous circumstances or the creativity of autonomous individuals, as was the case with the vibrancy of the *pasar malam*, the experience of buzz must be deliberately manufactured and curated to produce an aspired outcome.

Enticing large crowds to occupy a space, acquire a product, or experience an event, buzz carries the potential for exponential success. With its expanded conception of tourism, the "Tourism 21" report appears to be less concerned about increasing the number of tourists and the length of their visits than attracting the type of people who will magnify the vibrancy and excitement of its domain.[30] From the standpoint of the report, this vibrancy and excitement should assume a benign form that would not threaten the stability of its established order but would contribute to its spectacular branding for global competitiveness.

Desiring Normalcy in the Megalopolis

Singapore's global branding was tied to its buzz as a model world city. Together with other cities in the Global South such as Jakarta, Nairobi, Dhaka, and Mumbai, Manila was frequently cited in the international media as the foremost example of an ungovernable megalopolis whose seemingly insurmountable problems hampered the Philippines' prospects as a site for investment and development. Based on normative measures of economic growth and social order such as those of Singapore, the international media tended to describe burgeoning megacities as being beset by overcrowding, crime, unrest, and underdevelopment.[31] The incapacity of government and the despondency of the population would be captured in the predominance of a grittier and more cynical type of film noir in the Philippines during this historical period—films such as Jeffrey Jetturian's *Kubrador* (The Bet Collector) (2006), Brillante Mendoza's *Kinatay* (2009), Erik Matti's *On the Job* (2013), and Dodo Dayao's *Violator* (2014), which disclosed the pervasive corruption of the megalopolis and its institutions by reinterpreting audiovisual horror tropes. Highlighting the entrenchment of the cycle of poverty and exploitation, these films focus on the inescapable corruption of the morality of individuals seeking a better livelihood who are left without any choice but to resort to crime to survive. While Mendoza's *Kinatay* is characterized by the remorseless brutality and impunity of its criminal characters, *Violator* explores how the depravity of the city could produce the figuration of the devil. The cynicism and horror of this urban imaginary were what prompted many Filipinos to vote for Davao mayor Rodrigo Duterte because he supposedly possessed the track record and political will to improve the order and livability of Metropolitan Manila along the lines of Davao and Singapore. The ideal of normalcy for which Manila aspired was epitomized by the exceptionalism of Singapore as a model of progress in the region,[32] which was propagated by tourists and migrants who shared this indelible, legible image in their social media networks.

Before the 1960s, EDSA was officially called Highway 54, a two-lane circumferential thoroughfare that cut through fields of wild cogon grass.[33] Shaping the idea of Manila in the public culture, the gradual relocation of the urban population from the congested center of Greater Manila to the flourishing *arrabales* or suburbs of Rizal province elevated the importance of EDSA, after Calle Escolta in the 1930s and Avenida Rizal in the 1960s, as the metropolis's main boulevard. From the assemblage of different cities and municipalities, which EDSA interconnected, President Ferdinand Marcos established Metropolitan Manila, the National Capital Region, in 1975, consolidating power by placing it under the governorship of his spouse, Imelda Marcos, who subjected it to her personal norms of morality and beauty. EDSA became inscribed in the collective imaginary as the site of two popular revolutions in 1986 and 2001, which overthrew the corrupt, despotic administrations of Ferdinand Marcos and Joseph Estrada. During these mass uprisings, sections of the boulevard were emptied of vehicles in transit and occupied by bodies in protest as multitudes of Filipinos fought to translate their utopian ideals of democracy into reality.

The uncontrolled development and overpopulation of Metro Manila resulted in deficient infrastructure that strained to accommodate the relentless overabundance of vehicles and commuters. The air in the metropolis hovered at hazardous levels because of combined pollution from the mobility of vehicles, the construction of buildings, and the operation of factories.[34] Characterized by the sensorial profusion of congestion, heat, and pollution without much greenery, the built environment proved inhospitable to pedestrians who, unlike in the past, were deterred from browsing for products or congregating with friends on the streets but nonetheless traversed its topography. As the congested metropolis expanded with a swelling population, public commercial and leisure activity were driven indoors within clean, air-conditioned enclosures, where the experience of urban life was more manageable, pleasant, and utopian.

In *The Quiet Ones*, his acclaimed English-language novel about the precarity of middle-class professionals in call centers, Glenn Diaz writes about Metro Manila's "monochrome of dreary survival" and "suffocating concrete."[35] Winner of the Palanca Grand Prize, National Book Award, and Madrigal-Gonzalez First Book Award, the novel portrays the metropolis as a wearied, overburdened organism that perpetuates an established order of poverty and complacency with little possibility for upward social mobility. Comprising several entwined narratives that transpire at different temporal moments, the novel documents the listless and meandering trajectories of middle-class customer service representatives who stumble upon a criminal scheme to steal their company's earnings, which present them with a miraculous opportunity to transcend their seemingly fated routine of "dreary" and "suffocating" everyday life.

Signifying their immobility and entrapment through a recurrent trope of listless bus rides north of the megalopolis, the novel culminates with the mastermind behind the scheme being unspectacularly arrested by the police at the Ninoy Aquino International Airport before he can abscond by plane. Permeated by a customary sense of unfulfilled expectations in which future projects inevitably end in failure, even their escape from their given conditions is met less with excitement than resignation. The language of the novel captures this experience of helpless futility by seamlessly mixing reality, aspiration, and fantasy through sentence fragments that trail off to abruptly form new thoughts or impressions, which never find concrete realization. Waiting for a form of deliverance that never arrives, their acquiescence to the impotence of upheaval is encapsulated by the novel in its description of the shift in the neon lights of the metropolis to a "sallow hue."

An overburdened metropolis without adequate infrastructure and employment represented a microcosm of the state of the nation in which

Filipinos were driven to seek opportunities from outside its domain amid seemingly insurmountable government corruption and incompetence. Outsourcing value production, the enormous revenue from the remittances of overseas Filipino workers significantly contributed to the economic boom of the early 2010s. Constituting nearly 10 percent of its Gross Domestic Product,[36] overseas remittances were extolled by the state as the safeguard of the Philippine economy against the volatility of the world market. Fueling an increase in purchasing power among its expanding middle class, the steady influx of remittances from OFWs enabled domestic consumption to bolster two-thirds of the national economy.

Now the principal hubs of public life in the megalopolis, Metropolitan Manila's shopping malls cultivated emergent modes of spatial practice and social transcendence that, rooted in neoliberal cosmopolitanism, aligned local rhythms with global temporalities. A decade into the new millennium, the burgeoning Philippine economy was characterized by the increased purchasing power of a broader range of the population, whose members had developed a greater awareness of cosmopolitan lifestyles from budget air travel and viral social media. Their demands for a more orderly and livable urban environment, which would emulate that of global cities in other parts of Asia, exerted pressure on the established order to improve the conditions of everyday life. Whereas no such reality previously existed in the megalopolis, shopping malls furnished a rezoned space where utopian aspirations for the normalcy of future prosperity could be incarnated in the present milieu.

Call Center Consumption

In addition to the increased domestic consumption from overseas remittances, the short-lived economic boom in the Philippines at the start of the new millennium resulted from the rise of the multibillion-dollar Business Process Outsourcing industry with its 20 percent annual growth.[37] The global expansion of the BPO service industry resulted when companies headquartered in industrialized nations, seeking to reduce their expenses, transplanted parts of their operations to more affordable offshore locations. Outsourcing could be defined as a company's minimization or closure of business functions and departments and their delegation or consignment to local subsidiaries and independent companies, which, external to its corporate structure, perform this work at a lower cost.[38] Such outsourced functions have typically included customer service, technical support, legal advice, accounting, advertising, public relations, and graphic design. Intrinsic to the twenty-four-hour workings of global capitalism, outsourcing delegates vital functions to labor in a distant location by giving it autonomy to produce output without reducing its identity and autonomy to the coherence of the larger configuration.

Overtaking India, the Philippines had developed into the principal global hub for call centers by 2011.[39] As rezoned spatial and temporal enclosures that provide client care and technical support across geographic and cultural boundaries, call centers exemplify the interconnectivity of the world in the period of transnational capitalism. Although their unique selling point is to supply technological know-how for the consumers of innovative goods, call centers perform an affective function by helping them manage their anxiety and anger over the contingency and uncertainty of advanced modern technology.[40] Representing a form of migration without mobility,[41] call center agents are required by their job to possess the talent and skill of mimicry in adapting themselves to the language, customs, and etiquette of a distant location without ever being transplanted overseas. With 70 percent of them concentrated in Metro Manila, call centers were staffed with hundreds of thousands of Filipinos whose cosmopolitan sophistication enabled them to address the product-related questions and issues of English-speaking consumers as though they were educated and located in North America.

Outsourcing the problem of unemployment to multinational companies in the service industry, call centers helped the Philippine government address its precarious job market by incorporating the labor of individuals who had been trained as doctors, physical therapists, and engineers but ended up working as customer service representatives because of the higher salary.[42] As Wendy Brown writes about the expansion of economic calculation of cost and benefit to private and social life,[43] their cosmopolitan identities as customer service representatives derived from their technological knowledge, cultural sophistication, and purchasing power.[44] As consumer spaces, call centers evoked the atmosphere of a college campus with the youthful energy and aspirational life of computer terminals, karaoke machines, game tables, and fast-food kiosks.[45] Earned from their technical and affective assistance for international consumers, call center agents' increased purchasing power allowed them to become regular consumers themselves.[46] Because their work shifts usually extended past midnight into the early morning, commercial and leisure spaces in the surrounding environment such as retail stores, restaurants, gyms, and coffee shops reconfigured their daily schedules to cater to their needs. With their increased purchasing power, call center agents cultivated the public perception of having extravagant lifestyles by expending their salaries on laptop computers, brand-name clothes, and digital cameras.[47] Targeted by credit card companies, these neoliberal consumers, who behaved without concern for the financial consequences of their actions, were often heavily in debt.[48]

The Quiet Ones highlights how many urban residents of Metropolitan Manila subsisted on the purchasing power of their monthly paychecks. In the novel, their everyday life is marked by minor tragedies such as illnesses and muggings, which characters are no longer surprised to experience, but form part of the quotidian trajectories and rhythms of the tropical metropolis under neoliberal capitalism. Working as call center agents in the tiny office of the Business Process Outsourcing (BPO) company Magellan Solutions for the client UTelCo with scarce opportunity for career advancement, the protagonists have accustomed their bodies to the mundane rituals of their work regime: "His years at the call center had coalesced into an inert choreography. His index finger would dance over the keypad of his desk phone and, by instinct rather than thought, push the precise buttons of his employee number and password. His tongue, once docile and lazy, had routinely unfurled to produce English sentences even before they registered in his mind."[49] The call center agents in *The Quiet Ones* log on to their customer service calls only at the last minute. Bored with the repetitiveness of their work regime, they play online backgammon or search for sexy photos while responding to the questions and complaints of disgruntled consumers.

The call center in *The Quiet Ones* is pictured as a cosmopolitan workplace with employees of different genders, ethnicities, and cultures. Several of the protagonists across the novel's multiple plotlines identify as "gay," which captures how the BPO industry in the Philippines is open to service workers with a queer orientation.[50] The Filipino characters in *The Quiet Ones* become involved in precarious sexual affairs with Americans and Australians, who reveal their fascination or bewilderment about the Philippines. Exploring the complex connections between local professionals who aspire for transcendence and foreign migrants who are perplexed by their failure, the novel highlights how they became hospitable to the transformative potential of external flows without effacing their autonomous capacities.

The Quiet Ones describes how Magellan Solutions is located on the thirty-second floor with thirty teams of twelve call center agents each working eleven-hour shifts without any windows that would enable them to tell the difference between night and day. Operating with multiple shifts, call centers reconfigured the routines of the work regime and everyday life into a twenty-four-hour cycle. When the workday in North America concluded, that in Southeast Asia commenced. While this temporality disrupted the circadian rhythms of employees and curtailed their social interactions with family,[51] it permitted them to form professional and affective bonds with colleagues. Illustrating the extension of David Harvey's concept of time-space compression,[52] this perpetual twenty-four-hour workday could be seen to align with the universalizing circular time of neoliberal globalization.

The call center's mode of relational labor could be understood as an engagement with the outside.[53] Often young, impressionable fresh college graduates, call center agents are valued for their openness and adaptability to the norms and rhythms of different cultures and environments.[54] As depicted in movies like *That Thing Called Tadhana* (2014) and *English Only, Please* (2014) popular in supermall cinemaplexes, millennial Filipinos derived social value from their familiarity with world cities such as Rome and New York and their facility with the global language of English. One prevalent source of distinction during the 2000s was the financial capacity to vacation in tourist destinations geographically proximate to the Philippines, like Hong Kong, Bangkok, and Singapore, which would be circulated through digital photos shared via social networks like Facebook or Instagram. Another important source of distinction in millennial Metropolitan Manila was the demonstration of a proficiency in American English, evident among agents of call centers and graduates of exclusive schools. English became a necessity at the turn of the millennium because it was the lingua franca of the world market, which permitted traders to conduct financial transactions and computer users to navigate the Internet. Now defined by the flexibility of cosmopolitan sophistication, distinction and transcendence rested on the ability to negotiate the influence of external realities in the form of global styles and trends. Dealing with external realities in an overseas location by adjusting their temporality obliged workers to synchronize the mundane rhythms of their urban life with the economic cycle of the world market.

One-Stop Shopping and the Outsourced Axiomatic

The desire for cosmopolitan sophistication among middle-class Filipinos with increased purchasing power was accommodated by the architecture of shopping malls. Oriented toward the incorporation of its outside, the configuration of Metropolitan Manila's malls was an assemblage of different typologies of commercial and leisure space that had been distinct and autonomous in previous historical periods. Through its everyday use by ordinary residents as a hub for urban flows of goods and services, the shopping mall became the center of public life where different social practices, identities, and relations were reproduced, negotiated, and redefined with the norms of neoliberal cosmopolitanism. The convenience and security from their circumscribed, zoned enclosures allowed them to perform an array of vital functions for their visitors that would have been administered by governmental institutions or private companies elsewhere in the city. In Metro Manila's malls, the responsibility for incarnating the model world city in the urban milieu of the Global South megalopolis became outsourced to private business, which was commonly perceived to be more efficient at translating this utopian ideal into local reality.

Straddling the border between the cities of Pasig and Mandaluyong in the Ortigas Center, the blank utilitarian monumentality of the popular SM Megamall was distinguished by its two massive, rectangular blocks. Designated Mega A and Mega B, these two extensive six-story buildings were adjoined by a new annex, the Mega Atrium, which was an expansion of the multilevel bridge connecting the two wings. In the early 2010s, two additional annexes were constructed on the sites of the open-air parking areas fronting each block with offices for multinational BPO companies. In the mid-2010s, a new Fashion Wing was added, featuring stores and restaurants that could previously be found only in Hong Kong and Singapore, two nearby prosperous cities where hundreds of thousands of Filipinos worked. Critic and activist Rolando Tolentino describes how the shopping mall is the neoliberal reconfiguration of the plaza, which assimilates [*nilamon*] all previously existing commercial and leisure spaces.[55] Expanding on this idea, Deleuze and Guattari explain that neoliberal capitalism operates as an axiomatic that constantly adds external elements with disparate logics to its existing configurations.[56] Characterized by capitalist expansion, the shopping mall likewise subjects its enclosure to constant rezoning as it outsources and incorporates multiple spaces and objects external to its configuration, maximizing their potential for profit while retaining the integrity of their identity.

The configuration of the shopping mall epitomizes the inherent tendency of capitalism to subsume every possible reality within its twenty-four-hour universal circular time. The family corporations that owned most of the shopping malls in the Philippines during this historical period had accumulated assets extending into various areas of investment including banking, real estate, and telecommunications. The most popular shopping malls in Metropolitan Manila were enormous structures christened "supermalls" by the Henry Sy family's SM Prime Holdings, which operated approximately forty-five shopping malls throughout the archipelago, in addition to retail stores, banking services, and residential developments.[57] Set in a giant shopping mall where the seat of government has been transplanted, Charlson Ong's award-winning turn-of-the-millennium novel *An Embarrassment of Riches* narrates how the overthrow of a twenty-year dictatorship leads to the consolidation of capitalist sovereignty amid the weakening of state institutions and factionalism among political actors.[58] Allegorizing the dystopic future of the tropical megalopolis, it discloses the rise to dominance of neoliberal capitalism in the synecdoche of the mall.

Proclaiming "We've Got It All for You," the official SM slogan packaged and circulated its unique selling point as a catchy jingle that became inscribed in the public culture. Advertised as a destination for "one-stop shopping," SM Supermalls presented a "complete" selection of products and services within a single, expansive enclosure that its owners described as being integral to their success as commercial spaces.[59] In earlier historical periods, Manila's residents needed to face the undesirable realities of the tropical urban environment such as heat, humidity, and congestion when traveling to different districts to obtain a variety of items. Victor Gruen, the architect who designed the original shopping mall in the Midwestern United States in the 1950s, envisaged it as a utopian sanctuary, a city-into-itself that, isolated from its urban surroundings, stood out from it. Gruen called for modern

FIGURE 13. Combining previously separate commercial and leisure spaces and practices within its safe and comfortable enclosure, SM Megamall incarnates the utopian normalcy of a world city. (Photo by author)

individuals to be liberated from the "unsightliness" of realities characteristic of the metropolis such as signs, billboards, garbage, alleyways, loading docks, smokestacks, telephone poles, and electric wires.[60] For Gruen, the shopping mall transcended the clutter and debris of modernization by reproducing the city without these undesirable realities. Sheltering its visitors from the urban blight of poverty, disease, crime, and violence, the shopping mall transported them to a safe, convenient, and pleasant air-conditioned utopia that retained the modern sophistication of metropolitan life.

In his 2001 book *Sa Loob at Labas ng* Mall *kong Sawi / Kaliluha'y Siyang Nangyayaring Hari*, Rolando Tolentino wrote, "*walang brownout, maaliwalas ang kapaligiran: pantay ang ilaw, parang parating tanghaling tapat; malinis, walang basura sa kalye; malamig; may mga puno rin naman; nagfla-flush ang toilet; maayos ang serbisyo; at walang krimen.*"[61] For Tolentino, this spatial sanitization of the mall includes effacing traces, from public sight and knowledge, of the exploitation, impoverishment, and oppression of human labor through contractualization or *endo*, short-term employment without personal leave and medical insurance. Instead of being "ahistorical" and "artificial" as Tolentino claims,[62] however, the bright, polished, and air-conditioned interiors of the mall in millennial Manila were experienced as ordinary and routine. Not simply an enclosure that improved on its surrounding environment, utopia was now defined by its mundane incorporation of the entirety of the world in a geographic location that had previously seemed isolated from the transnational flows of capital. Permitting the residents of burgeoning metropolitan areas in the Global South to experience this entirety, the mall proffered them a concrete, legible model of the utopian normalcy of a prosperous world city.

A utopia is typically imagined to be a spatial enclosure that transcends its undesirable surroundings as the fullest realization of ideals of order and community.[63] In the eyes of modernist architects and urban planners such as Robert Moses and Le Corbusier who helped design North American and Western European cities, utopian visions radically addressed the problems of industrialization and capitalism that had rendered the city unlivable to ordinary people.[64] Among Filipinos, utopia might have been difficult to conceive of as a concretely achievable reality, given the historical failure of efforts at economic growth as a result of corrupt and incompetent governance. For most of the twentieth century, utopia bore the religious resonance of a

Promised Land, whether it was the undeveloped hinterland of Mindanao under the U.S. regime or the bountiful capital of Manila after the Pacific War. By the turn of the millennium, utopia had come to connote a home within a gated residential subdivision far from the more congested, squalid, and crime-ridden areas of Metropolitan Manila. Equating it to a desire for utopia, Lauren Berlant explains that the aspiration for normalcy is the primary mode of agency under conditions of economic insecurity and social immobility,[65] such as in a megalopolis where the state has failed to provide adequate infrastructure and opportunity for its residents to subsist in a livable manner. Writing about the right to the city, Harvey describes how it has been articulated as a demand to share in the equitable distribution of the city's productive surplus, which would afford its residents proper access to facilities, services, and resources.[66] In the period of neoliberal capitalism, this desire for the right to utopian normalcy transpired as an aspiration to experience an everyday life no different from that in the world cities of industrialized nations, which Filipinos had become acquainted with as tourists and migrants. Because of its geographic location in Southeast Asia, where it offered employment opportunities to Filipino families who met its racial quotas, Singapore resonated as a model world city in the collective imagination with its orderly public spaces and hypermodern commercial structures.

Marketed as "cities," shopping malls strove to become the central public space in the megalopolis by incorporating business and domestic activities that in previous historical periods would not have been performed in sites of commercial exchange and consumption. Hardt and Negri explain how the management of difference in the period of neoliberal capitalism shifted from exclusion, which was inscribed through the authority of legal norms, to inclusion, which was negotiated through the contingency of everyday practices.[67] Instead of aiming to transform all who occupied its domain into a consumer, which would require it to allocate more resources for social production, the shopping mall enacted a neoliberal mode of zoning to attract and accommodate flows of non-shoppers.[68] The business establishments housed inside SM Megamall included medical clinics and fitness gyms, which guaranteed that the bodies of corporate employees stayed healthy and energetic for the twenty-four-hour work regime. Illustrating the possibilities of utopian normalcy in a prosperous world city, both languid and delinquent practices became incorporated into the economy of the mall, which, despite their seeming lack of economic utility, permitted urban residents to leisurely stroll through its air-conditioned corridors or restlessly play in its amusement centers without necessarily accumulating any material possessions.

The customer service counter at SM's Department Store served as a more efficient, miniature community center that processed payments for public utilities, insurance plans, and credit cards alongside applications for birth, marriage, and death certificates. Amid a congested and polluted urban environment, supermalls like SM Megamall adopted governmental functions that the state failed to perform competently, such as monitoring and authenticating the life cycle of its citizens. On weekends, a vacant section of the shopping mall was cordoned off so that Mass could be celebrated for devout Catholics who wished to practice their religion. Although the church represented the city center in earlier periods, it now existed as a supplement to the shopping mall, which exceeded it in influence on the population and importance to the cityscape. Because of the shopping mall's popularity and centrality, formerly dominant institutions such as state and church acknowledged the diminution of their authority by outsourcing their facilities to its enclosure, which became the principal site where the population was administered. If utopia had been regarded as an ideal that required the resources of an overarching authority to implement,[69] its outsourcing to private business signaled the acceptance by the government of its incapacity in the face of the profit-oriented, free-market logic of neoliberal capitalism.

The shopping mall superseded the ungovernable disorder of a third-world megalopolis with the enclosed, consumable utopia of a world-class city but without completely transcending it. Instead of realizing a sanctuary that existed at a transcendent remove from everyday life, this outsourced form of utopia domesticated the contingency of the megapolis by recreating and managing its urban flows with greater legibility. Especially in the case of shopping malls in Metro Manila, where many crimes occurred with impunity due to the ineffectiveness of the police and the judiciary, its enclosure, guarded by private security agencies, guaranteed safety to wary business and shoppers from the threat of unexpected and uncontrollable violence. Consumers effortlessly navigated its atriums and corridors without ever having to deal with the inconvenience of cramped stalls or the danger of speeding vehicles. More effective than visionary blueprints for building a new capital, which had been repeatedly frustrated by entrenched incompetence and corruption, the shopping mall represented an ideal, aspirational domain where residents could experience future progress and prosperity as concrete, achievable, and quotidian realities in the present time. Its utopian normalcy derived from this legible distillation of the cosmopolitan values and rhythms of a model world-class city that otherwise would have stayed incomprehensible due to the diversity of the megalopolis but were now rendered routine. While Tolentino suggests that the shopping mall is a "rehearsal space" for the *"palatag ng hinaharap"* [future foretold] of progress,[70] I would argue that the mall does not simply rehearse or anticipate utopian progress but makes legible and routine its normalcy.

Neoliberal Zoning and Super-Rich Prestige

Representing a legible model of a world-class city, Singapore branded itself with the buzz of livable, cosmopolitan utopia to attract an influx of not only migrant professionals but also super-rich investors. Spread across the island of Singapore, shopping malls of different sizes and shapes stood as monuments to the tropical island city-state's progress. While many of them were concentrated in the commercial districts of the city center as tourist destinations, they acted as hubs of social life for public housing estates in the urban outskirts where residents congregated, gossiped, and shopped. If neoliberal zoning in Manila was defined by the stark juxtaposition of exclusive gated communities and poor informal settlements in the free market of an elite democracy, the democratic centralism of Singapore aspired to be more appropriately egalitarian in its distribution of racial quotas among its public housing estates. Accommodating transnational flows of products, migrants, and innovations in Singapore, the abundance and variety of shopping malls in Singapore demonstrated the management of difference through neoliberal zoning, whose inclusive classification and organization of urban space based on productive use allowed businesses to target different segments of its multinational, multilinguistic, and multiethnic population.

To construct its infrastructure and improve its livability as a world city, Singapore depended on construction and service workers from Bangladesh, India, China, Myanmar, Indonesia, and the Philippines, whose abruptly increased number fomented popular discontent among its longtime residents.

The cosmopolitan sophistication of Singaporean citizens rested on low-wage migrant labor, whose participation in their national economy would enable them to elevate their job level, salary scale, and professional capacity. Made more manageable without access to legal and economic protections in the form of permanent residency, union membership, and a minimum wage, the presence of migrant workers in Singapore was contrastingly more transient and precarious than that of professionals and investors because their contractual employment was determined by the volatility of the world market. Illustrating the logic of neoliberal cosmopolitanism, which bound the robustness of prosperity to the influx of migration, the precarity of their livelihood relied on the hospitality of the state.

Neoliberal zoning in Singapore's shopping malls entailed the targeting of the diversity of consumers among its multinational population. Instead of being demolished or even refurbished, many obsolete or decaying shopping malls were converted to commercial spaces that catered to marginal niche markets. Outsourcing mass consumption to the urban periphery amid the reluctance of the state to intervene in the economy, they served as hubs of capitalist exchange, public leisure, and social life for the different segments of Singapore's migrant workforce: Golden Mile Complex on Beach Road for Thais, Peninsula Plaza on North Bridge Road for Burmese, City Plaza in the Katong district for Indonesians, and Lucky Plaza on Orchard Road for Filipinos. Standing on the opposite side of Orchard Road from luxury malls Ion Orchard and Takashimaya-Ngee Ann City, Lucky Plaza housed employment agencies, provision stores, beauty salons, and remittance centers for Filipino migrants. As depicted in social melodramas about Filipino migrants by Singaporean filmmakers such as *Ilo-Ilo* (2013) and *Unlucky Plaza* (2014), the surrounding environment of Lucky Plaza would teem with the surplus of activity of the thousands of domestic helpers who would congregate there on Sundays. Their vibrant presence in the main commercial street disclosed Singapore's historical identity as a cosmopolitan hub for intraregional migration, dating to the nineteenth century, that had often been concealed from the "out-of-bounds" or "OB Markers" of state-owned print and television news organizations the *Straits Times* and Channel News Asia, which emphasized its official Han Chinese character.[71]

With the highest per capita income in the world,[72] Singapore likewise possessed the highest income disparity among industrialized nations.[73] Harvey asserts that the rise to dominance of neoliberal capitalism resulted in an exponential increase in wealth for the elite alongside an intensified condition of poverty for the marginalized.[74] Under neoliberal capitalism's regime of immaterial production, Mezzadra and Neilson highlight that the paradigmatic modes of transnational labor constituted not only the affective care of domestic helpers but also the speculative risk-taking of financial traders,[75] which together comprised a significant part of Singapore's migrant workforce. One-third of Singapore's robust financial services industry consisted of expatriate professionals, a large majority of whom earned more than U.S. $300,000 per annum.[76] Already outnumbering those in Europe, Southeast Asian multibillionaires, who owned more than U.S. $10 billion in assets, were projected to overtake those in the United States by the early 2020s.[77] According to the Knight-Frank Wealth Report, Singapore hosted the third-largest number of ultra-high-net-worth individuals, many of whom had relocated from China, India, Indonesia, and Switzerland.[78] Aspiring to tap into the global capital flows of super-rich investors to contribute to its economy, Singapore differed in its treatment of low-wage migrant labor by privileging the migration of elite consumers from overseas with special visa and citizenship schemes such as its Global Investor Programme, which awarded Permanent Residency to foreign nationals who invested U.S. $1.75 million.[79]

The fascination in the public culture with the extravagant, carefree lifestyles of the transnational super-rich reveals how excess became the basis of social value for global prestige in the period of neoliberal capitalism.[80] Instead of being founded on material abundance, distinction could be said to be defined by the capacity to transcend the necessity of given conditions. In previous historical periods distinction had derived its value from the visible possession of luxury goods, to which the majority lacked access because of the exclusivity of the commercial street and the limit to their purchasing power. When these luxury goods started to be exhibited in glass store displays and shelves, the sight of these objects was made more public and democratic. Dissociated from the practice of owning inaccessible objects, social value became rooted in the activity of occupying the commercial street. Particularly in 1960s Manila, with the rapid growth of its urban population, the dominant value of social distinction in the metropolis shifted to popularity, the shared commonality of participating in an amorphous mass. Distinction in this milieu rested on imitating the gestures, appearances, and lifestyles

of popular movie stars, who, despite the allure of their transcendent standing, continued to bear traces of their mundane origins. Epitomized by the
extravagant everyday life of the super-rich, distinction had come to rest not
on the visible possession of material wealth but on the legible performance
of social superiority, which far exceeded the bounds of normative behavior.
Occupying the top tier of the established hierarchy, members of the super-
rich no longer even bothered to negotiate such norms. With the characteristic impunity of neoliberal capitalism, they conducted themselves as though
their abundant wealth had exempted them from the mundane concerns and
constraints that afflicted the majority.

The disparities between elite and marginalized, between the prosperity
of the world city and the precarity of the local population, were configured
into the spatial zoning of Singapore's shopping malls. Targeted toward mass
consumers, the inclusive basement levels of luxury malls such as Ion Orchard
and Takashimaya-Ngee Ann City were the most crowded sections because
the retail stores with the most reasonably priced items were located there.
Connected via underground, air-conditioned corridors to the Mass Transit Railway (MTR) and adjacent shopping malls, the built environments of
these basement levels were characterized by the swarming mobility of bodies through its fast-moving escalators and labyrinthine corridors. Concealed
from the public sight of shoppers above street level, their architecture was
less palatial than that of the luxury malls' upper floors with their low ceilings
and plastic flooring. More spacious and less crowded, the upper floors of Ion
Orchard and Takashimaya-Ngee Ann City featured the boutiques of Gucci,
Louis Vuitton, Cartier, Tiffany & Co., Hermes, and Chanel, high-end fashion
brands favored by the global elite as symbols of their excess. Juxtaposed with
marbled floors, posts, and walls, their soaring ceilings were characterized by
soft lighting and glittering chandeliers to magnify the spectacular grandeur of
their interiors. Complementing their glass window displays, boutiques daz-
zled with illuminated patterns or video screens. Oriented toward attracting
and managing the influx of global capital, the interiors of these luxury malls
were designed to evoke a buzz of elegance and prestige that would appeal to
the affluent tourists with increased purchasing power who frequented them.

Featuring the flagship boutiques of high-end fashion brands, the Marina Bay Sands Shoppes in Singapore's new Marina Bay financial district
outsourced domestic consumption by targeting the super-rich tourists who
gambled at its casino. Disclosing the borderless autonomy of transnational

FIGURE 14. Through its spectacular, deconstructivist architecture, Ion Orchard aspires to contribute to Singapore's buzz of elite prestige. (Photo by author)

capital, members of the global super-rich from other geographic locations were reported in the local news media to fly in on their private jets
to party at exclusive clubs at the Marina Bay Sands casino complex, where
bills frequently exceeded U.S. $100,000. Representing a different mode of
tourism that did not focus on visiting tourist attractions and buying brand-
name clothes, this type of mobility approximated what Zygmunt Bauman
described as the mobility of the jet-setting super-rich flying from location
to location to attend parties.[81] In millennial Singapore, excess was defined
by the superfluous expenditure of exorbitant sums of money for the sole
purpose of private pleasure.

Kevin Kwan's *New York Times* Best Seller *Crazy Rich Asians* visualizes the
excessive lifestyles of the super-rich in East and Southeast Asia. With its
short, fragmentary chapters briskly shifting between Singapore, Shanghai,
Taipei, Shenzhen, and Hong Kong, the novel depicts its wealthy characters effortlessly traveling back and forth across different world cities. Their
seamless mobility illustrates how the twenty-four-hour cycle of neoliberal

capitalism brazenly transcends national borders and laws. Knight-Frank Wealth Reports published during the 2010s revealed the importance for members of the global elite to be based in world cities where they could maintain intimate connections with individuals of equivalent financial wealth and social standing.[82]

Highlighting the importance to them of financial wealth and social standing, *Crazy Rich Asians* portrays its characters as obsessing over the relationships and networks that would guarantee individuals inclusion in this exclusive clique. For instance, the matriarch of the family is described as knowing how to situate each person she meets within a social hierarchy: "Every single person occupied a specific space in the elaborately constructed social universe in her mind ... within thirty seconds of learning their name and where they lived, she would implement her social algorithm and calculate precisely where they stood in her constellation based on who their family was, who else they were related to, what approximate net worth might be, how the fortune was derived, and what family scandals might have occurred within the past fifty years."[83] Featuring revolving groups of protagonists, the novel's multiple narratives alternate and intertwine to trace the hidden linkages among them formalized by money, kinship, and gossip.

Instead of unfolding as a romantic Bildungsroman of a female Asian-American migrant professional in the knowledge production industry of academia, as is the case with the 2018 film adaptation, the original novel is interested in unveiling the exclusive connections of the Asian super-rich, which remain invisible to public knowledge. The Young family, whose enormous wealth the Taiwanese-American university professor Rachel Chu is gradually introduced to, is described in the novel as being "richer than *God*."[84] Highlighting the norms and expectations among members of the elite about their necessary pursuit of a superfluous lifestyle, the various episodes detail the many luxury acquisitions of its characters including diamonds, mansions, hotels, paintings, watches, sportscars, yachts, and jets. Revealing the importance of appearing in the high society pages and top ten lists of Fortune Asia and Hong Kong Tattle magazines as the "richest" or "most invited," the characters underscore their belief that the only way for them to gain respect is through lavish spending.[85] Expanding on the conceptions of delinquency and excess during this historical period, the novel captures how even affluent individuals consider the opulent behavior of characters like Nick Young and Pek-lin Goh to be exorbitant and excessive because of their impulsive spending devoid of any fear of consequences. While unjust to the majority of the population, the novel's image of extravagance in Singapore helped enhance the buzz of its spectacular branding as an attractive destination for speculative investment from overseas.

Disclosed through fragments of gossip about their secrets, the luxurious everyday life of the characters in *Crazy Rich Asians* unfolds in a rarefied private sphere far removed from the mundane concerns and activities of the majority of the population. Its alluring prestige derives from the brazen languor of their enormous wealth, which appears to effortlessly regenerate and increase through unknown sources. As depicted in the novel, affluent individuals value the forbidding opaqueness of their privacy by selecting to mingle solely with each other in exclusive social clubs such as the Pulau Club, Colonial Club, Churchill Club, and Chinese Athletic Association. The super-rich in *Crazy Rich Asians* travel first-class by private plane to attend extravagant bachelorette parties and wedding banquets with Asian celebrities in hidden, remote resorts like Samsara Island and Pulau Samsara. Secluded from the rest of the urban environment despite being situated next to Singapore's UNESCO Heritage Site the Botanic Gardens, the palatial domestic spaces of the Young family's fifty-acre Tyersall Avenue are unknown to real estate agents and hidden from Google Maps.[86] The use of footnotes in the novel to provide background knowledge about the vernacular terms and conditions, which the super-rich insouciantly appropriate and exceed beyond the bounds of significance and consequence, emphasize this sheer disparity in access.

Representing a different form of "OB Markers," the extravagance of the super-rich in millennial Singapore was commonly visible only through sensationalized media representations in the international press, which generated a type of buzz centered on the unattainable allure of excess. Among local social media networks, posts spread virally of the impunity of Chinese migrant professionals whose expensive sports cars would crash and explode on the nighttime streets of the city-state without their arrest or punishment. Instead of publicly flaunting this material wealth, the global elite reportedly hid and stored their luxury possessions in freeport storage facilities under high surveillance and security as they accrued in value. Restricted to members of their exclusive class, their activities and lifestyles were not physically accessible to ordinary people, who, frequenting disparate public spaces, never interacted with them. Inscribed in the print and audiovisual cultures of the time, everyday life at the top tier of the established hierarchy, which occurred at a transcendent distance from national laws and local norms, remained invisible and forbidden.

Encapsulated by the slogan of the Urban Redevelopment Authority, the Singapore government's plans for the built environment of a model world city aimed to refashion and rezone its public spaces into sites "to live, work, and play." While evoking the spectatorial experience of an amusement park according to Frederic Thompson's conception of the carnival spirit, play in millennial Singapore under neoliberal capitalism transpired in two forms, according to the poles of its economic and social disparities. On the one hand, play denoted the restless movement of ordinary people, who, stressed from their precarity in a work regime that privileged transnational capital and talent, were in search of sources of relaxation and revitalization. On the other hand, play could refer to the excess and impunity of the lifestyle of the super-rich, which was not bound by norms of legality or propriety. Defined by wealth inequality and unregulated capital, these two forms of play comprised modes of leisure that, affording people reprieve from the stress of adhering to the demands of prevailing conditions, characterized the practices and process of cosmopolitan sophistication in a model world city.

Unlike amusement parks, whose spectatorial experience of abundance and variety anticipated their logic, shopping malls were configured less toward reinvigorating bodies for the work regime than toward aligning their rhythms and temporalities with those of the world market under the regime of neoliberal capitalism. Without developing economic linkages with global flows, which permitted these flows to maintain their autonomy without submitting them to an overarching framework or narrative, local territories would be unable to attain international standards of progress and prosperity. Dependent on their management of the influx of foreign capital, the governments of Singapore and the Philippines were compelled to rezone their urban environments to comply with the world market's prerequisites for investment for the maintenance of their populations. Cultivating the cosmopolitan sophistication of air-conditioned, sanitary modernity among urban residents, the outsourced contribution to the economy of call center agents, migrant workers, and super-rich investors highlights the centrality of external realities to the constitution of national sovereignty under neoliberal capitalism, which exceeds its aspiration to harness and control them.

Conclusion: Lost Modernities

Juxtaposing the vernacular print and audiovisual cultures of two Southeast Asian cities during three historical periods, *Monsoon Marketplace* has sought to uncover the multiple variations and transformations of capitalism, modernity, consumerism, and spectatorship across different urban environments and media ecologies.

Instead of occupying evolutionary stages in a linear hierarchy of civilization and progress, postcolonial Southeast Asian metropolises such as Manila and Singapore bear multiple trajectories and temporalities that have overlapped, diverged, and meandered at different historical moments. The various chapters in *Monsoon Marketplace* explore how capitalist modernity, mass consumption, and media spectatorship have unfolded not as overarching processes that homogeneously produce docility, atomization, and alienation but as vernacular experiences that ambivalently facilitate and delimit agency, community, and revolution.

During important periods in the 1930s, 1960s, and 2000s, Manila and Singapore's popular commercial and leisure spaces redefined the possibilities of mass entertainment, visual perception, public life, and collective activity. *Monsoon Marketplace* has explored how print and audiovisual media representations trace the vernacular imagination of shifts in the cultures of production, distribution, exchange, and consumption in the marginalized subregion of Southeast Asia. Such changes have corresponded with transitions in the political, economic, and social conditions of colonial occupation, national development, and neoliberal globalization. If, in the current period of populist authoritarianism, class inequality, and fake news, opportunities for transcending the seeming permanence of the established order appear to be marked by impasse and failure, excavating the entanglements of trajectories and temporalities in spatial and social landscapes might be able to reveal the nascence of future frictions and upheavals.

In their introduction to their special issue for *positions: asia critique* entitled *End of Area*, Naoki Sakai and Gavin Walker highlight the collusion of Area Studies in North American universities with the U.S. government's goals of imperial and military capitalism to divide the world into controllable geographic areas. Sakai and Walker critique disciplinary fields such as Southeast Asian Studies for apprehending their areas as objects of knowledge, whose classification of their prevailing conditions and speculation about their future trends have led to the diminution and domination of their complexity and difference.[1] This complicity, they argue, has brought about the poverty of Southeast Asia as a sociological category. Insisting on the urgency of Southeast Asia as a provisional frame of reference, *Monsoon Marketplace* explores how affinities, variances, and disparities among entangled trajectories and temporalities across different urban environments and media ecologies might create an opening for overturning these long-standing hierarchies and injustices.

Differentiating cities and their populations with various degrees of economic and material growth according to a global division of labor, the discourses of modernization theory produced and circulated by international news organizations and policy institutes tend to equate postcoloniality with scarcity, primordialism, tradition, and inertia. From this exclusionary standpoint determined by a corporate and geopolitical elite, any form of order, prosperity, or civilization attained in these locations is the outcome of colonial influence, political intervention, or business investment originating from elsewhere.

In the wake of the decline of the United States as an imperial power in the twenty-first century, one of the goals of the book is to examine the decline of empire through print and audiovisual media representations of languid expatriates seeking refuge by withdrawing to their tropical bungalows and vigorous locals driving development by sanitizing their urban surroundings. While the legacy of colonialism has continued to uphold the dominance of the English language and white masculinity, this book describes how youthful activists who benefitted from the colonial system of public education harnessed its knowledge practices and social networks to protest the efforts by postcolonial leaders to impose their homogeneous vision of progress. Instead of dwelling on imperialist conquest and violence, it analyzes urban plans and public speeches to see how nationalist politicians seized the opportunities created by sovereignty to experiment with innovative modes of administration and control for the purposes of industrial development that would benefit the welfare of the entire population. Whereas some blueprints of visions succeeded because of the ruthless suppression of difference and dissent through the mechanisms of the state, others failed because their implementation was deterred by the corruption and incompetence of officials regardless of colonial or local allegiance.

Monsoon Marketplace maps interconnections among seemingly unrelated discourses, objects, and images to uncover how commercial, administrative, infrastructural, and technological innovations in public spaces of capitalist distribution, exchange, and consumption have shaped the prevailing practices of consumerism and spectatorship in Manila and Singapore across different periods. Defining the multiplicity of modernity in the postcolonial metropolis, the print and audiovisual cultures surrounding such innovations articulate the vernacular experiences of urban residents of the dynamic flows, processes, and changes of tropical milieus as they strive to harness opportunities for transcendence and self-determination.

Diverging from the interactivity and malleability of theater genres such as the *bangsawan* and vaudeville, glass windows and movie theaters of 1930s Manila and Singapore facilitated the shift to a standardized, non-reciprocal mode of visual apprehension that isolated consumers from their busy urban surroundings through a focused gaze of cognitive absorption. Confronted by pluralistic and debilitating flows of bodies and goods in trading ports under U.S. and British occupation, cognitive absorption in the photographs of colonial newspapers and souvenir postcards from the detached standpoint of bungalow verandahs helped manage this uncertainty. Extending physical capacities through their abundance and variety, the entertainment attractions and sporting events in carnivals and amusement parks from this same period revitalized entrepôt labor through the spectatorial experience of sensorial immersion.

Embodying their restless energy, the bustling movie theaters, coffee shops, and street bazaars of 1960s Singapore and Manila gathered the youthful crowds of these postcolonial metropolises under the spectatorial experience of virtual infinitude of neon signs and lights. Negotiating governmental discourses about the rapid linearity of national development and urban renewal with contrasting degrees of achievement and failure, the ambivalent characters and hybrid narratives of popular fantasy and noir films visualized imaginaries of vigorous mobility and transformation. Collectively idling in public spaces, urban residents exchanged gossip about the seemingly mythic personas of actors and politicians who, conveying traces of their prosaic origins, represented models of mimicry for transcending and unsettling the entrenchment of the established hierarchy.

In millennial Manila and Singapore, the distinct typologies of commercial and leisure spaces such as movie theaters, coffee shops, and street bazaars, which had previously been located throughout the urban environment, became concentrated and incorporated within the axiomatic typology of shopping malls. Offering a safe and comfortable enclosure from the tropical heat and congestion of the developing metropolis, their bright, polished, air-conditioned interiors incarnated the utopian normalcy of model world cities. Shaped by intensifying wealth inequality and market competition in the face of the twenty-four-hour cycle of neoliberal capitalism, call center agents and overseas migrant workers fashioned their cosmopolitan sophistication based on their capacities to accommodate the autonomous conditions of external flows.

The multiplicity of commercial and leisure spaces in different locations and periods reveals the significance of innovations in facilitating and delimiting the changes brought about by colonial, vernacular, regional, national, global flows of modernity. Seminal Southeast Asian Studies scholar Benedict Anderson famously highlighted how the emergence of modernity in the form of a nationalist consciousness was facilitated through the innovative dissemination and consumption of print media that evoked the image of simultaneity among shared activities across distant milieus.[2] Expanding on this idea, *Monsoon Marketplace* explores how both foreign and local corporations and investors in Manila and Singapore experimented with commercial, administrative, infrastructural, and technological innovations in street bazaars, department stores, amusement parks, movie theaters, and shopping malls to shape and reshape the parameters of social identity and relations in their distinct urban environments and media ecologies. The contrasting spatial configurations of enclosure in bungalows and supermarkets managed the transformative potential of dynamic modern urban flows. Despite the languor of the tropical heat and humidity, the spectatorial experience of carnival rides, entertainment attractions, and sports events in amusement parks extended the physical capacities for the work regime of an entrepôt economy through sensorial immersion. In expanding metropolises with tentative goals of economic development, glass displays, neon advertisements, and movie screens have enabled consumers and spectators to explore the alternate worlds of their ideal lifestyles, fantasies, and communities.

Looking at how commercial, administrative, technological, and infrastructural innovations in sites of capitalist exchange and mass consumption were described in print and audiovisual media representations produced and circulated in different historical periods, I explored how these innovations point to contingencies, tensions, and ruptures in the prevailing regimes of knowledge and practice. In corporate discourse, innovations are conventionally defined as improvements or enhancements to existing structures, products, technologies, and practices for the purposes of greater profitability and efficiency.[3] The same logic could be discerned in the innovations that governments and businesses introduce to the consumer spaces of postcolonial metropolises. For instance, with the goal of establishing public order, administrative and technological innovations reconfigure urban environments and social practices by instilling norms of sanitation, discipline, and cosmopolitanism. Designed to attract shoppers and encourage purchases, commercial and infrastructural innovations impact not only their personal identity but their collective agency by modulating their aspirations, energies, and movements. While innovations enable regimes of sovereignty and capitalism to enhance their operation, they likewise create openings for alternative practices and lifestyles that depart from the trajectories and temporalities of progress.

Reinhart Koselleck highlights how historical transitions are mediated by innovations that shape their conditions of possibility.[4] I uncovered how the introduction of innovations and the encounter with them entail adjustments and transformations that must be made in the face of the uncertainties and anxieties of changing conditions. Redefining personal and collective agency without necessarily leading to their diminution or suppression, new spaces and infrastructures of capitalist exchange and mass entertainment create opportunities for dominant and emerging modes of visual perception, social behavior, and collective activity to be instantiated or refashioned. Signaling the passage between regimes of knowledge and practice, innovations manage, harness, contain, or delay their imminent possibilities.

Across the disparate spatial environments and media ecologies of Singapore and Manila during the 1930s, 1960s, and 2000s, *Monsoon Marketplace* has aimed to map the multiplicity of the possibilities of modernity by focusing on three distinct, vernacular forms that, undergoing variation and transformation through commercial, administrative, technological, and infrastructural innovations, have interacted, overlapped, and conflicted with each other at different historical moments.

First, *air-conditioned, sanitary modernity* is a regime of health, morality, beauty, and order that intervenes in the spatial configuration and social practice of the city and its population through the discourses and initiatives of governments and businesses. In Southeast Asian metropolises, which colonial administrations regarded as uncontrollably sordid and filthy, the introduction and maintenance of sanitation has been entangled with fantasies of progress against the threat of contagion.

In colonial 1930s Manila, for example, the configuration and experience of air-conditioned modernity were permeated by the sweeping, transcendent force of divine intervention that only government and business were supposedly able to harness through their construction of durable infrastructure, stylistic architecture, and innovative technology in their commercial streets and department stores. Glass window displays and souvenir postcard photographs inscribed the logic of air-conditioned modernity in sanitizing the complexity of the objects they presented. In postcolonial 1960s Singapore, air-conditioned modernity was driven by a resolute, incremental process of national development and urban renewal that pragmatically incorporated and refashioned all the contents of its domain for the sake of industrial productivity and economic growth. Regulating and eliminating street bazaars and rural villages where crowds leisurely and boisterously gathered, the state rearranged and regimented social relations for the discipline of factory work. Millennial Southeast Asian cities during the 2000s were characterized by the aspirations of their governments, citizens, and migrants to attain the utopian normalcy of progress, which was incarnated in the shopping malls of top-ranked, model world cities.

Second, *languid modernity* expresses a tentativeness toward air-conditioned modernity that is marked by a sense of resignation about its inevitability. Whereas air-conditioned modernity is sweeping, resolute, and rapid in character, languid modernity acquiesces to a slower, more hesitant temporality that is not necessarily characterized by more traditional, primitive, or rural conditions. In the canon of critical theories, consumerism and spectatorship are typically understood to be leisure practices of docility and languor. Instead of being a withdrawal from development and self-determination, languid modernity could be seen to assume a different form of agency.

In colonial 1930s Singapore, for instance, the languid consumption of weeks-old newspapers from the metropole in the verandahs of tropical bungalows enabled debilitated expatriate officials and managers to manage contagion and degeneracy from their exposure to the local milieu. In postcolonial 1960s Singapore, the discourses of the newly independent government strove to degrade and dismantle the spatial and social landscapes of rural villages and informal settlements for being communal sources of disorder and languor that resisted the industrial productivity of a developing nation. In millennial Southeast Asia, languor became subsumed under the neoliberal economy of the shopping mall as a quotidian, cosmopolitan activity of leisurely browsing and strolling that intensified the entanglement of mass consumption with public life.

Last, *delinquent, fugitive modernity* is divergent from or resistant to the linear trajectories and temporalities of air-conditioned modernity. Denigrated by state discourses for contravening or disrupting its visions and operations of social order and economic productivity, fugitives and delinquents exhibit ambivalence and antagonism toward the established order but often without any definite object or goal.

In 1930s Manila and Singapore, undesirable, unmanageable realities banished to the outside of the urban domain were called delinquent and fugitive. The fringes of city limits were imagined in the public culture to be sources of vice, crime, violence, and sin. Carnivals and amusement parks allowed a sanitized form of delinquency to be reproduced in their enclosures through the spectatorial experience of sensorial immersion in their thrilling attractions and rides, which captivated audiences on the innocuous threshold of physicality and death. In 1960s Singapore, street hawkers and night markets refused the state's uncompromising visions of industrial productivity and material progress by pursuing their own flexible terms of spatial occupation and mobility. In 1960s Manila, genre narratives featuring delinquents and fugitives on movie screens offered models of mimicry and metamorphosis for spectators. The delinquent languor of restless youth hanging out in movie theaters and corner stores was believed to translate to mass protests calling for a revolutionary upheaval of the established order. In millennial Southeast Asia, the restless energies of urban crowds became dispersed by the architecture and mobility of mass leisure and consumerism in shopping malls. Instead of espousing an antagonistic lifestyle, the delinquency of youthful play rehearsed the market competition and innovation of neoliberal capitalism.

The uncertainties and anxieties during the COVID-19 pandemic accelerated the transformation of the entangled configurations, uses, and significations of capitalism, modernity, consumption, and spectatorship. Marked by a reduction in spatial mobility, social interaction, and sensorial immersion, the onset of the novel coronavirus outbreak in 2020 furthered the dominance of the technological innovations of smartphones, whose media convergence transformed norms of political sovereignty, commercial exchange, and mass consumption. Movie theaters and retail boutiques found their earnings decrease as urban residents departed from the exhaustion of the work regime to spend their idle, languid time watching films and purchasing goods using commercial apps. Through their cognitive absorption by smartphone screens in public spaces, spectators became engrossed by videos and livestreams on YouTube and TikTok. Instead of browsing through the glass displays at brick-and-mortar stores, consumers relied on online marketplaces and delivery services such as Grab, Foodpanda, Carousell, Shopee, and Lazada to acquire products that were directly shipped to their homes. Restricted from meeting in person, family and friends in disparate locations communicated with each other through the virtual communities of social media networks, where fake news easily and uncritically circulated. Inducing cognitive absorption in echo chambers of opinion, the monetization of spreadability by digital platforms like Facebook and Instagram facilitated the rise of populist authoritarianism by enabling interest groups to target users and influencers with similar interests and sentiments who were more amenable to liking or sharing the paid content regardless of its veracity. Sanitary modernity was reconfigured as an assemblage of social restrictions and travel quarantines to fight the spread of the virus, which continued to mutate beyond the firm biopolitical control of state authorities and their health strategies. While understood to provide a comparative advantage for the innovation economy, the delinquency of speculative investors, creative professionals, and foreign migrants became perceived by governments and corporations as a necessary risk that the algorithmic mechanisms of neoliberal capitalism should learn how to manage and harness.

Calle Escolta experienced a resurgence in the 2010s with the innovative restoration of the First United Building at the entrance to the commercial street from Plaza Goiti (renamed Plaza Lacson after the former Manila mayor in 2003). Designed by the architect of the Crystal Arcade, Andres Luna de San Pedro, the Art-Deco Perez-Samanillo Building had housed Berg's Department Store, which thrived after the Pacific War under the proprietorship of the Sylianteng family. While the upper floors host offices for the Business Process Outsourcing industry, the cavernous ground floor of the First United Building contains a coffee shop, craft brewery, bespoke barbershop, and coworking space. Driving the revival of the memory of the Escolta as the "Queen of the Streets," the First United Building has become a creative hub through the initiative of the 98B COLLABoratory art collective, which organizes the Saturday X Future Market (SXFM), a weekly bazaar for local artists and designers. Staged by The Manila Creative Exchange (TMCX) initiative from 2016 until the onset of the COVID-19 pandemic, the annual Escolta Block Festival would include film screenings, DJ sets, cultural exhibits, crafts workshops, popup libraries, and heritage tours. In the face of endemic corruption and inequality, these various efforts to reimagine the established order through the arts signified an aspiration to evoke the lost promise of Manila, which had diminished with the failure of liberal democracy in the long aftermath of the two EDSA People Power Revolutions.

The Great World and New World amusement parks had been redeveloped into the Great World and City Square shopping malls by the 2010s in line with the construction of adjacent Mass Rail Transit stations. MediaCorp Raintree Pictures, a studio owned by the sovereign wealth fund Temasek Holdings, produced a 2011 commercial movie, *It's a Great, Great World*, to capitalize on the trendy nostalgia for the past in the runup to Singapore's Golden Jubilee or SG50. While one of the first local films to use multiple minority Chinese languages including Hokkien, Cantonese, Teochew, Hakka, and Shanghainese, its portrayal of nightclub singers, game operators, and food vendors was criticized for failing to capture the multiracial and multicultural atmosphere of the parks. Entitled "New World," the third edition of the Singapore Night Festival in 2011 was curated by the independent theatre company TheatreWorks to evoke the carnival spirit. More innovative and radical in conceptualization, it featured boxers, strongmen, acrobats, taxi dancers, shadow puppeteers, and drag queens, together with music and video events from regional contemporary art collectives such as Jakarta's Forum Lenteng, Manila's Green Papaya, and Vietnam's Propeller Group. Organized by the government's National Heritage Board, however, the subversive charm of this mass event was eventually abandoned for a more benignly consumable form of art oriented toward families to generate more buzz in the urban environment. While the small city-state has reinvented itself to become the leading global financial hub in Asia in place of its troubled rival Hong Kong, this fleeting moment of artistic experimentation represented a nostalgia for a lost creativity and vibrancy that had been sacrificed in its relentless drive for prosperity.

An archipelago could be understood to bring together incongruous, marginalized imaginaries to trace accidental and unexpected commonalities, interconnections, and possibilities. In a time of rising authoritarianism, this book has hoped to offer a map of shifting archipelagos of trajectories and temporalities that depart from the overarching fantasy of progress and control.

NOTES

INTRODUCTION: METHODS OF ARCHIPELAGIC CAPITALISM

1. *Riding the ASEAN Elephant: How Business Is Responding to the Unusual Animal* (Economist Corporate Network, 2013).

2. Richard Dobbs et al., *Urban World: Mapping the Economic Power of Cities* (McKinsey Global Institute, 2011).

3. Jonathan Woetzel et al., *Southeast Asia at the Crossroads: Three Paths to Prosperity* (McKinsey Global Institute, 2014), 7.

4. Jennifer Robinson, "Global and World Cities: A View from off the Map," *International Journal of Urban and Regional Research* 26, no. 3 (2002): 531–54.

5. Sidney Mintz, *Sweetness and Power: The Place of Sugar in Modern History* (New York: Penguin, 1986); Carl A. Trocki, *Opium, Empire and the Global Political Economy: A Study of the Asian Opium Trade, 1750–1950* (London: Routledge, 1999); Sven Beckert, *Empire of Cotton: A Global History* (New York: Vintage, 2015); Andrew B. Liu, *Tea War: A History of Capitalism in China and India* (New Haven, Conn.: Yale University Press, 2020).

6. Rachel Bowlby, *Carried Away: The Invention of Modern Shopping* (New York: Columbia University Press, 2001); Sharon Zukin, *Points of Purchase: How Shopping Changed American Culture* (New York: Routledge, 2004).

7. Rolando B. Tolentino, *Sa Loob at Labas ng Mall kong Sawi, Kaliluhay Siyang Nangyayaring Hari: Ang Pagkatuto at Pagtatanghal ng Kulturang Popular* (Quezon City: University of the Philippines Press, 2001).

8. Chua Beng Huat, *Life Is Not Complete without Shopping: Consumption Culture in Singapore* (Singapore: Singapore University Press, 2003).

9. Ara Wilson, *The Intimate Economies of Bangkok: Tomboys, Tycoons, and Avon Ladies in the Global City* (Berkeley: University of California Press, 2004).

10. Wilson, *Intimate Economies*, 19.

11. T. J. Clark, *The Painting of Modern Life: Paris in the Art of Manet and His Followers*, rev. ed. (Princeton, N.J.: Princeton University Press, 1999); Vanessa R. Schwartz, *Spectacular Realities: Early Mass Culture in Fin-de-Siècle*

Paris (Berkeley: University of California Press, 1998); Leo Ou-Fan Lee, *Shanghai Modern: The Flowering of a New Urban Culture in China, 1930–1945* (Cambridge, Mass.: Harvard University Press, 1999); Zhang Zhen, *An Amorous History of the Silver Screen: Shanghai Cinema, 1897–1936* (Chicago: University of Chicago Press, 2006); Ravi Sundaram, *Pirate Modernity: Delhi's Media Urbanism* (London: Routledge, 2009); Ackbar Abbas, *Hong Kong: Culture and the Politics of Disappearance* (Minneapolis: University of Minnesota Press, 1997); Yomi Braester, *Painting the City Red: Chinese Cinema and the Urban Contract* (Durham, N.C.: Duke University Press, 2010); and Joshua Neves, *Underglobalization: Beijing's Media Urbanism and the Chimera of Legitimacy* (Durham, N.C.: Duke University Press, 2020).

12. Miriam Hansen, *Babel and Babylon: Spectatorship in American Silent Film* (Cambridge, Mass.: Harvard University Press, 1991).

13. Zhang, *Amorous History*, 11.

14. Zhang, *Amorous History*, xxix.

15. Chua Beng Huat, *Communitarian Ideology and Democracy in Singapore* (London: Routledge, 1995), and *Political Legitimacy and Housing: Stakeholding in Singapore* (London: Routledge, 1997).

16. Chua Beng Huat and Koichi Iwabuchi, eds. *East Asian Pop Culture: Analyzing the Korean Wave* (Hong Kong: Hong Kong University Press, 2008).

17. Kuan-Hsing Chen and Chua Beng Huat, eds., *The Inter-Asia Studies Reader* (London: Routledge, 2007).

18. Cristina Pantoja Hidalgo and Priscelina Patajo-Legasto, eds., *Philippine Postcolonial Studies: Essays in Language and Literature* (Quezon City: University of the Philippines Press, 1993).

19. E. San Juan Jr., *Beyond Postcolonial Theory* (New York: St. Martin's Press, 1998); E. San Juan Jr., *After Postcolonialism: Mapping Philippines–United States Confrontations* (Lanham, Md.: Rowan & Littlefeld, 2000).

20. Kuan-Hsing Chen, *Asia as Method: Toward Deimperialization* (Durham, N.C.: Duke University Press, 2010).

21. Reinhart Koselleck, *The Practice of Conceptual History: Timing History, Spatial Concepts*, trans. Todd Presner, Kerstin Behnke, and Jobst Welge (Stanford, Calif.: Stanford University Press, 2002), 167–69.

22. Michel Foucault, "Nietzsche, Genealogy, History" (1971), in *Aesthetics, Method, and Epistemology: Essential Works of Foucault, 1954–1984*, ed. James D. Faubion (New York: New Press, 1998), 369–91.

23. Su Lin Lewis, *Cities in Motion: Urban Life and Cosmopolitanism in Southeast Asia, 1920–1940* (Cambridge: Cambridge University Press, 2016).

24. Jini Kim Watson, *The New Asian City: Three-Dimensional Fictions of Space and Urban Form* (Minneapolis: University of Minnesota Press, 2011).

25. Dipesh Chakrabarty, *Provincializing Europe: Postcolonial Thought and Historical Difference* (Princeton, N.J.: Princeton University Press, 2000).

26. Benedict Anderson, *The Spectre of Comparisons: Nationalism, Southeast Asia, and the World* (London: Verso, 2004), 2.

27. Partha Chatterjee, "Anderson's Utopia," and H. D. Harootunian, "Ghostly Comparisons: Anderson's Telescope," both in *Grounds of Comparison: Around the Work of Benedict Anderson*, ed. Pheng Cheah and Jonathan Culler (New York: Routledge, 2003), 161–90.

28. Chen, *Asia as Method*.

29. Raymond Williams, *Marxism and Literature* (New York: Oxford University Press, 1977), 131–32.

30. Lee, *Shanghai Modern*, 63.

31. Lee, *Shanghai Modern*, 45.

32. Lee, *Shanghai Modern*, 4–6.

33. Harry D. Harootunian, *Overcome by Modernity: History, Culture, and Community in Interwar Japan* (Princeton, N.J.: Princeton University Press, 2002).

34. Yolanda Mártinez-San Miguel and Michelle Stephens, "'Isolated Above, but Connected Below': Toward New, Global, Archipelagic Linkages," in *Contemporary Archipelagic Thinking: Towards New Comparative Methodologies and Disciplinary Formations*, ed. Michelle Stephens and Yolanda Mártinez-San Miguel (Lanham, Md.: Rowman & Littlefield, 2020), 3 and 5.

35. Édouard Glissant, *Introduction to a Poetics of Diversity*, trans. Celia Britton (Liverpool: Liverpool University Press, 2020), 54–55.

36. Walter Benjamin, *The Arcades Project*, ed. Rolf Tiedemann, trans. Howard Eiland and Kevin McLaughlin (Cambridge, Mass.: Belknap Press, 2002).

37. Benjamin, *Arcades Project*, 461.

1. WALLED STREET OF MODERNITY

1. "Escolta Lensmen," *Sunday Times Magazine*, June 25, 1950, 23.

2. "Modern Fairy Tale Palace Rises in Spite of Difficulties," *Tribune*, June 1, 1932, 11.

3. S. A. Pilar and R. D. Perez III, "Crystal Arcade," in *Cultural Center of the Philippines Encyclopedia of Philippine Art*, vol. III, *Philippine Architecture*, ed. Nicanor G. Tiongson (Manila: Cultural Center of the Philippines, 1994), 223–24.

4. *Manila Daily Bulletin*, June 1, 1932, 4.

5. Daniel Doeppers, *Manila, 1900–1941: Social Change in a Late Colonial Metropolis*, Southeast Asian Studies (New Haven, Conn.: Yale University Press, 1984).

6. Sylvia Mendez Ventura, "Earthquakes, Typhoons, Floods, and Other Acts of God," in *Turn of the Century*, ed. Gilda Cordero-Fernando and Nik Ricio (Quezon City, Philippines: GCF, 1978), 197–201.

7. José Rizal, *Noli Me Tangere* (1887), chapter 32, trans. Ma. Soledad Lacson-Locsin (Makati City, Philippines: Bookmark, 1996), 205–13.

8. Ian Morley, *Cities and Nationhood: American Imperialism and Urban Design in the Philippines, 1896–1916* (Honolulu: University of Hawaii Press, 2018), 76.

9. Morley, *Cities and Nationhood*, 117.

10. Rudolf Mrázek, *Engineers of Happy Land: Technology and Nationalism in a Colony* (Princeton, N.J.: Princeton University Press, 2002).

11. Eric Hobsbawm, *The Age of Empire, 1875–1914* (1987; repr. London: Abacus, 1994).

12. David E. Nye, *American Technological Sublime* (Cambridge, Mass.: MIT Press, 1994); Wolfgang Schivelbusch, *The Railway Journey: The Industrialization of Time and Space in the 19th Century* (Berkeley: University of California Press, 1986).

13. Warwick Anderson, *Colonial Pathologies: American Tropical Medicine, Race, and Hygiene in the Philippines* (Durham, N.C.: Duke University Press, 2006), 115–16.

14. *Gateway to Manila (Shopping in Old Manila): A Complete Practical Guide Book to the Orient's Most Charming City*, 6th ed. (1934), 43.

15. Anderson, *Colonial Pathologies*, 115.

16. W. L. Blakemore, "Air Conditioning," radio health talk (Singapore: Government Print Office, 1940).

17. Mary Douglas, *Purity and Danger: An Analysis of Concepts of Pollution and Taboo* (1966; repr. London: Routledge, 2002), 48–49.

18. Douglas, *Purity and Danger*, 48–49.

19. Lewis E. Gleeck Jr., *The Manila Americans* (Manila: Carmelo and Bauermann, 1977), 4–5.

20. Alfred McCoy and Alfredo Roces, *Philippine Cartoons: Political Caricature of the American Era* (Quezon City, Philippines: Vera-Reyes, 1985), 29.

21. Anders Stephanson, "Blessings of Civilization, 1865–1914," in *Manifest Destiny: American Expansionism and the Empire of Right* (New York: Hill and Wang, 1995), 66–111.

22. Jackson Lears, "Crisis and Regeneration," in *Rebirth of a Nation: The Making of Modern America, 1877–1920* (New York: HarperPerennial, 2009), 167–221.

23. *Inaugural Program January 8th, 1935: Capitol Theatre, Manila's new million peso show emporium* (Manila: n.p., 1935).

24. Edgar Wickberg, *The Chinese in Philippine Life: 1850–1898* (1965; Quezon City, Philippines: Ateneo de Manila University Press, 2000), 75.

25. Wickberg, *Chinese*, 107–8.

26. Teodoro Agoncillo, "Manila in the 1890s," in *History and Culture, Language and Literature: Selected Essays of Teodoro Agoncillo*, ed. Bernadita Reyes Churchill (Manila: University of Santo Tomas Publishing House, 2003), 330–31.

27. Lorelei D. C. de Viana, *Three Centuries of Binondo Architecture 1594–1898: A Socio-Historical Perspective* (Manila: University of Santo Tomas Publishing House, 2001), 50.

28. *The Tribune XIV Anniversary*, June 17, 1939, 49.

29. Genevieve Alva Clutario, *Beauty Regimes: A History of Power and Modern Empire in the Philippines, 1898–1941* (Durham, N.C.: Duke University Press, 2023), 21.

30. Wickberg, *Chinese*, 131.

31. Anthony Reid, *Southeast Asia in the Age of Commerce, 1450–1680*, vol. 1, *The Lands below the Winds* (New Haven, Conn.: Yale University Press, 1988).

32. Paul A. Kramer, *The Blood of Government: Race, Empire, the United States, & the Philippines* (Chapel Hill: University of North Carolina Press, 2006), 166–70, 201–3.

33. Matthew Isaac Cohen, *The Komedie Stamboel: Popular Theater in Colonial Indonesia, 1891–1903* (Athens: Ohio University Center for International Studies, 2006), 11.

34. Anderson, *Colonial Pathologies*; Kramer, *Blood of Government*.

35. "Esco Program over Station KZIB Getting Popular," *Tribune*, April 1, 1938, 11.

36. Patricia May B. Jurilla, *Tagalog Bestsellers of the Twentieth Century: A History of the Book in the Philippines* (Quezon City, Philippines: Ateneo de Manila University Press, 2008), 134.

37. Henry Jenkins, *What Made Pistachio Nuts? Early Sound Comedy and the Vaudeville Aesthetic* (New York: Columbia University Press, 1992), 224.

38. James T. Siegel, *Solo in the New Order: Language and Hierarchy in an Indonesian City* (Princeton, N.J.: Princeton University Press, 1986).

39. Ann McClintock, *Imperial Leather: Race, Gender, Sexuality in the Colonial Conquest* (New York: Routledge, 1995), 221–22.

40. Roland Marchand, *Advertising the American Dream: Making Way for Modernity, 1920–1940* (Berkeley: University of California Press, 1985); Vincent Vinikas, *Soft Soap, Hard Sell: American Hygiene in an Age of Advertisement* (Ames: Iowa State University Press, 1992).

41. Vinikas, *Soft Soap*, 97.

42. Anderson, *Colonial Pathologies*, 88.

43. Anderson, *Colonial Pathologies*, 4–5.

44. Anderson, *Colonial Pathologies*, 117.

45. Anderson, *Colonial Pathologies*, 71.

46. Jaime C. Bulatao, "*Hiya*," *Philippine Studies* 12, no. 3 (1964): 428.

47. Joy H. Alvarez, "*Hiya: Kahulugan, Manifestation, at Kadahilanan*," in *Pananaliksik sa Sikolohiya*, ed. Virgilio Enriquez and Lilia Antonio (Quezon City, Philippines: n.p., 1975), 122.

48. Carmen Guerrero Nakpil, *Women Enough and Other Essays* (Quezon City, Philippines: Ateneo de Manila University Press, 1999), 12.

49. Denise Cruz, *Transpacific Femininities: The Making of the Modern Filipina* (Durham, N.C.: Duke University Press, 2012), 69.

50. Guerrero Nakpil, *Women Enough*, 15.

51. Anne-Lise François, *Open Secrets: The Literature of Uncounted Experience* (Stanford, Calif.: Stanford University Press, 2008).

52. Claro M. Recto, *Vintage Recto: Memorable Speeches and Writings* (Quezon City, Philippines: Foundation for Nationalist Studies, 1986), 134.

53. Doeppers, *Manila*, 66.

54. Ma. Luisa Camagay, *Working Women of Manila of the 19th Century* (Quezon City: University of the Philippines Press/University Center for Women Studies, 1995), 23.

55. Camagay, *Working Women*, 5.

56. "The New Filipino Woman," *Graphic*, November 28, 1935.

57. "Confessions of a Beautiful Shopgirl," *Philippines Free Press*, September 24, 1932, 20–21.

58. "When a Woman Goes Shopping—," *Graphic*, August 31, 1932, 42.

59. "Bargain Sales and the Housewife," *Graphic*, August 17, 1932, 39.

60. *Tribune Anniversary*, 44.

61. Johann Friedrich Geist, *Arcades: The History of a Building Type* (Cambridge, Mass.: MIT Press, 1983), 36.

62. Robert MacMicking, *Recollections of Manila and the Philippines* (Manila: Filipiana Book Guild, 1967), 17.

63. Alison Adburgham, *Shops and Shopping 1800-1914: Where, and in What Manner the Well-Dressed Englishwoman Bought Her Clothes* (London: George Allen & Unwin, 1964), 96.

64. William Leach, *Land of Desire: Merchants, Power, and the Rise of a New American Culture* (New York: Vintage, 2004), 72.

65. Samuel F. Gaches, "38 Years of Progress," *American Chamber of Commerce Journal*, October 1938, 29.

66. "Confessions of a Beautiful Shop Girl," *Philippines Free Press*, September 24, 1932, 20.

67. *Manila Daily Bulletin* supplement on Capitol Theatre, June 1, 1932.

68. "Modern Fairy Tale Palace Rises in Spite of Difficulties," *Tribune*, June 1, 1932, 11.

69. "Attractive Features of Escolta Edifice Drive Away Depression," *Tribune*, June 1, 1932, 9.

70. Weihong Bao, *Fiery Cinema: The Emergence of an Affective Medium in China, 1915-1945* (Minneapolis: University of Minnesota Press, 2015), 223–24.

71. Leach, *Land of Desire*, 62–63.

72. Leach, *Land of Desire*, 64, 69.

73. John Berger, *Ways of Seeing* (London: British Broadcasting Corporation and Penguin, 1972), 88.

74. Otto von Simson, *The Gothic Cathedral: Origins of Gothic Architecture and the Medieval Concept of Order*, rev. ed. (Princeton, N.J.: Princeton University Press, 1962), 4, 123.

75. Jackson Lears, *Fables of Abundance: A Cultural History of Advertising in America* (New York: Basic Books, 1995).

76. Laling H. Lim, "At the Edge of Manila," in *The Manila We Knew*, ed. Erlinda Enriquez Panlilio (Pasig City, Philippines: Anvil, 2006), 22.

77. Luning B. Ira, Isagani R. Medina, and Nik Rios, *Streets of Manila* (Quezon City, Philippies: GCF, 1977), 61.

78. Nick Joaquin, *Almanac for Manileños* (Manila: Mr. & Ms. Publications, 1979), 311.

79. Wickberg, *Chinese*, 75.

80. Cruz, *Transpacific Femininities*, 36.

81. Cruz, *Transpacific Femininities*, 90.

82. Bao, *Fiery Cinema*, 216, 218.

83. Deogracias A. Rosario, "Greta Garbo," in *Philippine Literature: A History and Anthology*, ed. Bievenido Lumbera and Cynthia Nograles Lumbera, rev. ed. (Pasig City, Philippines: Anvil, 1997).

84. Helen Lopez, "The Outsider Within: The Cultural Representation of Women in Selected Tagalog Novelists from the 1920s," in *Women Reading: Feminist Perspectives on Philippine Literary Texts*, ed. Thelma B. Kintanar (Quezon City: University of the Philippines Press, 1992), 112.

85. Modern Girl Around the World Research Group, "The Modern Girl Around the World: Cosmetics Advertising and the Politics of Race and Style," in *The Modern Girl Around the World: Consumption, Modernity, and Globalization*, ed. Modern Girl Around the World Research Group (Durham, N.C.: Duke University Press, 2008), 35.

86. Modern Girl Around the World Research Group, "Modern Girl," 34.

87. "Greta Garbo is going up to Baguio!" Rosario, "Garbo," 138.

88. "Jesus!—Monina cries, but no one can tell if the cause is Octavio's kissing her or the carriage almost being hit by the zigzagging automobile." Rosario, "Garbo," 140.

89. Thorstein Veblen, *The Theory of the Leisure Class* (1899) (New York: Dover, 1994).

90. Clutario, *Beauty Regimes*, 96.

91. Vernadette Vicuña Gonzalez, *Empire's Mistress, Starring Isabel Rosario Cooper* (Durham, N.C.: Duke University Press, 2021), 31.

2. BETWEEN SPACES OF IMPERIAL LANGUOR

1. Chua Ai Lin, "Modernity, Popular Culture, and Urban Life: Anglophone Asians in Colonial Singapore, 1920–1940" (Ph.D. diss., University of Cambridge, 2007), 1.

2. "Malaya Wakes Up to Air-Conditioning," *Singapore Free Press and Mercantile Advertiser*, July 27, 1938, 4.

3. Tamara S. Wagner, *Occidentalism in Novels of Malaysia and Singapore, 1819–2004: Colonial and Postcolonial Financial Straits and Literary Style* (Lewiston, N.Y.: Edwin Mellen, 2005), 116–17.

4. Brenda S. A. Yeoh, *Contesting Space in Colonial Singapore: Power Relations and the Urban Built Environment*, 2nd ed. (Singapore: Singapore University Press, 2003).

5. Rotary Club and the Municipal Commissioners of the Town of Singapore, *A Handbook of Information* (Singapore: 1933), 53–54.

6. Wong Lin Ken, "Singapore: Its Growth as an Entrepôt Port, 1819–1941," *Journal of Southeast Asian Studies* 9, no. 1 (1978): 56.

7. David Harvey, *A Brief History of Neoliberalism* (London: Oxford University Press, 2007), 2.

8. Rotary Club, *Handbook*, 54.

9. Robert Bruce Lockhart, *Return to Malaya* (London: Putnam, 1936), 93.

10. W. Somerset Maugham, *The Casuarina Tree: Seven Stories* (Singapore: Oxford University Press, 1985), 47.

11. Anne McClintock, *Imperial Leather: Race, Gender, and Sexuality in the Colonial Conquest* (New York: Routledge, 1995), 24–25.

12. Geraldine Lowe-Ismail, *Chinatown Memories* (Singapore: Talisman, 2011), 43–45.

13. Yvonne Quahe, *We Remember: Cameos of Pioneer Life* (Singapore: Landmark, 1986), 58; Lowe-Ismail, *Chinatown Memories*, 43–45; Yeoh, *Contesting Space*, 45.

14. Maugham, *Casuarina Tree*, 88.

15. W. Somerset Maugham, *Ah King and Other Stories* (Singapore: Oxford University Press, 1986), 270–71.

16. Richard Dyer, *White* (New York: Routledge, 1997), 156.

17. McClintock, *Imperial Leather*, 47.

18. Abdul JanMohamed, "The Economy of Manichean Allegory: The Function of Racial Difference in Colonialist Literature," *Critical Inquiry* 12, no. 1 (1985): 59–87.

19. Philip Holden, *Orienting Masculinity, Orienting Nation: W. Somerset Maugham's Exotic Fiction* (Westport, Conn.: Greenwood, 1996), 48.

20. Dyer, *White*, 164.

21. Yeoh, *Contesting Space*.

22. Lai Chee Kien, "*Maidan* to *Padang*: Reinventions of Urban Fields in Malaysia and Singapore," *Traditional Dwellings and Settlements Review* 21 (2010): 55–70.

23. Thomas R. Metcalf, *An Imperial Vision: Indian Architecture and Britain's Raj* (Berkeley: University of California Press, 1989), 186, 202.

24. Metcalf, *Imperial Vision*, 16, 193.

25. Kevin Lynch, *The Image of the City* (Cambridge, Mass.: MIT Press, 1960).

26. J. L. Sert, F. Léger, and S. Giedion, "Nine Points of Monumentality," in *Architecture You and Me: The Diary of a Development*, ed. Sigfried Giedeon (Cambridge, Mass.: Harvard University Press, 1958), 48–51.

27. Lewis Mumford, *The City in History: Its Origins, Its Transformations, and Its Prospects* (New York: Harcourt, 1961), 65.

28. Yeoh, *Contesting Space*.

29. Julian Davison, *Black and White: The Singapore House, 1898–1941* (Singapore: Talisman, 2006), 42.

30. Davison, *Black and White*, 144.

31. Davison, *Black and White*, 3.

32. Norman Edwards, *The Singapore House and Residential Life, 1819–1939* (Oxford: Oxford University Press, 1991), 20.

33. Metcalf, *Imperial Vision*, 7.

34. Dyer, *White*, 156.

35. McClintock, *Imperial Leather*, 47.

36. Yeoh, *Contesting Space*, 87.

37. Kelly Hurley, *The Gothic Body: Sexuality, Materialism, and Degeneration at the Fin de Siècle* (Cambridge: Cambridge University Press, 1997), 69.

38. Yeoh, *Contesting Space*, 163.

39. Anthony D. King, *Colonial Urban Development: Culture, Social Power, and Environment* (London: Routledge; Boston: Kegan Paul, 1976), 125.

40. John Tosh, *A Man's Place: Masculinity and the Middle-Class Home in Victorian England* (New Haven, Conn.: Yale University Press, 1999), 30, 33.

41. Edwards, *Singapore House*, 143.

42. Ann Laura Stoler, *Carnal Knowledge and Imperial Power: Race and the Intimate in Colonial Rule* (Berkeley: University of California Press, 2002), 6.

43. Stephen Arata, *Fictions of Loss in the Victorian Fin de Siècle* (New York: Cambridge University Press, 1996), 158–59.

44. Maugham, *Casuarina Tree*, 76.

45. Maugham, *Casuarina Tree*, 278.

46. Stoler, *Carnal Knowledge*, 66.

47. Maugham, *Ah King*, 91–92.

48. Maugham, *Casuarina Tree*, 29.

49. Tosh, *Man's Place*, 32.

50. Deborah Cohen, *Household Gods: The British and their Possessions* (New Haven, Conn.: Yale University Press, 2006), xi.

51. Davison, *Black and White*, 144; Tosh, *Man's Place*, 32.

52. King, *Colonial Urban Development*, 156–79; Robert R. Reed, *City of Pines: The Origins of Baguio as a Colonial Hill Station and Regional Capital* (Berkeley: University of California Center for South and Southeast Asian Studies, 1976).

53. Michael D. Pante, "Peripheral Pockets of Paradise: Perceptions of Health and Geography in Early Twentieth-Century Manila and its Environs," *Philippine Studies* 59, no. 2 (2011): 187–212.

54. Davison, *Black and White*, 3.

55. Lee Kip Lin, *Singapore House, 1819–1942* (Singapore: Times Editions, 1988).

56. Davison, *Black and White*, 62.

57. Davison, *Black and White*, 12.

58. Maugham, *Casuarina Tree*, 131.

59. Maugham, *Ah King*, 57.

60. Eddie Tay, *Colony, Nation, and Globalization: Not at Home in Singaporean and Malaysian Literature* (Singapore: NUS Press, 2011), 53.

61. Patrick Collier, "Imperial/Modernist Forms in the *Illustrated London News*," *Modernism/Modernity* 19, no. 3 (2012): 490, 494.

62. Stuart Hall, "The Determinations of News Photographs," in *The Manufacture of News: Deviance, Social Problems, and the Mass Media*, ed. Stanley Cohen and Jock Young (London: Constable, 1981), 176–90.

63. Stuart Hall, Chas Critcher, Tony Jefferson, John Clarke, and Brian Roberts, *Policing the Crisis: Mugging, the State, and Law and Order* (London: Macmillan, 1978), 55.

64. Georg Simmel, "The Metropolis and Modern Life," in *The Sociology of Georg Simmel* (Glencoe, Ill.: Free Press, 1950), 410.

65. Simmel, "Metropolis," 410.

66. Maugham, *Casuarina Tree*, 292.

67. Rosalind C. Morris, "Imperial Pastoral: The Politics and Aesthetics of Translation in British Malaya," *Representations* 99, no. 1 (2007): 159.

68. Cheah Jin Seng, *Singapore: 500 Early Postcards* (Singapore: Editions Didier Millet, 2006).

69. Susan Stewart, *On Longing: Narratives of the Miniature, the Gigantic, the Souvenir, the Collection* (1987; repr. Durham, N.C.: Duke University Press, 1993), 137–38.

70. Howard Woody, "International Postcards: Their History, Production, and Distribution (Circa 1895 to 1915)," in *Delivering Views: Distant Cultures in Early Postcards*, ed. Christraud M. Geary and Virginia-Lee Webb (Washington, D.C.: Smithsonian Institution Press, 1998), 16.

71. King, *Colonial Urban Development*, 147.

72. Yeoh, *Contesting Space*, 143.

73. Yeoh, *Contesting Space*, 96.

74. Yeoh, *Contesting Space*, 86.

75. "Sin Taken Out of Singapore," *Sunday Times*, March 12, 1933, 9.

76. Kah-Wee Lee, "Vice and the City: Embarrassments of Nationalism in Singapore, 1960–1980," in *Asian Cities: Colonial to Global* (Amsterdam: Amsterdam University Press, 2015).

77. John Tagg, *The Burden of Representation: Essays on Photographies and Histories* (Minneapolis: University of Minnesota Press, 1993), 151.

78. Vicente L. Rafael, *White Love, and Other Events in Filipino History* (Durham, N.C.: Duke University Press, 2014), 83.

3. SPECTACLES BEYOND THE LIMITS OF EXHAUSTION

1. Alfred W. McCoy, "Philippine Commonwealth and the Cult of Masculinity," *Philippine Studies* 48, no. 3 (2000): 315–46; Genevieve Alva Clutario, *Beauty Regimes: A History of Power and Modern Empire in the Philippines, 1898–1941* (Durham, N.C.: Duke University Press, 2023), 100.

2. Tan Kar Lin, "The 'Worlds' Entertainment Parks of Singapore (1920s–1980s): New Urban Form and Social Space for Culture and Consumption" (Master's thesis, National University of Singapore, 2004).

3. Tom Gunning, "The Cinema of Attraction: Early Film, Its Spectator, and the Avant-Garde," *Wide Angle* 8 (1986): 63–70; Jonathan Crary, *Techniques of the Observer: On Vision and Modernity in the Nineteenth Century* (Cambridge, Mass.: MIT Press, 1990).

4. Warwick Anderson, *Colonial Pathologies: American Tropical Medicine, Race, and Hygiene in the Philippines* (Durham, N.C.: Duke University Press, 2006), 121–22.

5. Glenn Anthony May, "The Business of Education in the Colonial Philippines, 1909–1930," in *Colonial Crucible: Empire in the Making of the Modern American State*, ed. Alfred W. McCoy and Francisco A. Scarano (Madison: University of Wisconsin Press, 2009), 151–53.

6. Nick Joaquin, *Almanac for Manileños* (Manila: Mr. & Ms. Publications, 1979), 39.

7. Joaquin, *Almanac for Manileños*, 39.

8. *Manila Carnival Commercial and Industrial Fair January 27–February 11, 1934* (Manila: Philippine Carnival Association, 1934), 9.

9. Nick Joaquin, "Popular Culture: The American Years," in *Filipino Heritage*, ed. Alfredo Roces (Quezon City, Philippines: Lahing Pilipino, 1977), 10:2,734.

10. Quijano de Manila [Nick Joaquin], *Manila: Sin City? and Other Chronicles* (Quezon City, Philippines: National Bookstore, 1977), 258.

11. *Philippines Free Press*, April 28, 1934, 36.

12. "Carnival Sidelights," *Sunday Tribune*, February 12, 1933, 10.

13. *Rosenstock's Manila City Directory* (Manila: Philippine Education Co., 1934–35).

14. Alan Trachtenberg, *The Incorporation of America: Culture and Society in the Gilded Age* (New York: Hill and Wang, 1982), 231.

15. Joaquin, *Almanac for Manileños*, 39.

16. Clutario, *Beauty Regimes*, 66–67.

17. Anderson, *Colonial Pathologies*, 123.

18. *Manila Carnival Commercial and Industrial Fair* (Manila: Philippine Carnival Association, 1933), 9.

19. Tom Gunning, "The World as Object Lesson: Cinema Audiences, Visual Culture, and the St. Louis World's Fair, 1904," *Film History* 6, no. 4 (1994): 424–25.

20. Anderson, *Colonial Pathologies*, 123.

21. Robert M. Lewis, *From Traveling Show to Vaudeville: Theatrical Spectacle in America, 1830–1910* (Baltimore: Johns Hopkins University Press, 2003), 280.

22. Lauren Rabinovitz, *Electric Dreamland: Amusement Parks, Movies, and American Modernism* (New York: Columbia University Press, 2012), 8–9.

23. Tan, "'Worlds' Entertainment Parks," 24.

24. Yvonne Quahe, *We Remember: Cameos of Pioneer Life* (Singapore: Landmark, 1986), 83.

25. "Tamil Laborers Go to Evening Classes," *Sunday Times*, July 26, 1936, 15.

26. Tan, "'Worlds' Entertainment Parks," 5.

27. Frederic Wakeman Jr., *Policing Shanghai 1927–1937* (Berkeley: University of California Press, 1995), 105.

28. This thick description of New World Amusement Park is based on blueprints submitted to the Building Control Authority in 1923 and 1938, courtesy of the Singapore National Archives.

29. "Vaudeville and Kronchong Competition," The City Opera, *Malaya Tribune*, March 29, 1928, 10; "Attractive Programme for the Hari Raya Haji," The City Opera, *Malaya Tribune*, May 29, 1928, 10; "The New World," *Straits Times*, August 2, 1928, 10.

30. "When Night Falls in Singapore," *Sunday Times*, November 26, 1933, 10.

31. Wong Yunn Chii and Tan Kar Lin, "Emergence of a Cosmopolitan Space for Culture and Consumption: The New World Amusement Park-Singapore (1923–1970) in the Inter-War Years," *Inter-Asia Cultural Studies* 5, no. 2 (2004): 291.

32. Frederic Thompson, "Amusing the Million," *Everybody's Magazine*, September 1908, <nationalhumanitiescenter.org/pds/gilded/people/text2/thompson.pdf>.

33. Mikhail Bakhtin, *Rabelais and His World*, trans. Hélène Iswolsky (Bloomington: Indiana University Press, 1984).

34. Wong and Tan, "Emergence of a Cosmopolitan Space," 288–89.

35. Judith A. Adams, *The American Amusement Park Industry: A History of Technology and Thrills* (Boston: Twayne, 1991), 4.

36. Matthew Isaac Cohen, *The Komedie Stamboel: Popular Theater in Colonial Indonesia, 1891–1903* (Athens: Ohio University Press, 2006), 10.

37. Wong and Tan, "Emergence of a Cosmopolitan Space," 291.

38. Wong and Tan, "Emergence of a Cosmopolitan Space," 294.

39. "The Between Seasons Period," *Sunday Times*, February 18, 1934, 16.

40. Lim Kee Chan, "S'pore Forgets – But this Ring Idol Gets Cheers from Afar," *Straits Times*, March 30, 1980, 16.

41. Little Nene, "Ignacio Is Down—But Not Out," *New Nation*, May 11, 1973, 15.

42. "New Ring Role for Ignacio," *Straits Times*, November 5, 1949, 12.

43. Chan, "S'pore Forgets," 16.

44. Lee Kuan Yew, *The Papers of Lee Kuan Yew: Speeches, Interviews, Dialogues* (Singapore: National Archives of Singapore, 2012), 2:77.

45. Michel Foucault, *Discipline and Punish: The Birth of the Prison* (1978), trans. Alan Sheridan (repr. New York: Vintage, 1995), 216.

46. Joyce Carol Oates, *On Boxing* (Hopewell, N.J.: Ecco, 1995), 8.

47. Oates, *On Boxing*, 8.

48. Russell B. Nye, "Eight Ways of Looking at an Amusement Park," *Journal of Popular Culture* 15 (1981): 71.

49. Michael Fried, *Art and Objecthood: Essays and Reviews* (Chicago: University of Chicago Press, 1998), 159.

50. Nye, "Eight Ways of Looking at an Amusement Park," 71.

51. Qtd. in Tan, "'Worlds' Entertainment Parks," 83.

52. John Kasson, *Amusing the Million: Coney Island at the Turn of the Century* (New York: Hill and Wang, 1978), 15.

53. Kasson, *Amusing the Million*, 18–20.

54. Tan Sooi Beng, *Bangsawan: A Social and Stylistic History of Popular Malay Opera* (Singapore: Oxford University Press, 1993), 28.

55. Tan, *Bangsawan*, 20.

56. E. Mowbray Tate, *Transpacific Steam: The Story of Steam Navigation from the Pacific Coast of North America to the Far East and the Antipodes, 1867–1941* (New York: Cornwall, 1986), 39–40.

57. Gareth Curless, "The Triumph of the State: Singapore's Dockworkers and the Limits of Global History, c. 1920–1965," *Historical Journal* 60, no. 4 (2017): 1,100–1,101.

58. Deborah Cowen, *The Deadly Life of Logistics: Mapping Violence in Global Trade* (Minneapolis: University of Minnesota Press, 2014).

59. Cowen, *Deadly Life of Logistics*, 100.

60. Stephen Dobbs, *The Singapore River: A Social History, 1819–2002* (Singapore: Singapore University Press, 2003), 66.

61. William Leach, *Land of Desire: Merchants, Power, and the Rise of a New American Culture* (New York: Vintage, 1994), 73.

62. Alfred McCoy and Alfredo Roces, *Philippine Cartoons: Political Caricature of the American Era* (Quezon City, Philippines: Vera-Reyes, 1985), 140; Linda España-Maram, *Creating Masculinity in Los Angeles' Little Manila: Working-Class Filipinos and Popular Culture, 1920s–1950s* (New York: Columbia University Press, 2006), 83.

63. España-Maram, *Creating Masculinity*, 100–101.

64. William Roff, *The Origins of Malay Nationalism*, 2nd ed. (Kuala Lumpur: Oxford University Press, 1994), 183.

65. "Malayan Club News," *Straits Times*, March 24, 1935, 11.

66. "Malayan Correspondence Club," *Singapore Free Press and Mercantile Advertiser*, September 2, 1931, 7.

67. "Clubs Prepare to Challenge 'Black Ordinance,'" *Sunday Times*, July 5, 1936, 1.

68. Su Lin Lewis, *Cities in Motion: Urban Life and Cosmopolitanism in Southeast Asia, 1920–1940* (Cambridge: Cambridge University Press, 2016), 119.

69. John Tosh, *A Man's Place: Masculinity and the Middle-Class Home in Victorian England* (New Haven, Conn.: Yale University Press, 1999), 186.

70. "Around the Clubs in Malaya," *Sunday Tribune*, April 22, 1934, 16.

71. Lewis, *Cities in Motion*, 110.

72. "Malayan Clubs," *Malaya Tribune*, June 18, 1934, 10.

73. Richard Holt, "The Amateur Body and the Middle-Class Man: Work, Health, and Style in Victorian Britain," *Sport in History* 26, no. 3 (2006): 352.

74. Eric Hobsbawm, *The Age of Empire, 1875–1914* (1987; repr. London: Abacus, 1994), 182.

75. Tosh, *Man's Place*, 189.

76. Roberta J. Park, "Biological Thought, Athletics, and the Formation of a 'Man of Character,' 1830–1900," in *Manliness and Morality: Middle-Class Masculinity in Britain and America, 1800–1940*, ed. J. A. Mangan and James Walvin (Manchester: Manchester University Press, 1987), 29.

77. J. A. Mangan and James Walvin, Introduction, in *Manliness and Morality: Middle-Class Masculinity in Britain and America, 1800–1940* (Manchester: Manchester University Press, 1987), 1.

78. J. A. Mangan, *Athleticism in the Victorian and Edwardian Public School: The Emergence and Consolidation of an Educational Ideology* (London: F. Cass, 2000), 9.

79. Park, "Biological Thought," 23.

80. Andrew Smith, *Victorian Demons: Medicine, Masculinity, and the Gothic at the Fin-de-Siècle* (Manchester: Manchester University Press, 2004), 18.

81. *Singapore Cricket Club, 1852–1985* (Singapore: Singapore Cricket Club, 1985), 15.

82. "Cricket Club Philistines and Snobs!" *Singapore Free Press and Mercantile Advertiser*, November 19, 1935, 2.

83. Maurice Dekobra, "Marriage and the Modern Youth," *Sunday Times*, February 18, 1934, 2.

84. Patrick Khaw, "The Singapore Recreation Club, 1883–1963" (Bachelor's thesis, National University of Singapore, 1986–87), 18–19.

85. Park, "Biological Thought."

86. John T. Sidel, "Philippine Politics in Town, District, and Province: Bossism in Cavite and Cebu," *Journal of Asian Studies* 56, no. 4 (1997): 950–951.

87. "Shock for Colony's Clubs and Societies," *Singapore Free Press and Mercantile Advertiser*, July 6, 1936, 6.

88. Lewis, *Cities in Motion*, 120.

89. Carl Trocki, *Opium and Empire: Chinese Society in Colonial Singapore, 1800–1910* (Ithaca, N.Y.: Cornell University Press, 1990), 238.

90. Susan Brownell, "Sports in Britain and China, 1850–1920: An Explanatory Overview," *International Journal of the History of Sport* 8, no. 1 (1991): 284–90.

91. "Clubs and Their Members," *Singapore Free Press and Mercantile Advertiser*, July 28, 1925, 14.

92. "Around the Clubs in Malaya," *Sunday Tribune*, April 22, 1934, 16.

93. "Cricket Club Philistines and Snobs!," 2.

94. "Proposed New Chinese Sports Club," *Straits Times*, January 20, 1930, 17; "Equal Rights for Women," *Malaya Tribune*, August 3, 1936, 5.

95. Roff, *Origins of Malay Nationalism*, 182.

96. Lewis, *Cities in Motion*, 120.

4. TEMPORALITIES OF DEVELOPMENT AND DELINQUENCY

1. Meredith L. Weiss and Edward Aspinall, eds., *Student Activism in Asia: Between Protest and Powerlessness* (Minneapolis: University of Minnesota Press, 2012).

2. Carl A. Trocki and Michael D. Barr, Introduction, *Paths Not Taken: Political Pluralism in Post-War Singapore*, ed. Michael D. Barr and Carl A. Trocki (Singapore: NUS Press, 2008), 6.

3. T. N. Harper, *The End of Empire and the Making of Malaya* (New York: Cambridge University Press, 1998), 301.

4. Goh Keng Swee, *The Practice of Economic Growth* (1977; repr. Singapore: Marshall Cavendish Academic, 2004), 109.

5. S. Rajaratnam, *The Prophetic and the Political* (Singapore: Institute of Southeast Asian Studies and Graham Brash, 2007), 224–25.

6. Lee Kah-Wee, *Las Vegas in Singapore: Violence, Progress, and the Crisis of National Modernity* (Singapore: NUS Press, 2019), 96.

7. Yue-man Yeung, "Periodic Markets: Comments on Spatio-Temporal Relationships," *Professional Geographer* 26, no. 2 (1974): 147.

8. Yue-man Yeung, *Changing Cities of Pacific Asia: A Scholarly Interpretation* (Hong Kong: Chinese University of Hong Kong Press, 1990), 243.

9. *Papineau's Guide to Singapore and Spotlight on Malaysia*, 18th ed. (Singapore: André, 1965), 133; "Spores Barter Trade Bazaar," *Straits Times*, September 15, 1966, 11.

10. Hernando de Soto, *The Other Path: The Economic Answer to Terrorism* (New York: Basic Books, 1989), 63.

11. Tan Pin Ho, interview with Jesley Chua Chee Huan, *Special Project*, Oral History Centre, 001864/03, October 15, 1997.

12. "Lunchtime in Change Alley," *Straits Times*, July 1, 1950, 12.

13. Victor Chew Chin Aik, interview with Jesley Chua Chee Huan, *Special Project*, Oral History Centre, 001965/07, November 3, 1997.

14. *Tourist Treasure Log: Singapore, the Shopper's Paradise* (Singapore: Tecco, 1968), 73.

15. *Willis' Singapore Guide* (Singapore: A. C. Willis, 1934).

16. *Straits Times*, March 16, 1934, 15.

17. *Willis' Singapore Guide*, 47; "Change Alley," *Singapore Free Press and Mercantile Advertiser*, October 9, 1933, 8; Tessi Cornelius, "Change Alley Changes," *Singapore Free Press*, August 5, 1946, 4.

18. *Straits Times*, March 16, 1934, 15.

19. Yeo Kim Wah, *Political Development in Singapore, 1945–1955* (Singapore: Singapore University Press, 1973), 133; *Papineau's Guide*, 91.

20. R. March, "The Street of a Thousand Faces," *Singapore Free Press*, January 21, 1952, 7; Talking Shop, *Straits Times*, August 13, 1953, 9; "Shoppers' Paradise for Visitors," *Straits Times*, June 11, 1967, 5.

21. *Willis' Singapore Guide*, 47.

22. Tan, interview.

23. "Tourist on Change Alley: 'It's Incredible!,'" *Straits Times*, October 16, 1961, 7.

24. Clifford Geertz, *Peddlers and Princes: Social Change and Economic Modernization in Two Indonesian Towns* (Chicago: University of Chicago Press, 1963), 30–31.

25. Chua Beng Huat, *Political Legitimacy and Housing: Stakeholding in Singapore* (London: Routledge, 1997), 152–67.

26. "New Code for Pasar Malam," *Straits Times*, March 2, 1966, 4.

27. De Soto, *Other Path*, 11–12.

28. Quoted in Yeung, *Changing Cities*, 238.

29. Lee, *Las Vegas*, 96.

30. "Record Shoe Production," *Straits Times*, July 31, 1964, 13.

31. "Saturday Shoppers' Secret," *Straits Times*, April 7, 1960, 9.

32. Deborah A. Kapchan, *Gender on the Market: Moroccan Women and the Revoicing of Tradition* (Philadelphia: University of Pennsylvania Press, 1996), 3.

33. Victor W. Turner, *The Ritual Process: Structure and Anti-Structure* (New York: Aldine Transaction, 1997), 94.

34. Michael Fernandez and Loh Kah Seng, "The Left-Wing Trade Unions in Singapore, 1945–1970," in Barr and Trocki, *Paths Not Taken*, 213.

35. Yeo, *Political Development in Singapore*, 183–201, 238–50.

36. Kah Seng Loh, Edgar Liao, Cheng Tju Lim, and Guo-Quan Seng, *The University Socialist Club and the Contest for Malaya: Tangled Strands of Modernity* (Amsterdam: Amsterdam University Press, 2012), 61.

37. Huan Jianli, "The Young Pathfinders: Portrayal of Student Political Activism," in *Paths Not Taken: Political Pluralism in Post-War Singapore*, ed. Michael D. Barr and Carl A. Trocki (Singapore: NUS Press, 2008), 189–90.

38. Hong Lysa and Huan Jianli, *The Scripting of a National History: Singapore and its Past* (Singapore: NUS Press, 2008), 138.

39. Fernandez and Loh, "Left-Wing Trade Unions," 216–17.

40. "Strike Drama at Raffles Place," *Straits Times*, September 12, 1961, 13.

41. "Sit-down Strike by 180 Shaw Brothers Employees," *Straits Times*, September 22, 1961, 1.

42. "Sit-down Strike at Shaw Cinemas," *Singapore Free Press*, December 21, 1961, 1; "Shaw Strike: A Deadlock after 30-Minute Talks," *Straits Times*, December 23, 1961, 4; "Shaw Shows on Again," *Straits Times*, February 2, 1962, 1.

43. "200 Pasar Malam Hawkers Go on Strike," *Straits Times*, May 18, 1966, 5.

44. Sidney G. Tarrow, *Power in Movement: Social Movements and Contentious Politics*, 3rd ed. (New York: Cambridge University Press, 2011), 111.

45. Tarrow, *Power*, 101.

46. Joshua Clover, *Riot. Strike. Riot: The New Era of Uprisings* (London: Verso, 2016), 16.

47. Clover, *Riot*, 84.

48. Gustave Le Bon, *The Crowd: A Study of the Popular Mind* (New York: Macmillan, 1896), 128–29.

49. T. N. Harper, "Lim Chin Siong and the 'Singapore Story,'" in *Our Comet in the Sky: Lim Chin Siong in History*, ed. Tan Jing Quee and Jomo K. S. (Kuala Lumpur, Malaysia: ISAN, 2001), 35.

50. Lee Kuan Yew, *The Papers of Lee Kuan Yew: Speeches, Interviews, and Dialogues* (Singapore: National Archives of Singapore, 2012), 2:351.

51. United Nations Industrial Survey Mission, *A Proposed Industrialization Programme for the State of Singapore* (New York: United Nations Programme of Technical Assistance, 1963), 83.

52. Lee, *Papers*, 4:93.

53. Goh, *Practice of Economic Growth*, 11.

54. United Nations Industrial Survey Mission, *Proposed Industrialization Programme*, xxi.

55. Le Bon, *Crowd*, 18.

56. Le Bon, *Crowd*, xxii.

57. William Mazzarella, "The Myth of the Multitude, or, Who's Afraid of the Crowd?," *Critical Inquiry* 36, no. 4 (2010): 700.

58. Le Bon, *Crowd*, 6.

59. Le Bon, *Crowd*, xix.

60. Le Bon, *Crowd*, 10.

61. Le Bon, *Crowd*, xix.

62. Le Bon, *Crowd*, 10.

63. Huan, "Young Pathfinders," 190–91.

64. Geoff Wade, "Operation Coldstore: A Key Event in the Creation of Modern Singapore," in *The 1963 Operation Coldstore in Singapore: Commemorating 50 Years*, ed. Poh Soo Kai, Tan Kok Fang, and Hong Lysa (Malaysia: SIDRC/Pusat Sejarah Rakyat, 2013), 15–69.

65. Article 8, number 3 of Singapore, Parliament, *Internal Security Act* (Singapore: Attorney-General's Chambers Legislative Division, 1963).

66. Chua Beng Huat, *Communitarian Ideology and Democracy in Singapore* (London: Routledge, 1995), 19.

67. Ping Tjin Thum, "Independence: The Further Stage of Colonialism in Singapore," in *The Limits of Authoritarian Governance in Singapore's Developmental State*, ed. Lily Zubaidah Ibrahim and Michael D. Barr (Singapore: Palgrave Macmillan, 2019), 49–69.

68. *Straits Times*, May 2, 1967, 4.

69. *Keep Singapore Clean, 1 October 1968* (Singapore: Television Corporation of Singapore, 1988).

70. "Ministry Warning to the 'Incorrigibles,'" *Straits Times*, October 10, 1968, 10.

71. "'Clean' Drive Is Now Crusade: Chua," *Straits Times*, October 31, 1968, 4.

72. "Follow the law for our liberation."

73. Cherian George, *Air-Conditioned Nation Revisited: Essays on Singapore Politics* (Singapore: Ethos, 2020), 40–43.

74. Lee, *Papers*, 4:171.

75. Michel Foucault, "Governmentality," in *Power: Essential Works of Foucault, 1954–1984* (New York: New Press, 2000), 210.

76. Foucault, "Governmentality," 216–17.

77. Tania Murray Li, *The Will to Improve: Governmentality, Development, and the Practice of Politics* (Durham, N.C.: Duke University Press, 2007), 8.

78. Lee, *Papers*, 4:171.

79. Goh, *Practice of Economic Growth*, 161.

80. Lee, *Papers*, 3:363–64.

81. Lee, *Papers*, 3:458.

82. Lee, *Las Vegas*, 73.

83. Hawker's Inquiry Commission, Report (Singapore Government Printing Office, 1950), 45.

84. "Pasar Malam Fee Fixed," *Straits Times*, March 5, 1966, 7

85. Chua, *Communitarian Ideology*, 58.

86. Chua, *Communitarian Ideology*, 68.

87. Singapore Ministry of National Development, Central Area Programme Map, *1958 Master Plan* (Singapore: Ministry of National Development, 1958).

88. James C. Scott, "Cities, People, and Language," in *Seeing Like a State: How Certain Schemes to Improve the Human Condition Have Failed* (New Haven, Conn.: Yale University Press, 1998), 53–83.

89. Ernest Gellner, *Nations and Nationalism*, 2nd ed. (Oxford: Blackwell, 2006), 28.

90. Li, *Will to Improve*, 9.

91. Chua, *Communitarian Ideology*, 69.

92. Lee, *Papers*, 4:80 and 83.

93. "New Code for Pasar Malam," *Straits Times*, March 2, 1966, 4.

94. "The Public Must Co-operate," *Straits Times*, October 1, 1968, 10.

95. Lee, *Papers*, 3:384.

96. Geertz, *Peddlers*, 28–29.

97. De Soto, *Other Path*, 246.

98. Y. T. Khoo, "Three Words Spell Success," *Singapore Free Press*, September 30, 1959, 4.

99. Clifford Geertz, "Suq: The Bazaar Economy in Sefrou," in *Meaning and Order in a Moroccan Society: Three Essays in Cultural Analysis*, ed. Clifford Geertz, Hildred Geertz, and Lawrence Rosen (Cambridge: Cambridge University Press, 1979), 124.

100. "Change Alley 'A Fascinating Place to Study Human Behavior,'" *Straits Times*, April 30, 1968, 30.

101. Geertz, *Peddlers*, 35.

102. Jennifer Alexander and Paul Alexander, "Striking a Bargain in Javanese Markets," *Man* (New Series) 22, no.1 (1987): 42–68.

103. *Willis' Singapore Guide*, from 1934, *Papineau's Guide*, from 1965, and *Tourist Treasure Log: Singapore, the Shopper's Paradise* (Singapore: Tecco Organization), from 1968.

104. "Talking Shop," *Straits Times*, August 13, 1953.

5. PANORAMIC POPULARITY IN THE NEON STREETS

1. Patricio N. Abinales and Donna J. Amoroso, *State and Society in the Philippines*, 2nd ed. (Lanham, Md.: Rowman and Littlefield, 2017), 121.

2. Talitha Espiritu, *Passionate Revolutions: The Media and the Rise and Fall of the Marcos Regime* (Athens: Ohio University Press, 2017), 28.

3. William E. McIntyre, "The Retail Pattern of Manila," *Geographical Review* 45, no. 1 (1955): 69.

4. Nick Joaquin, "Popular Culture: The American Years," in *Filipino Heritage: The Making of a Nation*, ed. Alfredo Roces (Quezon City, Philippines: Lahing Pilipino, 1977-1978), 8:2,735.

5. *The Fookien Times Philippines Yearbook* (Manila: Fookien Times, 1967), 193.

6. Paulo Alcazaren, Luis Ferrer, and Benvenuto Icamina, *Lungsod Iskwater: The Evolution of Informality as a Dominant Pattern in Philippine Cities* (Mandaluyong City, Philippines: Anvil, 2011), 61–62.

7. Luning B. Ira, Isagani R. Medina, and Nik Rios, *Streets of Manila* (Quezon City, Philippines: GCF, 1977), 99.

8. Sylvia L. Mayuga, *The Spy in My Own Country: Essays* (Manila: Sylvia L. Mayuga, 1981), 107–8.

9. Ira, Medina, and Rios, *Streets of Manila*, 109.

10. "Bookstore, bookstore, restaurant, bookstore, restaurant, bakery, tailor, restaurant, restaurant, restaurant, cinema, hotel, restaurant, restaurant, shoe store, restaurant. The city dominates the appetites of the body." Edgardo M. Reyes, *Sa Mga Kuko ng Liwanag* (Manila: De La Salle University Press, 1986), 143.

11. Benedict Anderson, *The Spectre of Comparisons: Nationalism, Southeast Asia, and the World* (London: Verso, 2004), 29–45.

12. "In the rugged faces of the sidewalks, multitudes of shoes drag and rise. Gangster. Doctor. Mistress. Professor. Barber. Cripple. Thief. Priest. Tomboy. Whore. Beggar. Pimp. Detective. Millionaire. Witch. All, all of them are here on the sidewalk. On the sidewalk floods all types of souls." Reyes, *Sa Mga Kuko ng Liwanag*, 143.

13. Anderson, *Spectre of Comparisons*, 37.

14. Ira, Medina, and Rios, *Streets of Manila*, 99.

15. Jose F. Lacaba, "Notes on '*Bakya*': Being an Apologia of Sorts for Filipino Masscult," in *Readings in Philippine Cinema*, ed. Rafael Ma. Guerrero (Manila: Experimental Cinema of the Philippines, 1983), 117

16. Lacaba, "Notes on '*Bakya*,'" 117.

17. Lacaba, "Notes on '*Bakya*,'" 120.

18. Anderson, "Nationalism, Identity, and the Logic of Seriality," 42–43.

19. *Philippines Free Press*, March 4, 1967, 51.

20. David E. Nye, *American Technological Sublime* (Cambridge, Mass.: MIT Press, 1994), 173.

21. Harry Chia, "S'pore Nights Now an Unmatched Spectacle of Colour in Whole of S-East Asia," *Singapore Free Press*, June 1, 1960, 9

22. Nye, *American Technological Sublime*, 196–97.

23. "No More Flashing Neon Lights," *New Nation*, April 13, 1972, 2.

24. "The neon lights have blinked open. Red, blue, yellow, and colors in between. The city is radiant, the city is colorful. If the world were an immense metropolis, without forest and without sea and without desert, the moon and the stars might as well extinguish themselves." Reyes, *Sa Mga Kuko ng Liwanag*, 142–43.

25. Guy Debord, *The Society of the Spectacle* (1967), trans. Donald Nicholson-Smith (New York: Zone, 1994), 12.

26. Quijano de Manila [Nick Joaquin], "The Nation: 1965," *Philippines Free Press*, June 12, 1965, 2.

27. *Philippines Free Press*, January 1962, 32–33, 36.

28. De Manila, "The Nation: 1965," 2.

29. *Philippine Graphic*, August 16, 1967.

30. De Manila, "The Nation: 1965," 2.

31. Quijano de Manila [Nick Joaquin], "The Unkindest Cut," *Philippines Free Press*, February 17, 1968, 5.

32. Quijano de Manila [Nick Joaquin], *Reportage on Crime: Thirteen Horror Happenings That Hit the Headlines* (1977; Manila: Anvil, 2009), 28–29.

33. De Manila, *Reportage on Crime*, 18.

34. De Manila, *Reportage on Crime*, 53.

35. Stuart Hall, Chas Critcher, Tony Jefferson, John Clarke, and Brian Roberts, "The Social Production of News," in *Policing the Crisis: Mugging, the State, and Law and Order* (London and Basingstroke: Macmillan, 1978), 53–77.

36. Ranajit Guha, *Elementary Aspects of Peasant Insurgency in Colonial India* (Durham, N.C.: Duke University Press, 1999).

37. P. A. Zapanta, "In the National Headcount, the Youths Have It," *Sunday Times Magazine*, October 30, 1966, 46.

38. "Manila: Its Needs and Resources" (Manila: Social Welfare Department, 1967), 91.

39. De Manila, *Reportage on Crime*, 63.

40. Vicente L. Rafael, *White Love, and Other Events in Filipino History* (Durham, N.C.: Duke University Press, 2000), 154.

41. De Manila, *Reportage on Crime*, 67.

42. De Manila, *Reportage on Crime*, 25.

43. Rafael, *White Love*, 155.

44. Felix M. Caliwag, "Manila's Swinging Tin Pan Alley," *Sunday Times Magazine*, June 6, 1965, 26.

45. The Tagalog word "*kanto*" means "street corner." The slang term "*istambay*" is a transliteration of the English phrasal verb "stand by."

46. Jose F. Lacaba, *Days of Disquiet, Days of Rage: The First Quarter Storm and Related Events*, new ed. (1983; repr. Manila: Anvil, 2003), 17.

47. James M. Mayo, *The American Grocery Store: The Business Evolution of an Architectural Space* (Westport, Conn.: Greenwood, 1993).

48. Rachel Bowlby, *Carried Away: The Invention of Modern Shopping* (New York: Columbia University Press, 2001), 8.

49. "Happy Confusion," *Singapore Free Press*, January 27, 1960, 3.

50. "Supermarts Change our Shopping Habits," *Straits Times*, December 8, 1967, 27.

51. "Supermarket Sensations," *Sunday Times Magazine*, March 14, 1965, 42.

52. Bowlby, *Carried Away*, 8.

53. Sharon Zukin, *Points of Purchase: How Shopping Changed American Culture* (New York: Routledge, 2004), 70–71.

54. Victoria de Grazia, *Irresistible Empire: America's Advance through 20th Century Europe* (Cambridge, Mass.: Harvard University Press, 2006), 383.

55. De Grazia, *Irresistible Empire*, 172.

56. Bowlby, *Carried Away*, 176.

57. Mayo, *American Grocery Store*, 159.

58. Packard, *Hidden Persuaders* (London: Longmans, Green, 1957), 110.

59. Maryr Tague, "Supermarkets: The New Retailing Revolution," *Philippines Free Press*, January 23, 1965, 34.

6. PUBLIC SPHERES OF POSTCOLONIAL FANTASY

1. Jan Uhde and Yvonne Ng Uhde, *Latent Images: Film in Singapore*, 2nd ed. (Singapore: NUS Press, 2009), 10.

2. Poshek Fu, "The Shaw Brothers Diasporic Cinema," in *China Forever: The Shaw Brothers and Diasporic Cinema*, ed. Poshek Fu (Champaign: University of Illinois Press, 2008), 1–25.

3. Sai-shing Yung, "Territorialization and the Entertainment Industry of the Shaw Brothers in Southeast Asia," in Fu, *China Forever*, 149.

4. *Philippine Graphic*, June 2, 1965, 53; *Philippines Free Press*, February 11, 1967, 43.

5. Gaik Cheng Khoo, *Reclaiming Adat: Contemporary Malaysian Film and Literature* (Vancouver: University of British Columbia Press, 2006), 91; Timothy P. Barnard, "The Shaw Brothers' Malay Films," in Fu, *China Forever*, 167–68.

6. Quijano de Manila, "Philippine Movies—In Crisis?" *Philippines Free Press*, February 11, 1967, 44.

7. Wong Yunn Chii and Tan Kar Lin, "Emergence of a Cosmopolitan Space for Culture and Consumption: The New World Amusement Park-Singapore (1923–1970) in the Inter-War Years," *Inter-Asia Cultural Studies* 5, no. 2 (2004): 281.

8. Nick Deocampo, *Film: American Influences on Philippine Cinema* (Manila: Anvil, 2011), 527–34.

9. Rosalie Matilac and Joel David, with notes from Pio de Castro III, Bienvenido Lumbera, and Nicanor G. Tiongson, "Distribution," in *Cultural Center of the Philippines Encyclopedia of Philippine Art*, vol. VIII, *Philippine Film*, ed. Nicanor G. Tiongson (Manila: Cultural Center of the Philippines, 1994), 112.

10. Kim Cheng Boey, *Between Stations: Essays* (Artarmon, New South Wales, Australia: Giramondo, 2009), 150.

11. "Singapore is moving forward.... Times are already changing...."

12. Joel S. Kahn, *Other Malays: Nationalism and Cosmopolitanism in the Modern Malay World* (Singapore: Asian Studies Association of Australia in association with Singapore University Press and NIAS Press, 2006), 126.

13. Kahn, *Other Malays*, xvi.

14. Kahn, *Other Malays*, 128.

15. Kahn, *Other Malays*, 164.

16. Matthew Isaac Cohen, *The Komedie Stamboel: Popular Theater in Colonial Indonesia, 1891–1903* (Athens: Ohio University Center for International Studies, 2006), 4.

17. "Malay Film Stars Are So Versatile," *Singapore Free Press,* July 27, 1959, 3; "Two Film Festival Awards Won by Malaya," *Straits Times,* April 20, 1963, 1.

18. Tan Sooi Beng, *Bangsawan: A Social and Stylistic History of Popular Malay Opera* (Singapore: Oxford University Press, 1993), 18–20.

19. Tan, *Bangsawan,* 35.

20. Tan, *Bangsawan,* 40–41.

21. Tan, *Bangsawan,* 16–18.

22. Tan, *Bangsawan,* 26–27.

23. Susan J. Napier, *Anime from* Akira *to* Princess Mononoke: *Experiencing Contemporary Japanese Animation* (New York: Palgrave Macmillan, 2000).

24. Napier, *Anime,* 12.

25. Timothy P. Barnard, "Decolonization and the Nation in Malay Film, 1955–1965," *South East Asia Research* 17, no. 1 (2009): 85.

26. Jini Kim Watson, *The New Asian City: Three-Dimensional Fictions of Space and Urban Form* (Minneapolis: University of Minnesota Press, 2011).

27. Teh Cheang Wan, "Public Housing in Singapore: An Overview," in *Public Housing in Singapore: A Multi-Disciplinary Study,* ed. Stephen H. K. Yeh (Singapore: Singapore University Press Housing and Development Board, 1975), 4.

28. Aline K. Wong and Stephen H. K. Yeh, eds. *Housing a Nation: 25 Years of Public Housing in Singapore* (Singapore: Maruzen Asia and Housing and Development Board, 1985), 40–41.

29. Aprodicio A. Laquian, *The City in Nation-Building* (Quezon City: University of the Philippines School of Public Administration, 1966), 53.

30. Loh Kah Seng, *Squatters into Citizens: The 1961 Bukit Ho Swee Fire and the Making of Modern Singapore* (Singapore: Asian Studies Association of Australia with NUS Press and NIAS Press, 2013), 99.

31. Quoted in Aprodicio A. Laquian, *Slums Are for People: The Barangay Magsaysay Pilot Project in Urban Community Development* (Manila: University of the Philippines College of Public Administration, 1969), 2-3.

32. Martin Perry, Lily Kong, and Brenda Yeoh, *Singapore: A Developmental City State* (Chichester: John Wiley and Sons, 1997), 166.

33. Kahn, *Other Malays,* 12–14.

34. Rosalind Galt, *Alluring Monsters: The Pontianak and Cinemas of Decolonization* (New York: Columbia University Press, 2021), 160, 162.

35. Goh Keng Swee, *The Economics of Modernization* (1972; repr. Singapore: Marshall Cavendish Academic, 2004), 18.

36. ". . . like jobless monkeys pushing dust. . . ."

37. Watson, *New Asian City,* 192.

38. Emanuel Levy, "Social Attributes of American Movie Stars," *Media, Culture, and Society* 12 (1990): 247–67.

39. Altman, *Film/Genre* (London: BFI, 1999), 149.

40. Altman, *Film/Genre,* 154–55.

41. Quijano de Manila [Nick Joaquin], *Reportage on Crime: Thirteen Horror Happenings That Hit the Headlines* (1977; Manila: Anvil, 2009), 20.

42. De Manila, *Crime*, 73.

43. Quijano de Manila [Nick Joaquin], *Gloria Diaz and Other Delineations* (Quezon City, Philippines: National Bookstore, 1977), 34.

44. Quijano de Manila [Nick Joaquin], *Reportage on Politics* (Manila: National Bookstore, 1981, 90.

45. Quijano de Manila [Nick Joaquin], "The Manila of His Affections," *Philippines Free Press*, June 26, 1965, 50.

46. Antonio J. Villegas, *Building a Better Manila* (Manila: n.p., 1963).

47. Felix M. Caliwag, "Go," *Sunday Times Magazine*, January 31, 1965, 27.

48. Napoleon G. Rama, "Go! Go! Go!" *Philippines Free Press*, March 30, 1968, 2.

49. See Villegas, *Building a Better Manila*.

50. Michael Pinches, "Modernization and the Quest for Modernity: Architectural Form, Squatter Settlements, and the New Society in Manila," in *Cultural Identity and Urban Change in Southeast Asia: Interpretative Essays*, ed. Marc Askew and William S. Logan (Victoria, Australia: Deakin University Press, 1994), 26.

51. Aprodicio A. Laquian, *Slums Are for People: The Barangay Magsaysay Pilot Project in Urban Community Development* (Manila: University of the Philippines College of Public Administration, 1969), 11.

52. Laquian, *Slums Are for People*, 11.

53. F. M. Caliwag, "Headline-Making Coffeetalk," *Sunday Times Magazine*, February 21, 1965, 18–21.

54. James C. Scott, *Domination and the Arts of Resistance: Hidden Transcripts* (New Haven, Conn.: Yale University Press, 1992).

55. Scott, *Domination*, 142.

56. Ranajit Guha, *Elementary Aspects of Peasant Insurgency in Colonial India* (Durham, N.C.: Duke University Press, 1999), 261.

57. Scott, *Domination*, 142.

58. Paulo Freire, *Pedagogy of the Oppressed* (New York: Continuum, 2000).

59. Freire, *Pedagogy*, 53.

60. Jürgen Habermas, *The Structural Transformation of the Public Sphere: An Inquiry into a Category of Bourgeois Society* (Cambridge, Mass.: MIT Press, 1989).

61. Caroline S. Hau, *Elites and Ilustrados in Philippine Culture* (Quezon City, Philippines: Ateneo de Manila University Press, 2017), 2, 6.

62. Khairudin Aljunied, "Coffee-shops in Colonial Singapore: Domains of Contentious Publics," *History Workshop Journal* (2013).

63. Lee Kah-Wee, *Las Vegas in Singapore: Violence, Progress, and the Crisis of National Modernity* (Singapore: NUS Press, 2019), 98, 100.

64. Lai Ah Eng, "The Kopitiam in Singapore: An Evolving Story about Migration and Cultural Diversity" (Working Paper, Asia Research Institute, 2010), 8.

65. Jean Duruz and Gaik Cheng Khoo, eds., *Eating Together: Food, Space, and Identity in Malaysia and Singapore* (Lanham, Md.: Rowman and Littlefield, 2015), 31.

66. Chua Beng Huat, *Political Legitimacy and Housing: Stakeholding in Singapore*. (London: Routledge, 1997), 79.

67. Duruz and Khoo, *Eating Together*, 32–33.

68. Chua, *Political Legitimacy and Housing*, 152–67.

69. Erik Harms, "Eviction Time in the New Saigon: Temporalities of Displacement in the Rubble of Development," *Cultural Anthropology* 28, no. 2 (2013): 357.

70. Harms, "Eviction Time," 360–61.

7. NEOLIBERAL COSMOPOLITANISM IN THE TROPICAL WORLD CITY

1. Martin Perry, Lily Kong, and Brenda Yeoh, *Singapore: A Developmental City State* (Chichester: John Wiley and Sons, 1997).

2. Kenneth Paul Tan, "The Ideology of Pragmatism: Neo-liberal Globalization and Political Authoritarianism in Singapore," *Journal of Contemporary Asia* 42, no. 1 (2012): 67–92.

3. David Harvey, *A Brief History of Neoliberalism* (Oxford: Oxford University Press, 2007).

4. *Foreign Policy*, September/October 2010.

5. Singapore, Economic Strategies Committee, "Making Singapore a Leading Global City" (Report, Economic Strategies Committee, 2011).

6. Goh Chok Tong, "First-World Economy, World-Class Home" (Speech, Singapore, 1999), http://www.nas.gov.sg/archivesonline/speeches/view-html?filename=1999082202.htm.

7. Pheng Cheah, *Inhuman Conditions: On Cosmopolitanism and Human Rights* (Cambridge, Mass.: Harvard University Press, 2006), 18.

8. Cheah, *Inhuman Conditions*, 3.

9. Jacques Derrida, "Hostipitality," *Angelaki* 5, no. 3 (2000): 3–18.

10. Aihwa Ong, *Neoliberalism as Exception: Mutations in Citizenship and Sovereignty* (Durham, N.C.: Duke University Press, 2006), 6–7.

11. Aihwa Ong, *Flexible Citizenship: The Cultural Logics of Transnationality* (Durham, N.C.: Duke University Press, 1999), 19.

12. Ong, *Neoliberalism as Exception*, 97–118.

13. Singapore Tourism Board, "i'mpact: Annual Report 2010/2011" (Report, Singapore Tourism Board, 2010/2011), 35.

14. Singapore, Economic Strategies Committee, "Highly Skilled People, Innovative Economy, Distinctive Global City" (Report, Economic Strategies Committee, 2010).

15. Richard Florida, *The Rise of the Creative Class* (New York: Basic Books, 2003).

16. "This Is a True City of Shops," *Straits Times*, May 30, 1975, 5.

17. Singapore 21 Committee, "Singapore 21: Together, We Make the Difference" (Report, Singapore 21 Committee, 1999), 5.

18. Rem Koolhaas and Bruce Mau, *S,M,L,XL*, 2nd ed. (New York: Monacelli, 1995); William Gibson, "Disneyland with the Death Penalty," *Wired*, April 1, 1993, https://www.wired.com/1993/04/gibson-2/; Nicole-Marie Ng, "Time Out City Index 2018: Apparently Singapore Is Boring?," *TimeOut*, January 31, 2018, https://www.timeout.com/singapore/news/time-out-city-index -2018-apparently-singapore-is-boring-013118.

19. Simon Anholt, *Competitive Identity: The New Brand Management for Nations, Cities, and Regions* (New York: Palgrave Macmillan, 2007), 22.

20. Anholt, *Competitive Identity*, 5-7.

21. Singapore Tourism Board, "Street of Singapore: Remaking Orchard Road" (Report, Singapore Tourism Board, 2003).

22. Anholt, *Competitive Identity*, 60–61.

23. "Buzz, *n.*," *OED Online*, Oxford University Press.

24. Renee Dye, "The Buzz on Buzz," *Harvard Business Review* 78, no. 6 (2000): 140.

25. Malcolm Gladwell, *The Tipping Point: How Little Things Can Make a Big Difference* (Boston: Little, Brown, 2000), 89–132.

26. Victor Gruen and Larry Smith, *Shopping Towns U.S.A.: The Planning of Shopping Centers* (New York: Reinhold, 1960), 147.

27. Henry Jenkins, Sam Ford, and Joshua Green, *Spreadable Media: Creating Value and Meaning in a Networked Culture* (New York: NYU Press, 2013), 198–99.

28. Frederic Thompson, "Amusing the Million," *Everybody's Magazine*, September 1908, <nationalhumanitiescenter.org/pds/gilded/people/text2/thompson.pdf>.

29. Dye, "Buzz," 140.

30. Singapore 21 Committee, "Singapore 21," 22.

31. Jenny Kleeman, "Manila: A Megacity Where the Living Must Share with the Dead," *Guardian*, October 15, 2010, http://www.theguardian.com/world/2010/oct/15/philippines-overpopulation-crisis.

32. Chua Beng Huat, "Singapore as Model: Planning Innovation, Knowledge Experts," in *Worlding Cities: Asian Experiments and the Art of Being Global*, ed. Ananya Roy and Aihwa Ong (Malden, Mass.: Wiley-Blackwell, 2011), 29–54.

33. Sylvia Mendez Ventura, "The E.D.S. in Edsa," in *Ragtime in Kamuning: Sari-Sari Essays* (Manila: Anvil, 1993), 43.

34. Evangeline C. Santiago, "The Air in Manila Could Be Cancerous," *Philippine Daily Inquirer*, July 16, 2013, http://lifestyle.inquirer.net/114205/ the-air-in-metro-manila-could-be-cancerous.

35. Glenn Diaz, *The Quiet Ones: A Novel* (Quezon City, Philippines: Ateneo de Manila University Press, 2017), 52.

36. Kathleen A. Martin, "OFW Inflows Seen to Hit $23.6 B in 2014," *Philippine Star*, December 23, 2013, http://www.philstar.com/business/2013/12/23/1271095/ofw-inflows-seen-hit-23.6-b-2014.

37. "Booming PH Outsourcing Industry Faces Worker Shortage," *Philippine Daily Inquirer*, October 8, 2013, http://business.inquirer.net/146547/booming-ph-outsourcing-industry-faces-worker-shortage.

38. "Outsourcing, *n.*," *OED Online*, Oxford University Press.

39. Vikas Bajaj, "A New Capital for Call Centers," *New York Times*, November 25, 2011.

40. Jan M. Padios, *A Nation on the Line: Call Centers as Postcolonial Predicaments in the Philippines* (Durham, N.C.: Duke University Press, 2018), 57.

41. Zygmunt Bauman, *Globalization: The Human Consequences* (New York: Columbia University Press, 1998), 78.

42. Padios, *Nation on the Line*, 66.

43. Wendy Brown, "Neo-liberalism and the End of Liberal Democracy," *Theory & Event* 7, no. 1 (2003), https://muse.jhu.edu/article/48659.

44. Padios, *Nation on the Line*, 4.

45. Padios, *Nation on the Line*, 49.

46. Emmanuel David, "Outsourced Heroes and Queer Incorporations: Labor Brokerage and the Politics of Inclusion in the Philippine Call Center Industry," *GLQ: A Journal of Lesbian and Gay Studies* 22, no. 3 (2016): 391.

47. Padios, *Nation on the Line*, 136–37.

48. Padios, *Nation on the Line*, 148.

49. Diaz, *Quiet Ones*, 30.

50. Jeffrey J. Sallaz, *Lives on the Line: How the Philippines Became the World's Call Center Capital* (New York: Oxford University Press, 2019), 135, 151.

51. Purnima Mankekar and Akhil Gupta, "Intimate Encounters: Affective Labor in Call Centers," *positions: east asia cultures critique* 24, no. 1 (2016): 30.

52. David Harvey, *The Condition of Postmodernity: An Enquiry into the Origins of Social Change* (Oxford: Blackwell, 1990).

53. Padios, *Nation on the Line*, 9.

54. Ma. Regina Hechanova-Alampay, *1-800-Philippines: Understanding and Managing the Filipino Call Center Worker* (Quezon City: Institute of Philippine Culture, 2010), 13–15.

55. Rolando Tolentino, *Sa Loob at Labas ng* Mall *kong Sawi, Kaliluha'y Siyang Nangyayaring Hari: Ang Pagkatuto at Pagtatanghal ng Kulturang Popular* (Quezon City: University of the Philippines Press, 2001), 24.

56. Gilles Deleuze and Félix Guattari, *A Thousand Plateaus: Capitalism and Schizophrenia*, trans. Brian Massumi (Minneapolis: University of Minnesota Press, 1987), 461–62.

57. SM Prime Holdings, http://www.smprime.com/; SM Supermalls, http://www.smsupermalls.com/information.

58. Charlson Ong, *An Embarrassment of Riches* (Quezon City: University of the Philippines Press, 2000).

59. Jennee Grace U. Rubrico, "Supermalls Gain Popularity, but Retailers Not Favoring One Format," *Business World*, September 14, 2009, S1/1.

60. Gruen and Smith, *Shopping Towns*, 75; Jeffrey M. Hardwick, *Mall Maker: Victor Gruen, Architect of an American Dream* (Philadelphia: University of Pennsylvania Press, 2004), 128.

61. ". . . no brownouts, the environment is bright: the lighting is even, almost like a perpetual noontime; clean, with no garbage on the street; cool; a few trees are actually present; the toilets flush; the service is good; and no crime"; Tolentino, *Sa Loob at Labas ng* Mall *kong Sawi*, 21.

62. Tolentino, *Sa Loob at Labas ng* Mall *kong Sawi*, 21 and 183.

63. Robert Fishman, *Urban Utopias in the Twentieth Century: Ebenezer Howard, Frank Lloyd Wright, Le Corbusier* (Cambridge, Mass.: MIT Press, 1982), 6.

64. Fishman, *Urban Utopias*, 4.

65. Lauren Berlant, *Cruel Optimism* (Durham, N.C.: Duke University Press, 2011).

66. David Harvey, "The Right to the City," *New Left Review* 53 (2008): 23–40.

67. Michael Hardt and Antonio Negri, *Empire* (Cambridge, Mass.: Harvard University Press, 2000), 194–95.

68. Paco Underhill, *The Call of the Mall* (New York: Simon and Schuster, 2004), 67.

69. Fishman, *Urban Utopias*.

70. Tolentino, *Sa Loob at Labas ng* Mall *kong Sawi*, 20 and 185.

71. Kenneth Paul Tan, "Racial Stereotypes in Singapore Films: Commercial Value and Critical Possibilities," in *Race and Multiculturalism in Malaysia and Singapore*, ed. Daniel P. S. Goh, Matilda Gabrielpillai, Philip Holden, and Gaik Cheng Khoo (Oxford: Routledge, 2009), 124–40.

72. Knight-Frank Research, *The Wealth Report 2012: A Global Perspective on Prime Property and Wealth* (Knight Frank and Citi Private Bank, 2012), 10.

73. Tom Benner, "Singapore Poverty in the Spotlight," *Al Jazeera*, November 9, 2013, http://www.aljazeera.com/indepth/features/2013/11/singapore-poverty-spotlight-20131178362669442.html.

74. Harvey, *Brief History of Neoliberalism*.

75. Sandro Mezzadra and Brett Neilson, *Border as Method, or, the Multiplication of Labor* (Durham, N.C.: Duke University Press, 2013), 111–30.

76. HSBC Expat, *Expat Explorer Survey 2013* (HSBC Expat, 2013).

77. Knight-Frank Research, *Wealth Report 2012*, 11.

78. Knight-Frank Research, *The Wealth Report 2016: A Global Perspective on Prime Property and Wealth* (Knight Frank, 2016), 37.

79. Singapore, Economic Development Board, "Global Investor Programme," https://www.edb.gov.sg/en/how-we-help/global-investor-pro gramme.html.

80. Kevin Kwan, *Crazy Rich Asians* (New York: Doubleday, 2013).

81. Bauman, *Globalization*, 92–93.

82. Knight-Frank Research, *The Wealth Report 2015: A Global Perspective on Prime Property and Wealth* (Knight Frank, 2015), 42.

83. Kwan, *Crazy Rich Asians*, 144.

84. Kwan, *Crazy Rich Asians*, 123.

85. Kwan, *Crazy Rich Asians*, 326.

86. Kwan, *Crazy Rich Asians*, 147.

CONCLUSION: LOST MODERNITIES

1. Gavin Walker and Naoki Sakai, "A Genealogy of Area Studies," *positions: asia critique* 27, no. 1 (2019): 2–3.

2. Benedict Anderson, *Imagined Communities: Reflections on the Origin and Spread of Nationalism*, 2nd ed. (London: Verso, 1991).

3. Joseph A. Schumpeter, *Capitalism, Socialism, and Democracy*, 3rd ed. (1950; repr. New York: Harper, 1978.)

4. Reinhart Koselleck, *The Practice of Conceptual History: Timing History, Spatial Concepts* (Stanford, Calif.: Stanford University Press, 2002).

REFERENCES

Periodicals
Al Jazeera
American Chamber of Commerce Journal
Business World
Foreign Policy
Guardian
Liwayway
Malaya Tribune
Manila Chronicle
Manila Times
Manila Daily Bulletin
New York Times
Philippines Free Press
Philippine Graphic
Philippines Herald
Philippine Magazine
Philippine Panorama
Singapore Free Press and Mercantile Advertiser
Straits Times
Sunday Chronicle Magazine
Sunday Times Magazine
Sunday Tribune Magazine
Tribune

Books and Articles

Abbas, Ackbar. *Hong Kong: Culture and the Politics of Disappearance.* Minneapolis: University of Minnesota Press, 1997.
Abinales, Patricio N., and Donna J. Amoroso. *State and Society in the Philippines.* 2nd ed. Lanham, Md.: Rowman and Littlefield, 2017.

Adams, Judith A. *The American Amusement Park Industry: A History of Technology and Thrills.* Boston: Twayne, 1991.

Adburgham, Alison. *Shops and Shopping 1800–1914: Where, and in What Manner the Well-Dressed Englishwoman Bought Her Clothes.* London: George Allen and Unwin, 1964.

Agoncillo, Teodoro. "Manila in the 1890s." In *History and Culture, Language and Literature: Selected Essays of Teodoro Agoncillo*, edited by Bernadita Reyes Churchill, 317–37. Manila: University of Santo Tomas Publishing House, 2003.

Alcazaren, Paulo, Luis Ferrer, and Benvenuto Icamina. *Lungsod Iskwater: The Evolution of Informality as a Dominant Pattern in Philippine Cities.* Mandaluyong City, Philippines: Anvil, 2011.

Alexander, Jennifer, and Paul Alexander. "Striking a Bargain in Javanese Markets." *Man (New Series)* 22, no. 1 (1987): 42–68.

Aljunied, Khairudin. "Coffee-shops in Colonial Singapore: Domains of Contentious Publics." *History Workshop Journal* (2013).

Altman, Rick. *Film/Genre.* London: BFI, 1999.

Anholt, Simon. *Competitive Identity: The New Brand Management for Nations, Cities, and Regions.* New York: Palgrave Macmillan, 2007.

Alvarez, Joy H. "Hiya: Kahulugan, Manifestation, at Kadahilanan." In *Pananaliksik sa Sikolohiya*, edited by Virgilio Enriquez and Lilia Antonio, 115–26. Quezon City, Philippines: n.p., 1975.

Anderson, Benedict. *Imagined Communities: Reflections on the Origin and Spread of Nationalism.* 2nd ed. London: Verso, 1991.

———. *The Spectre of Comparisons: Nationalism, Southeast Asia, and the World.* London: Verso, 2004.

Anderson, Warwick. *Colonial Pathologies: American Tropical Medicine, Race, and Hygiene in the Philippines.* Durham, N.C.: Duke University Press, 2006.

Arata, Stephen. *Fictions of Loss in the Victorian Fin de Siècle.* New York: Cambridge University Press, 1996.

Bakhtin, Mikhail. *Rabelais and His World.* Translated by Hélène Iswolsky. Bloomington: Indiana University Press, 1984.

Bao, Weihong. *Fiery Cinema: The Emergence of an Affective Medium in China, 1915–1945.* Minneapolis: University of Minnesota Press, 2015.

Barnard, Timothy P. "Decolonization and the Nation in Malay Film, 1955–1965." *South East Asia Research* 17, no. 1 (2009): 65–86.

———. "The Shaw Brothers' Malay Films." In Fu, *China Forever*, 154–73.

Barr, Michael D., and Carl A. Trocki. *Paths Not Taken: Political Pluralism in Post-War Singapore.* Singapore: NUS Press, 2008.

Bauman, Zygmunt. *Globalization: The Human Consequences.* New York: Columbia University Press, 1998.

Bayat, Asef. "From 'Dangerous Classes' to 'Quiet Rebels': Politics of the Urban Subaltern in the Global South." *International Sociology* 15, no. 3 (2000): 533–57.

Bazin, André. *What Is Cinema?* Vol. 1. Translated by Hugh Gray. Berkeley: University of California Press, 1967.

Beckert, Sven. *Empire of Cotton: A Global History*. New York: Vintage, 2015.

Benjamin, Walter. *The Arcades Project*. Edited by Rolf Tiedemann. Translated by Howard Eiland and Kevin McLaughlin. Cambridge, Mass.: Belknap Press, 2002.

Berger, John. *Ways of Seeing*. London: British Broadcasting Corporation and Penguin, 1972.

Berlant, Lauren. *Cruel Optimism*. Durham, N.C.: Duke University Press, 2011.

Bernards, Brian. *Writing the South Seas: Imagining the Nanyang in Chinese and Southeast Asian Postcolonial Literature*. Seattle: University of Washington Press, 2015.

Blakemore, W. L. "Air Conditioning." Radio health talk, Singapore Government Print Office, 1940.

Bowlby, Rachel. *Carried Away: The Invention of Modern Shopping*. New York: Columbia University Press, 2001.

Braester, Yomi. *Painting the City Red: Chinese Cinema and the Urban Contract*. Durham, N.C.: Duke University Press, 2010.

Brown, Wendy. "Neo-liberalism and the End of Liberal Democracy." *Theory & Event* 7, no. 1 (2003). https://muse.jhu.edu/article/48659.

Brownell, Susan. "Sports in Britain and China, 1850–1920: An Explanatory Overview." *International Journal of the History of Sport* 8, no. 2 (1991): 284–90.

Bulatao, Jaime C. "*Hiya*." *Philippine Studies* 12, no. 3 (1964): 424–38.

Camagay, Ma. Luisa. *Working Women of Manila of the 19th Century*. Quezon City: University of the Philippines Press / University Center for Women Studies, 1995.

Caoli, Manuel A. *The Origins of Metropolitan Manila: A Political and Social Analysis*. Quezon City, Philippines: New Day, 1988.

Chakrabarty, Dipesh. *Habitations of Modernity: Essays in the Wake of Subaltern Studies*. Chicago: University of Chicago Press, 2002.

———. *Provincializing Europe: Postcolonial Thought and Historical Difference*. Princeton, N.J.: Princeton University Press, 2000.

Chang Cheng-Tung. "A Sociological Study of Neighbourliness." In Yeh, *Public Housing in Singapore*, 281–301.

Chatterjee, Partha. "Anderson's Utopia." In Cheah and Culler, *Grounds of Comparison*, 161–70.

Cheah Jin Seng. *Singapore: 500 Early Postcards*. Singapore: Editions Didier Millet, 2006.

Cheah, Pheng. *Inhuman Conditions: On Cosmopolitanism and Human Rights*. Cambridge, Mass.: Harvard University Press, 2006.

Cheah, Pheng, and Jonathan Culler, eds. *Grounds of Comparison: Around the Work of Benedict Anderson*. New York: Routledge, 2003.

Chen, Kuan-Hsing. *Asia as Method: Toward Deimperialization*. Durham, N.C.: Duke University Press, 2010.

Chen, Kuan-Hsing, and Chua Beng Huat, eds. *The Inter-Asia Studies Reader*. London: Routledge, 2007.

Chew, Victor Chin Aik. Interview with Jesley Chua Chee Huan. *Special Project*. Oral History Centre, 001965/07, November 3, 1997.

Chua Ai Lin. "Modernity, Popular Culture, and Urban Life: Anglophone Asians in Colonial Singapore, 1920–1940." Ph.D. dissertation, University of Cambridge, 2007.

Chua Beng Huat. *Communitarian Ideology and Democracy in Singapore*. London: Routledge, 1995.

———. *Life Is Not Complete without Shopping: Consumption Culture in Singapore*. Singapore: Singapore University Press, 2003.

———. *Political Legitimacy and Housing: Stakeholding in Singapore*. London: Routledge, 1997.

———. "Singapore as Model: Planning Innovation, Knowledge Experts." In *Worlding Cities: Asian Experiments and the Art of Being Global*, edited by Ananya Roy and Aihwa Ong, 29–54. Malden, Mass.: Wiley-Blackwell, 2011.

Chua Beng Huat, and Koichi Iwabuchi, eds. *East Asian Pop Culture: Analyzing the Korean Wave*. Hong Kong: Hong Kong University Press, 2008.

Clancey, Gregory. "Toward a Spatial History of Emergency: Notes from Singapore." Working Paper, Asia Research Institute, 2003.

Clark, T. J. *The Painting of Modern Life: Paris in the Art of Manet and His Followers*. Rev. ed. Princeton, N.J.: Princeton University Press, 1999.

Clover, Joshua. *Riot. Strike. Riot: The New Era of Uprisings*. London: Verso, 2016.

Clutario, Genevieve Alva. *Beauty Regimes: A History of Power and Modern Empire in the Philippines, 1898–1941*. Durham, N.C.: Duke University Press, 2023.

Cohen, Deborah. *Household Gods: The British and their Possessions*. New Haven, Conn.: Yale University Press, 2006.

Cohen, Matthew Isaac. *The Komedie Stamboel: Popular Theater in Colonial Indonesia, 1891–1903*. Athens: Ohio University Center for International Studies, 2006.

Collier, Patrick. "Imperial/Modernist Forms in the *Illustrated London News*." *Modernism/Modernity* 19, no. 3 (2012): 487–514.

Cordero-Fernando, Gilda, and Nik Ricio. *Turn of the Century*. Quezon City, Philippines: GCF, 1978.

Cowen, Deborah. *The Deadly Life of Logistics: Mapping Violence in Global Trade*. Minneapolis: University of Minnesota Press, 2014.

Crary, Jonathan. *Techniques of the Observer: On Vision and Modernity in the Nineteenth Century*. Cambridge, Mass.: MIT Press, 1990.

Cruz, Denise. *Transpacific Femininities: The Making of the Modern Filipina*. Durham, N.C.: Duke University Press, 2012.

Curaming, Rommel A. "Postcolonial Studies and *Pantayong Pananaw* in Philippine Historiography: A Critical Engagement." *Kritika Kultura* 26 (2016): 63–91.

Curless, Gareth. "The Triumph of the State: Singapore's Dockworkers and the Limits of Global History, c. 1920–1965." *Historical Journal* 60, no. 4 (2017): 1,097–1,123.

David, Emmanuel. "Outsourced Heroes and Queer Incorporations: Labor Brockerage and the Politics of Inclusion in the Philippine Call Center Industry." *GLQ: A Journal of Lesbian and Gay Studies* 22, no. 3 (2016): 381–408.

Davison, Julian. *Black and White: The Singapore House, 1898–1941*. Singapore: Talisman, 2006.

de Certeau, Michel. "Vocal Utopias: Glossolalias." *Representations* 56, no. 1 (1996): 29–47.

Debord, Guy. *The Society of the Spectacle*. 1967. Translated by Donald Nicholson-Smith. New York: Zone, 1994.

de Grazia, Victoria. *Irresistible Empire: America's Advance through 20th Century Europe*. Cambridge, Mass.: Harvard University Press, 2006.

Deleuze, Gilles, and Félix Guattari. *A Thousand Plateaus: Capitalism and Schizophrenia*. Translated by Brian Massumi. Minneapolis: University of Minnesota Press, 1987.

de Manila, Quijano [Nick Joaquin]. *Gloria Diaz and Other Delineations*. Quezon City, Philippines: National Bookstore, 1977.

———. *Joseph Estrada and Other Sketches*. Quezon City, Philippines: National Bookstore, 1977.

———. *Language of the Streets and Other Essays*. Quezon City, Philippines: National Bookstore, 1977.

———. *Manila: Sin City? And Other Chronicles*. Quezon City, Philippines: National Bookstore, 1977.

———. *Reportage on Crime: Thirteen Horror Happenings That Hit the Headlines*. Manila: Anvil, 2009. Originally published in 1977.

———. *Reportage on Politics*. Manila: National Bookstore, 1981.

———. *Ronnie Poe and Other Silhouettes*. Quezon City, Philippines: National Bookstore, 1977.

Deocampo, Nick. *Film: American Influences on Philippine Cinema*. Manila: Anvil, 2011.

Derrida, Jacques. "Hostipitality." *Angelaki* 5, no. 3 (2000): 3–18.

de Soto, Hernando. *The Other Path: The Economic Answer to Terrorism*. New York: Basic Books, 1989.

de Viana, Lorelei D.C. *Three Centuries of Binondo Architecture 1594–1898: A Socio-Historical Perspective*. Manila: University of Santo Tomas Publishing House, 2001.

Diaz, Glenn. *The Quiet Ones: A Novel*. Quezon City, Philippines: Ateneo de Manila University Press, 2017.

Dobbs, Richard, et al. *Urban World: Mapping the Economic Power of Cities*. McKinsey Global Institute, 2011.

Dobbs, Stephen. *The Singapore River: A Social History, 1819–2002*. Singapore: Singapore University Press, 2003.

Doeppers, Daniel F. *Manila, 1900–1941: Social Change in a Late Colonial Metropolis*. Southeast Asia Studies. New Haven, Conn.: Yale University, 1984.

Douglas, Mary. *Purity and Danger: An Analysis of Concepts of Pollution and Taboo*. New York: Routledge, 2002. Originally published in 1966.

Duruz, Jean, and Gaik Cheng Khoo, eds. *Eating Together: Food, Space, and Identity in Malaysia and Singapore*. Lanham, Md.: Rowman and Littlefield, 2015.

Dye, Renee. "The Buzz on Buzz." *Harvard Business Review* 78, no. 6 (2000): 139–46.

Dyer, Richard. *Stars*. New ed. London: British Film Institute, 1998.

———. *White*. New York: Routledge, 2007.

Edwards, Norman. *The Singapore House and Residential Life, 1819–1939*. Oxford: Oxford University Press, 1991.

España-Maram, Linda. *Creating Masculinity in Los Angeles' Little Manila: Working-Class Filipinos and Popular Culture, 1920s–1950s*. New York: Columbia University Press, 2006.

Espiritu, Talitha. *Passionate Revolutions: The Media and the Rise and Fall of the Marcos Regime*. Athens: Ohio University Press, 2017.

Fernandez, Michael, and Loh Kah Seng. "The Left-Wing Trade Unions in Singapore, 1945–1970." In Barr and Trocki, *Paths Not Taken*, 206–26.

Fishman, Robert. *Urban Utopias in the Twentieth Century: Ebenezer Howard, Frank Lloyd Wright, Le Corbusier*. Cambridge, Mass.: MIT Press, 1982.

Florida, Richard. *The Rise of the Creative Class*. New York: Basic Books, 2003.

Fookien Times Philippines Yearbook. Manila, Philippines: Fookien Times, 1967.

Foucault, Michel. *Discipline and Punish: The Birth of the Prison*. 1978. Translated by Alan Sheridan. New York: Vintage, 1995.

———. "Governmentality." In *Power: Essential Works of Foucault, 1954–1984*, edited by James D. Faubion, 201–22. New York: New Press, 2000.

———. "Nietzsche, Genealogy, History." In *Aesthetics, Method, and Epistemology: Essential Works of Foucault, 1954–1984*, edited by James D. Faubion, 369–91. New York: New Press, 1998. Originally published in 1971.

François, Anne-Lise. *Open Secrets: The Literature of Uncounted Experience*. Stanford, Calif.: Stanford University Press, 2008.

Freire, Paulo. *Pedagogy of the Oppressed*. New York: Continuum, 2000. Originally published in 1968.

Fried, Michael. *Art and Objecthood: Essays and Reviews*. Chicago: University of Chicago Press, 1998.

Fu, Poshek, ed. *China Forever: The Shaw Brothers and Diasporic Cinema.* Champaign: University of Illinois Press, 2008.

———. "The Shaw Brothers Diasporic Cinema." In Fu, *China Forever*, 1–25.

Galt, Rosalind. *Alluring Monsters: The Pontianak and Cinemas of Decolonization.* New York: Columbia University Press, 2021.

Garcia, Jessie B. "The Golden Age of Filipino Movies." In *Readings in Philippine Cinema*, edited by Rafael Ma. Guerrero, 39–54. Manila: Experimental Cinema of the Philippines, 1983.

Gateway to Manila (Shopping in Old Manila): A Complete Practical Guide Book to the Orient's Most Charming City. 6th ed. 1934.

Geertz, Clifford. *Peddlers and Princes: Social Change and Economic Modernization in Two Indonesian Towns.* Chicago: University of Chicago Press, 1963.

———. "Suq: The Bazaar Economy in Sefrou." In *Meaning and Order in a Moroccan Society: Three Essays in Cultural Analysis*, edited by Clifford Geertz, Hildred Geertz, and Lawrence Rosen, 123–313. Cambridge: Cambridge University Press, 1979.

Geist, Johann Friedrich. *Arcades: The History of a Building Type.* Cambridge, Mass.: MIT Press, 1983.

Gellner, Ernest. *Nations and Nationalism.* 2nd ed. Oxford: Blackwell, 2006.

George, Cherian. *Air-Conditioned Nation Revisited: Essays on Singapore Politics.* Singapore: Ethos, 2020.

Gibson, William. "Disneyland with the Death Penalty." *Wired*, April 1, 1993. https://www.wired.com/1993/04/gibson-2/.

Gladwell, Malcolm. *The Tipping Point: How Little Things Can Make a Big Difference.* Boston: Little, Brown, 2000.

Gleeck, Lewis E., Jr. *The Manila Americans.* Manila: Carmelo and Bauermann, 1977.

Glissant, Édouard. *Introduction to a Poetics of Diversity.* Translated by Celia Britton. Liverpool: Liverpool University Press, 2020.

Goh Chok Tong. "First-World Economy, World-Class Home." Speech, Singapore, 1999. http://www.nas.gov.sg/archivesonline/speeches/view-html?filename=1999082202.htm.

Goh Keng Swee. *The Economics of Modernization.* Singapore: Marshall Cavendish Academic, 2004. Originally published in 1972.

———. *The Practice of Economic Growth.* Singapore: Marshall Cavendish Academic, 2004. Originally published in 1977.

Gruen, Victor, and Larry Smith. *Shopping Towns U.S.A.: The Planning of Shopping Centers.* New York: Reinhold, 1960.

Guerrero, Rafael Ma., ed. *Readings in Philippine Cinema.* Manila: Experimental Cinema of the Philippines, 1983.

Guerrero, Wilfrido Ma. *My Favorite 11 Plays.* Quezon City, Philippines: New Day, 1976.

Guerrero Nakpil, Carmen. *Woman Enough and Other Essays*. Quezon City, Philippines: Ateneo de Manila University Press, 1999.

Guha, Ranajit. *Elementary Aspects of Peasant Insurgency in Colonial India*. Durham, N.C.: Duke University Press, 1999.

Gunning, Tom. "The Cinema of Attraction: Early Film, Its Spectator, and the Avant-Garde." *Wide Angle* 8 (1986): 63–70.

———. "The World as Object Lesson: Cinema Audiences, Visual Culture, and the St. Louis World's Fair, 1904." *Film History* 6, no. 4 (1994): 422–44.

Habermas, Jürgen. *The Structural Transformation of the Public Sphere: An Inquiry into a Category of Bourgeois Society*. Cambridge, Mass.: MIT Press, 1989.

Hall, Stuart. "The Determinations of News Photographs." In *The Manufacture of News: Deviance, Social Problems, and the Mass Media*, edited by Stanley Cohen and Jock Young, 176–90. London: Constable, 1981.

Hall, Stuart, Chas Critcher, Tony Jefferson, John Clarke, and Brian Roberts. *Policing the Crisis: Mugging, the State, and Law and Order*. London: Macmillan, 1978.

Hansen, Miriam. *Babel and Babylon: Spectatorship in American Silent Film*. Cambridge, Mass.: Harvard University Press, 1991.

Hardt, Michael, and Antonio Negri. *Empire*. Cambridge, Mass.: Harvard University Press, 2000.

Hardwick, Jeffrey M. *Mall Maker: Victor Gruen, Architect of an American Dream*. Philadelphia: University of Pennsylvania Press, 2004.

Harms, Erik. "Eviction Time in the New Saigon: Temporalities of Displacement in the Rubble of Development." *Cultural Anthropology* 28, no. 2 (2013): 344–68.

Hau, Caroline S. *Elites and Ilustrados in Philippine Culture*. Quezon City, Philippines: Ateneo de Manila University Press, 2017.

Harootunian, Harry. *Overcome by Modernity: History, Culture, and Community in Interwar Japan*. Princeton, N.J.: Princeton University Press, 2002.

Harootunian, H. D. "Ghostly Comparisons: Anderson's Telescope." In Cheah and Culler, *Grounds of Comparison*, 171–90.

Harper, T. N. *The End of Empire and the Making of Malaya*. New York: Cambridge University Press, 1998.

———. "Lim Chin Siong and the 'Singapore Story.'" In *Our Comet in the Sky: Lim Chin Siong in History*, edited by Tan Jing Quee and Jomo K. S., 3–55. Kuala Lumpur, Malaysia: ISAN, 2001.

Harvey, David. *A Brief History of Neoliberalism*. Oxford: Oxford University Press, 2007.

———. *The Condition of Postmodernity: An Enquiry into the Origins of Social Change*. Oxford: Blackwell, 1990.

———. "The Right to the City." *New Left Review* 53 (2008): 23–40.

Hawker's Inquiry Commission. Report, Singapore Government Printing Office, 1950.

Hechanova-Alampay, Ma. Regina. *1-800-Philippines: Understanding and Managing the Filipino Call Center Worker*. Quezon City: Institute of Philippine Culture, 2010.

Hidalgo, Cristina Pantoja, and Priscelina Patajo-Legasto, eds. *Philippine Postcolonial Studies: Essays in Language and Literature*. Quezon City: University of the Philippines Press, 1993.

Hobsbawm, Eric. *The Age of Empire, 1875–1914*. London: Abacus, 1994. Originally published in 1987.

———. *Industry to Empire: The Birth of the Industrial Revolution*. Rev. ed. New York: New Press, 1999.

Holden, Philip. *Orienting Masculinity, Orienting Nation: W. Somerset Maugham's Exotic Fiction*. Westport, Conn.: Greenwood, 1996.

Holston, James. *The Modernist City: An Anthropological Critique of Brasília*. Chicago: University of Chicago Press, 1989.

Holt, Richard. "The Amateur Body and the Middle-Class Man: Work, Health, and Style in Victorian Britain." *Sport in History* 26, no. 3 (2006): 352–69.

Hong, Lysa, and Huan Jianli. *The Scripting of a National History: Singapore and Its Past*. Singapore: National University of Singapore Press, 2008.

Horkheimer, Max, and Theodor W. Adorno. *Dialectic of Enlightenment: Philosophical Fragments*, edited by Gunzelin Schmidd Noer. Translated by Edmund Jephcott. Stanford, Calif.: Stanford University Press, 2002.

HSBC Expat. *HSBC Expat Explorer Survey 2013*. HSBC Expat, 2013.

Huang, Jianli. "The Young Pathfinders: Portrayal of Student Political Activism." In Barr and Trocki, *Paths Not Taken*, 188–205.

Hurley, Kelly. *The Gothic Body: Sexuality, Materialism, and Degeneration at the Fin de Siècle*. Cambridge: Cambridge University Press, 1997.

Ileto, Reynaldo C. *Filipinos and Their Revolution: Event, Discourse, and Historiography*. Quezon City, Philippines: Ateneo de Manila University Press, 1998.

———. *Pasyon and Revolution: Popular Movements in the Philippines, 1840–1910*. Quezon City, Philippines: Ateneo de Manila University Press, 1979.

Inaugural Program January 8th, 1935: Capitol Theatre, Manila's new million peso show emporium. Manila: n.p., 1935.

Ira, Luningning B. "Two Tickets to the Vod-a-vil." In *Filipino Heritage: The Making of a Nation*, vol. IX, edited by Alfredo Roces, 2,507–10. Quezon City, Philippines: Lahing Pilipino, 1978.

Ira, Luning B., Isagani R. Medina, and Nik Rios. *Streets of Manila*. Quezon City, Philippines: GCF, 1977.

Ira, Luning Bonifacio, and Isagani R. Medina. "What Will They Think of Next!" In *Turn of the Century*, edited by Gilda Cordero-Fernando and Nik Ricio, 206–25. Quezon City, Philippines: GCF, 1978.

JanMohamed, Abdul. "The Economy of Manichean Allegory: The Function of Racial Difference in Colonialist Literature." *Critical Inquiry* 12, no. 1 (1985): 59–87.

Jenkins, Henry. *What Made Pistachio Nuts? Early Sound Comedy and the Vaudeville Aesthetic*. New York: Columbia University Press, 1992.

Jenkins, Henry, Sam Ford, and Joshua Green. *Spreadable Media: Creating Value and Meaning in a Networked Culture*. New York: NYU Press, 2013.

Joaquin, Nick. *Almanac for Manileños*. Manila: Mr. & Ms. Publications, 1979.

———. *Manila, My Manila*. Makati City, Philippines: Bookmark, 1999.

———. "Pop Culture: The American Years." In *Filipino Heritage*, vol. IX, edited by Alfredo Roces, 2,732–44. Quezon City, Philippines: Lahing Pilipino, 1977.

———. *Reportage on Crime: Thirteen Horror Happenings That Hit the Headlines*. Manila: Anvil, 2009. Originally published in 1977.

Jurilla, Patricia May B. *Tagalog Bestsellers of the Twentieth Century: A History of the Book in the Philippines*. Quezon City, Philippines: Ateneo de Manila University Press, 2008.

Kahn, Joel S. *Other Malays: Nationalism and Cosmopolitanism in the Modern Malay World*. Singapore: Asian Studies Association of Australia in association with Singapore University Press and NIAS Press, 2006.

Kapchan, Deborah A. *Gender on the Market: Moroccan Women and the Revoicing of Tradition*. Philadelphia: University of Pennsylvania Press, 1996.

Kasson, John. *Amusing the Million: Coney Island at the Turn of the Century*. New York: Hill and Wang, 1978.

Keppy, Peter. "Southeast Asia in the Age of Jazz: Locating Popular Culture in the Colonial Philippines and Indonesia." *Journal of Southeast Asian Studies* 44, no. 3 (2013): 444–64.

Khaw, Patrick. "The Singapore Recreation Club, 1883–1963." Bachelor's thesis, National University of Singapore, 1986–87.

Khoo, Gaik Cheng. *Reclaiming Adat: Contemporary Malaysian Film and Literature*. Vancouver: University of British Columbia Press, 2006.

Kim Cheng Boey. *Between Stations: Essays*. Artarmon, New South Wales, Australia: Giramondo, 2009.

King, Anthony D. *Colonial Urban Development: Culture, Social Power, and Environment*. London: Routledge; Boston: Kegan Paul, 1976.

Knight-Frank Research. *The Wealth Report 2012: A Global Perspective on Prime Property and Wealth*. Knight Frank and Citi Private Bank, 2012.

Knight-Frank Research. *The Wealth Report 2015: A Global Perspective on Prime Property and Wealth*. Knight Frank, 2015.

Knight-Frank Research. *The Wealth Report 2016: A Global Perspective on Prime Property and Wealth*. Knight Frank, 2016.

Kong, Lily, and Brenda S. A. Yeoh. *The Politics of Landscapes in Singapore: Constructions of "Nation."* Syracuse, N.Y.: Syracuse University Press, 2003.

Koolhaas, Rem, and Bruce Mau. *S,M,L,XL.* 2nd ed. New York: Monacelli Press, 1995.

Koselleck, Reinhart. *The Practice of Conceptual History: Timing History, Spatial Concepts.* Translated by Todd Presner, Kerstin Behnke, and Jobst Welge. Stanford, Calif.: Stanford University Press, 2002.

Kramer, Paul A. *The Blood of Government: Race, Empire, the United States, & the Philippines.* Chapel Hill: University of North Carolina Press, 2006.

Kusno, Abidin. *The Appearances of Memory: Mnemonic Practices of Architecture and Urban Form in Indonesia.* Durham, N.C.: Duke University Press, 2010.

Kwan, Kevin. *Crazy Rich Asians.* New York: Doubleday, 2013.

Lacaba, Jose F. *Days of Disquiet, Days of Rage: The First Quarter Storm and Related Events.* New edition. Manila: Anvil, 2003. Originally published in 1983.

———. "Notes on '*Bakya*': Being an Apologia of Sorts for Filipino Masscult." In *Readings in Philippine Cinema*, edited by Rafael Ma. Guerrero, 117–23. Manila: Experimental Cinema of the Philippines, 1983.

Lai Ah Eng. "The Kopitiam in Singapore: An Evolving Story about Migration and Cultural Diversity." Working Paper, Asia Research Institute, 2010.

Lai Chee Kien. "*Maidan* to *Padang*: Reinventions of Urban Fields in Malaysia and Singapore." *Traditional Dwellings and Settlements Review* 21 (2010): 55–70.

Laquian, Aprodicio A. *The City in Nation-Building.* Quezon City: University of the Philippines School of Public Administration, 1966.

———. *Slums Are for People: The Barangay Magsaysay Pilot Project in Urban Community Development.* Manila: University of the Philippines College of Public Administration, 1969.

Leach, William. *Land of Desire: Merchants, Power, and the Rise of a New American Culture.* New York: Vintage, 1994.

Lears, Jackson. "Crisis and Regeneration." In *Rebirth of a Nation: The Making of Modern America, 1877–1920*, 167–221. New York: HarperPerennial, 2009.

———. *Fables of Abundance: A Cultural History of Advertising in America.* New York: Basic Books, 1995.

Le Bon, Gustave. *The Crowd: A Study of the Popular Mind.* New York: Macmillan, 1896.

Lee Kah-Wee. *Las Vegas in Singapore: Violence, Progress, and the Crisis of National Modernity.* Singapore: NUS Press, 2019.

———. "Vice and the City: Embarrassments of Nationalism in Singapore, 1960–1980." In *Asian Cities: Colonial to Global.* Amsterdam: Amsterdam University Press, 2015.

Lee Kip Lin. *The Singapore House, 1819–1942.* Singapore: Times Editions, 1988.

Lee Kuan Yew. *The Papers of Lee Kuan Yew: Speeches, Interviews, and Dialogues.* 10 volumes. Singapore: National Archives of Singapore, 2012.

Lee, Leo Ou-Fan. *Shanghai Modern: The Flowering of a New Urban Culture in China, 1930–1945.* Cambridge, Mass.: Harvard University Press, 1999.

Lee, Sangjoon. *Cinema and the Cultural Cold War: US Diplomacy and the Origins of the Asian Cinema Network.* Ithaca, N.Y.: Cornell University Press, 2020.

Levy, Emanuel. "Social Attributes of American Movie Stars." *Media, Culture, and Society* 12 (1990): 247–67.

Lewis, Oscar. "The Culture of Poverty." *Scientific American* 215, no. 4 (1966): 19–25.

Lewis, Robert M. *From Traveling Show to Vaudeville: Theatrical Spectacle in America, 1830–1910.* Baltimore: Johns Hopkins University Press, 2003.

Lewis, Su Lin. *Cities in Motion: Urban Life and Cosmopolitanism in Southeast Asia, 1920–1940.* Cambridge: Cambridge University Press, 2016.

Li, Tania Murray. *The Will to Improve: Governmentality, Development, and the Practice of Politics.* Durham, N.C.: Duke University Press, 2007.

Lim, Edna. *Celluloid Singapore: Cinema, Performance, and the National.* Edinburgh: Edinburgh University Press, 2018.

Lim, Laling H. "At the Edge of Manila." In *The Manila We Knew*, edited by Erlinda Enriquez Panlilio. Pasig City, Philippines: Anvil, 2006.

Liu, Andrew B. *Tea War: A History of Capitalism in China and India.* New Haven, Conn.: Yale University Press, 2020

Liu, Gretchen. *Singapore: A Pictorial History 1819–2000.* Singapore: Archipelago Press with National Heritage Board, 1999.

Lockhart, Robert Bruce. *Return to Malaya.* London: Putnam, 1936.

Loh, Kah Seng. *Squatters into Citizens: The 1961 Bukit Ho Swee Fire and the Making of Modern Singapore.* Singapore: Asian Studies Association of Australia with NUS Press and NIAS Press, 2013.

Loh, Kah Seng, Edgar Liao, Cheng Tju Lim, and Guo-Quan Seng. *The University Socialist Club and the Contest for Malaya: Tangled Strands of Modernity.* Amsterdam: Amsterdam University Press, 2012.

Lopez, Helen. "The Outsider Within: The Cultural Representation of Women in Selected Tagalog Novelists from the 1920s." In *Women Reading: Feminist Perspectives on Philippine Literary Texts*, edited by Thelma B. Kintanar, 90–117. Quezon City: University of the Philippines Press, 1992.

Lowe-Ismail, Geraldine. *Chinatown Memories.* Singapore: Talisman, 2011.

Lynch, Kevin. *The Image of the City.* Cambridge, Mass.: MIT Press, 1960.

MacMicking, Robert. *Recollections of Manila and the Philippines.* 1900. Manila: Filipiniana Book Guild, 1967.

Maglipon, Jo-Ann Q. *Primed: Selected Stories 1972–1992.* Manila: Anvil, 1993.

Manalansan, Martin F., IV, and Augusto F. Espiritu, eds. *Filipino Studies: Palimpsests of Nation and Diaspora.* New York: NYU Press, 2016.

Mangan, J. A. *Athleticism in the Victorian and Edwardian Public School: The Emergence and Consolidation of an Educational Ideology*. London: F. Cass, 2000.

Mangan, J. A., and James Walvin, eds. Introduction. In *Manliness and Masculinity: Middle-Class Masculinity in Britain and America, 1800–1940*. Manchester: Manchester University Press, 1987.

Manila Carnival Commercial and Industrial Fair. Manila: Philippine Carnival Association, 1933.

Manila Carnival Commercial and Industrial Fair January 27–February 11, 1934. Manila: Philippine Carnival Association, 1934.

"Manila: Its Needs and Resources." Manila: Social Welfare Department, 1967.

Mankekar, Purnima, and Akhil Gupta. "Intimate Encounters: Affective Labor in Call Centers." *positions: east asia cultures critique* 24, no. 1 (2016): 17–43.

Marchand, Roland. *Advertising the American Dream: Making Way for Modernity, 1920–1940*. Berkeley: University of California Press, 1985.

Martínez-San Miguel, Yolanda, and Michelle Stephens. "'Isolated Above, but Connected Below': Toward New, Global, Archipelagic Linkages." In *Contemporary Archipelagic Thinking: Towards New Comparative Methodologies and Disciplinary Formations*, edited by Michelle Stephens and Yolanda Martínez-San Miguel, 1–44. Lanham, Md.: Rowman & Littlefield, 2020.

Matilac, Rosalie, and Joel David, with notes from Pio de Castro III, Bienvenido Lumbera, and Nicanor G. Tiongson. "Distribution." In *Cultural Center of the Philippines Encyclopedia of Philippine Art*, vol. VIII, *Philippine Film*, edited by Nicanor G. Tiongson, 112–13. Manila: Cultural Center of the Philippines, 1994.

Maugham, W. Somerset. *Ah King and Other Stories*. Singapore: Oxford University Press, 1986.

———. *The Casuarina Tree: Seven Stories*. Singapore: Oxford University Press, 1985.

May, Glenn Anthony. "The Business of Education in the Colonial Philippines, 1909–1930." In *Colonial Crucible: Empire in the Making of the Modern American State*, edited by Alfred W. McCoy and Francisco A. Scarano, 151–62. Madison: University of Wisconsin Press, 2009.

Mayo, James M. *The American Grocery Store: The Business Evolution of an Architectural Space*. Westport, Conn.: Greenwood, 1993.

Mayuga, Sylvia L. *The Spy in My Own Country: Essays*. Manila: Sylvia L. Mayuga, 1981.

Mazzarella, William. "The Myth of the Multitude, or, Who's Afraid of the Crowd?" *Critical Inquiry* 36, no. 4 (2010): 697–727.

———. *Shoveling Smoke: Advertising and Globalization in Contemporary India*. Durham, N.C.: Duke University Press, 2003.

McClintock, Anne. *Imperial Leather: Race, Gender, and Sexuality in the Colonial Conquest*. New York: Routledge, 1995.

McCoy, Alfred W. "Philippine Commonwealth and the Cult of Masculinity." *Philippine Studies* 48, no. 3 (2000): 315–46.

McCoy, Alfred, and Alfredo Roces. *Philippine Cartoons: Political Caricature of the American Era.* Quezon City, Philippines: Vera-Reyes, 1985.

McIntyre, William E. "The Retail Pattern of Manila." *Geographical Review* 45, no. 1 (1955): 66–80.

Metcalf, Thomas R. *An Imperial Vision: Indian Architecture and Britain's Raj.* Berkeley: University of California Press, 1989.

Mezzadra, Sandro, and Brett Neilson. *Border as Method, or, the Multiplication of Labor.* Durham, N.C.: Duke University Press, 2013.

Miller, Angela. "The Panorama, the Cinema, and the Emergence of the Spectacular." *Wide Angle* 18, no. 2 (1996): 34–69.

Mintz, Sidney. *Sweetness and Power: The Place of Sugar in Modern History.* New York: Penguin, 1986.

Mitchell, Timothy. *Colonizing Egypt.* Berkeley: University of California Press, 1991.

Modern Girl Around the World Research Group. "The Modern Girl Around the World: Cosmetics Advertising and the Politics of Race and Style." In *The Modern Girl Around the World: Consumption, Modernity, and Globalization*, edited by Modern Girl Around the World Research Group, 25–54. Durham, N.C.: Duke University Press, 2008.

Mordden, Ethan. *The Hollywood Studios: House Style in the Golden Age of Movies.* New York: Simon & Schuster, 1989.

Morley, Ian. *Cities and Nationhood: American Imperialism and Urban Design in the Philippines, 1896–1916.* Honolulu: University of Hawaii Press, 2018.

Morris, Rosalind C. "Imperial Pastoral: The Politics and Aesthetics of Translation in British Malaya." *Representations* 99, no. 1 (2007): 159–94.

Mrázek, Rudolf. *Engineers of Happy Land: Technology and Nationalism in a Colony.* Princeton, N.J.: Princeton University Press, 2002.

Mulvey, Laura. "Visual Pleasure and Narrative Cinema." *Screen* 16, no. 3 (1975): 6–18.

Mumford, Lewis. *The City in History: Its Origins, Its Transformations, and Its Prospects.* New York: Harcourt, 1961.

Napier, Susan J. *Anime from* Akira *to* Princess Mononoke: *Experiencing Contemporary Japanese Animation.* New York: Palgrave Macmillan, 2000.

Neves, Joshua. *Underglobalization: Beijing's Media Urbanism and the Chimera of Legitimacy.* Durham, N.C.: Duke University Press, 2020.

Nye, David E. *American Technological Sublime.* Cambridge, Mass.: MIT Press, 1994.

Nye, Russell B. "Eight Ways of Looking at an Amusement Park." *Journal of Popular Culture* 15 (1981): 63–75.

Oates, Joyce Carol. *On Boxing.* Hopewell, N.J.: Ecco, 1995.

Ong, Aihwa. *Flexible Citizenship: The Cultural Logics of Transnationality*. Durham, N.C.: Duke University Press, 1999.

———. *Neoliberalism as Exception: Mutations in Citizenship and Sovereignty*. Durham, N.C.: Duke University Press, 2006.

Ong, Charlson. *An Embarrassment of Riches*. Quezon City: University of the Philippines Press, 2000.

Packard, Vance. *Hidden Persuaders*. London: Longmans, Green, 1957.

Padios, Jan M. *A Nation on the Line: Call Centers as Postcolonial Predicaments in the Philippines*. Durham, N.C.: Duke University Press, 2018.

Pante, Michael D. "Peripheral Pockets of Paradise: Perceptions of Health and Geography in Early Twentieth-Century Manila and Its Environs." *Philippine Studies* 59, no. 2 (2011): 187–212.

Papineau's Guide to Singapore and Spotlight on Malaysia. 18th ed. Singapore: André, 1965.

Park, Roberta J. "Biological Thought, Athletics, and the Formation of a 'Man of Character,' 1830–1900." In Mangan and Walvin, *Manliness and Morality*, 7–34.

Perry, Martin, Lily Kong, and Brenda Yeoh. *Singapore: A Developmental City State*. Chichester: John Wiley and Sons, 1997.

Phillips, Henry Albert. Review of *The Casuarina Tree*. In *W. Somerset Maugham: The Critical Heritage*, edited by Anthony Curtis and John Whitehead, 171–74. London: Routledge, 1997.

Pilar, S. A., and R. D. Perez III. "Crystal Arcade." In *Cultural Center of the Philippines Encyclopedia of Philippine Art*, vol. 3, *Philippine Architecture*, edited by Nicanor G. Tiongson, 223–24. Manila: Cultural Center of the Philippines, 1994.

Pinches, Michael. "Modernization and the Quest for Modernity: Architectural Form, Squatter Settlements, and the New Society in Manila." In *Cultural Identity and Urban Change in Southeast Asia: Interpretative Essays*, edited by Marc Askew and William S. Logan, 13–42. Victoria, Australia: Deakin University Press, 1994.

Quahe, Yvonne. *We Remember: Cameos of Pioneer Life*. Singapore: Landmark, 1986.

Rabinovitz, Lauren. *Electric Dreamland: Amusement Parks, Movies, and American Modernism*. New York: Columbia University Press, 2012.

Rafael, Vicente L. *Motherless Tongues: The Insurgency of Language amid Wars of Translation*. Durham, N.C.: Duke University Press, 2016.

———. "Welcoming What Comes: Sovereignty and Revolution in the Colonial Philippines." *Comparative Studies in Society and History* 52, no. 1 (2010): 157–79.

———. *White Love, and Other Events in Filipino History*. Durham, N.C.: Duke University Press, 2000.

Rajaratnam, S. *The Prophetic and the Political*. Singapore: Institute of Southeast
   Asian Studies and Graham Brash, 2007. Originally published in 1987.
Recto, Claro M. *Vintage Recto: Memorable Speeches and Writings*. Edited by
   Renato Constantino. Quezon City, Philippines: Foundation for Nationalist
   Studies, 1986.
Reed, Robert R. *City of Pines: The Origins of Baguio as a Colonial Hill Station and
   Regional Capital*. Berkeley: University of California Center for South and
   Southeast Asian Studies, 1976.
Reid, Anthony. *Southeast Asia in the Age of Commerce, 1450–1680*. Vol. 1, *The
   Lands below the Winds*. New Haven, Conn.: Yale University Press, 1988.
Reyes, Edgardo M. *Sa Mga Kuko ng Liwanag* [In the Claws of Neon]. Manila:
   De La Salle University Press, 1986.
Riding the ASEAN Elephant: How Business Is Responding to the Unusual Animal.
   Economist Corporate Network, 2013.
Rizal, José. *Noli Me Tangere*. 1887. Translated by Ma. Soledad Lacson-Locsin.
   Makati City, Philippines: Bookmark, 1996.
Robinson, Jennifer. "Global and World Cities: A View from off the Map." *Inter-
   national Journal of Urban and Regional Research* 26, no. 3 (2002): 531–54.
Roces, Alfredo, ed. *Filipino Heritage: The Making of a Nation*. 10 vols. Quezon
   City, Philippines: Lahing Pilipino, 1977–78.
Rodriguez, Robyn Magalit. *Migrants for Export: How the Philippine State Brokers
   Labor to the World*. Minneapolis: University of Minnesota Press, 2010.
Roff, William. *The Origins of Malay Nationalism*. 2nd ed. Kuala Lumpur, Malay-
   sia: Oxford University Press, 1994.
Rosario, Deogracias A. "Greta Garbo." In *Philippine Literature: A History and
   Anthology*, edited by Bienvenido Lumbera and Cynthia Nograles Lumbera,
   138–42. Rev. ed. Pasig City, Philippines: Anvil, 1997.
Rosenstock's Manila City Directory. Manila: Philippine Education Co.,
   1934–35.
Rostow, W. W. *The Stages of Economic Growth: A Non-Communist Manifesto*.
   Cambridge: Cambridge University Press, 1960.
Rotary Club and the Municipal Commissioners of the Town of Singapore. *A
   Handbook of Information*. Singapore: 1933.
Roy, Ananya, and Aihwa Ong, eds. *Worlding Cities: Asian Experiments and the Art
   of Being Global*. Malden, Mass.: Wiley-Blackwell, 2011.
Sallaz, Jeffrey J. *Lives on the Line: How the Philippines became the World's Call
   Center Capital*. New York: Oxford University Press, 2019.
San Juan, E., Jr. *After Postcolonialism: Mapping Philippines–United States Confron-
   tations*. Lanham, Md.: Rowman & Littlefield, 2000.
———. *Beyond Postcolonial Theory*. New York: St. Martin's Press, 1998.
Schivelbusch, Wolfgang. *The Railway Journey: The Industrialization of Time and
   Space in the 19th Century*. Berkeley: University of California Press, 1986.

Schumpeter, Joseph A. *Capitalism, Socialism, and Democracy*. 3rd ed. New York: Harper, 1978. Originally published in 1950.

Schwartz, Vanessa R. *Spectacular Realities: Early Mass Culture in Fin-de-Siècle Paris*. Berkeley: University of California Press, 1998.

Scott, James C. "Cities, People, and Language." In *Seeing Like a State: How Certain Schemes to Improve the Human Condition Have Failed*, 53–83. New Haven, Conn.: Yale University Press, 1998.

———. *Domination and the Arts of Resistance: Hidden Transcripts*. New Haven, Conn.: Yale University Press, 1992.

Sert, J. L., F. Léger, and S. Giedion. "Nine Points of Monumentality." In *Architecture You and Me: The Diary of a Development*, edited by Sigfried Giedeon, 48–51. Cambridge, Mass.: Harvard University Press, 1958. Originally published in 1943.

Sidel, John T. "Philippine Politics in Town, District, and Province: Bossism in Cavite and Cebu." *Journal of Asian Studies* 56, no. 4 (1997): 947–66.

Siegel, James T. *Solo in the New Order: Language and Hierarchy in an Indonesian City*. Princeton, N.J.: Princeton University Press, 1986.

Simmel, Georg. "The Metropolis and Modern Life." In *The Sociology of Georg Simmel*, edited by Kurt H. Wolff, 409–24. Glencoe, Ill.: Free Press, 1950. Originally published in 1903.

Singapore. Economic Strategies Committee. "Highly Skilled People, Innovative Economy, Distinctive Global City." Report, Economic Strategies Committee, 2010.

Singapore. Economic Strategies Committee. "Making Singapore a Leading Global City." Report, Economic Strategies Committee, 2010.

Singapore. Ministry of National Development. Central Area Programme Map. *1958 Master Plan*. Singapore: Ministry of National Development, 1958.

Singapore. Parliament. *Internal Security Act*. Singapore: Attorney-General's Chambers Legislative Division, 1963.

Singapore. Singapore 21 Committee. "Singapore 21: Together, We Make the Difference." Report, Singapore 21 Committee, 1999.

Singapore Cricket Club, 1852–1985. Singapore: Singapore Cricket Club, 1985.

Singapore Tourism Board. "i'mpact: Annual Report 2010/2011." Report, Singapore Tourism Board, 2011.

Singapore Tourism Board. "Street of Singapore: Remaking Orchard Road." Report, Singapore Tourism Board, 2003.

Singapore Tourist Promotion Board. "Tourism 21: Vision of a Tourism Capital." Report, Singapore Tourist Promotion Board, 1996.

Singapore: The First Ten Years of Independence, 1965–1975. Singapore: National Library Board / National Archives of Singapore, 2007.

Smith, Andrew. *Victorian Demons: Medicine, Masculinity, and the Gothic at the Fin-de-Siècle*. Manchester: Manchester University Press, 2004.

Stephanson, Anders. "Blessings of Civilization, 1865–1914." In *Manifest Destiny: American Expansionism and the Empire of Right*, 66–111. New York: Hill and Wang, 1995.

Stewart, Susan. *On Longing: Narratives of the Miniature, the Gigantic, the Souvenir, the Collection*. Durham, N.C.: Duke University Press, 1993. Originally published in 1987.

Stoler, Ann Laura. *Along the Archival Grain: Epistemic Anxieties and Colonial Common Sense*. Princeton, N.J.: Princeton University Press, 2009.

———. *Carnal Knowledge and Imperial Power: Race and the Intimate in Colonial Rule*. Berkeley: University of California, Press, 2002.

Sundaram, Ravi. *Pirate Modernity: Delhi's Media Urbanism*. London: Routledge, 2009.

Tadiar, Neferti Xina M. *Fantasy-Production: Sexual Economies and Other Philippine Consequences for the New World Order*. Hong Kong: Hong Kong University Press, 2004.

Tagg, John. *The Burden of Representation: Essays on Photographies and Histories*. Minneapolis: University of Minnesota Press, 1993.

Tan Kar Lin. "The 'Worlds' Entertainment Parks of Singapore (1920s–1980s): New Urban Form and Social Space for Culture and Consumption." Master's thesis, National University of Singapore, 2004.

Tan, Kenneth Paul. "The Ideology of Pragmatism: Neo-liberal Globalization and Political Authoritarianism in Singapore." *Journal of Contemporary Asia* 42, no. 1 (2012): 67–92.

———. "Racial Stereotypes in Singapore Films: Commercial Value and Critical Possibilities." In *Race and Multiculturalism in Malaysia and Singapore*, edited by Daniel P. S. Goh, Matilda Gabrielpillai, Philip Holden, and Gaik Cheng Khoo, 124–40. Oxford: Routledge, 2009.

Tan Pin Ho. Interview with Jesley Chua Chee Huan. *Special Project*. Oral History Centre, 001864/03, October 15, 1997.

Tan Sooi Beng. *Bangsawan: A Social and Stylistic History of Popular Malay Opera*. Singapore: Oxford University Press, 1993.

Tarrow, Sidney G. *Power in Movement: Social Movements and Contentious Politics*. 3rd ed. New York: Cambridge University Press, 2011.

Tate, E. Mowbray. *Transpacific Steam: The Story of Steam Navigation from the Pacific Coast of North America to the Far East and the Antipodes, 1867–1941*. New York: Cornwall, 1986.

Tay, Eddie. *Colony, Nation, and Globalization: Not at Home in Singaporean and Malaysian Literature*. Singapore: NUS Press, 2011.

Teh Cheang Wan. "Public Housing in Singapore: An Overview." In Yeh, *Public Housing in Singapore*, 1–21.

Teo, Stephen. "Malay Cinema's Legacy of Cultural Materialism: P. Ramlee as Historical Mentor." In *Singapore Cinema: New Perspectives*, edited by Liew Kai Khiun and Stephen Teo, 3–19. London: Routledge, 2006.

Thompson, Frederic. "Amusing the Million." *Everybody's Magazine*. September 1908. <nationalhumanitiescenter.org/pds/gilded/people/text2/thompson.pdf>.

Thum, Ping Tjin. "Independence: The Further Stage of Colonialism in Singapore." In *The Limits of Authoritarian Governance in Singapore's Developmental State*, edited by Lily Zubaidah Ibrahim and Michael D. Barr, 49–69. Singapore: Palgrave Macmillan, 2019.

Tolentino, Rolando B. *Sa Loob at Labas ng Mall kong Sawi, Kaliluha'y Siyang Nangyayaring Hari: Ang Pagkatuto at Pagtatanghal ng Kulturang Popular*. Quezon City: University of the Philippines Press, 2001.

Tosh, John. *A Man's Place: Masculinity and the Middle-Class Home in Victorian England*. New Haven, Conn.: Yale University Press, 1999.

Tourist Treasure Log: Singapore, the Shopper's Paradise. Singapore: Tecco, 1968.

Trachtenberg, Alan. *The Incorporation of America: Culture and Society in the Gilded Age*. New York: Hill and Wang, 1982.

Trentman, Frank. *Empire of Things: How We Became a World of Consumers, from the Fifteenth Century to the Twenty-First*. New York: HarperPerennial, 2017.

Trocki, Carl A. *Opium and Empire: Chinese Society in Colonial Singapore, 1800–1910*. Ithaca, N.Y.: Cornell University Press, 1990.

———. *Opium, Empire, and the Global Political Economy: A Study of the Asian Opium Trade, 1750–1950*. London: Routledge, 1999.

Turner, Victor. *The Ritual Process: Structure and Anti-Structure*. New York: Aldine Transaction, 1997.

Uhde, Jan, and Yvonne Ng Uhde. *Latent Images: Film in Singapore*, 2nd ed. Singapore: NUS Press, 2009.

Underhill, Paco. *The Call of the Mall*. New York: Simon and Schuster, 2004.

United Nations Industrial Survey Mission. *A Proposed Industrialization Programme for the State of Singapore*. New York: United Nations Programme of Technical Assistance, 1963.

Veblen, Thorstein. *The Theory of the Leisure Class*. 1899. New York: Dover, 1994.

Ventura, Sylvia Mendez. "Earthquakes, Typhoons, Floods, and Other Acts of God." In *Turn of the Century*, edited by Gilda Cordero-Fernando and Nik Ricio, 196–205. Quezon City, Philippines: GCF, 1978.

———. "The E.D.S. in Edsa." In *Ragtime in Kamuning: Sari-Sari Essays*. Manila: Anvil, 1993.

Vicuña Gonzalez, Vernadette. *Empire's Mistress, Starring Isabel Rosario Cooper*. Durham, N.C.: Duke University Press, 2021.

Villegas, Antonio J. *Building a Better Manila*. Manila: n.p., 1963.

Vinikas, Vincent. *Soft Soap, Hard Sell: American Hygiene in an Age of Advertisement*. Ames: Iowa State University Press, 1992.

von Simson, Otto. *The Gothic Cathedral: Origins of Gothic Architecture and the Medieval Concept of Order*. Rev. ed. Princeton, N.J.: Princeton University Press, 1962.

Wade, Geoff. "Operation Coldstore: A Key Event in the Creation of Modern Singapore." In *The 1963 Operation Coldstore in Singapore: Commemorating 50 Years*, edited by Poh Soo Kai, Tan Kok Fang, and Hong Lysa, 15–69. Malaysia: SIDRC/Pusat Sejarah Rakyat, 2013.

Wagner, Tamara S. *Occidentalism in Novels of Malaysia and Singapore, 1819–2004: Colonial and Postcolonial Financial Straits and Literary Style*. Lewiston, N.Y.: Edwin Mellen, 2005.

Wakeman, Frederic Jr. *Policing Shanghai 1927–1937*. Berkeley: University of California Press, 1995.

Walker, Gavin, and Naoki Sakai. "A Genealogy of Area Studies." *positions: asia critique* 27, no. 1 (2019): 1–31.

Watson, Jini Kim. *The New Asian City: Three-Dimensional Fictions of Space and Urban Form*. Minneapolis: University of Minnesota Press, 2011.

Weber, Max. *The Theory of Social and Economic Organization*. 1947. Translated by A. H. Henderson and Talcott Parsons. New York: Free Press of Glencoe/Collier-Macmillan, 1964.

Weiss, Meredith L., and Edward Aspinall, eds. *Student Activism in Asia: Between Protest and Powerlessness*. Minneapolis: University of Minnesota Press, 2012.

Wickberg, Edgar. *The Chinese in Philippine Life: 1850–1898*. Quezon City, Philippines: Ateneo de Manila University Press, 2000. Originally published in 1965.

Williams, Raymond. *Marxism and Literature*. New York: Oxford University Press, 1977.

Willis' Singapore Guide. Singapore: A. C. Willis, 1934.

Wilson, Ara. *The Intimate Economies of Bangkok: Tomboys, Tycoons, and Avon Ladies in the Global City*. Berkeley: University of California Press, 2004.

Woetzel, Jonathan, et al. *Southeast Asia at the Crossroads: Three Paths to Prosperity*. McKinsey Global Institute, 2014.

Wong, Aline E., and Stephen H. K. Yeh, eds. *Housing a Nation: 25 Years of Public Housing in Singapore*. Singapore: Maruzen Asia and Housing and Development Board, 1985.

Wong Lin Ken. "Singapore: Its Growth as an Entrepôt Port, 1819–1941." *Journal of Southeast Asian Studies* 9, no. 1 (1978): 50–84.

Wong Yunn Chii and Tan Kar Lin. "Emergence of a Cosmopolitan Space for Culture and Consumption: The New World Amusement Park-Singapore (1923–1970) in the Inter-War Years." *Inter-Asia Cultural Studies* 5, no. 2 (2004): 279–304.

Woody, Howard. "International Postcards: Their History, Production, and Distribution (Circa 1895 to 1915)." In *Delivering Views: Distant Cultures in Early Postcards*, edited by Christraud M. Geary and Virginia-Lee Webb, 13–46. Washington, D.C.: Smithsonian Institution Press, 1998.

Yeh, Stephen Hua Kuo ed. *Public Housing in Singapore: A Multi-Disciplinary Study*. Singapore: Singapore University Press Housing and Development Board, 1975.

Yeo Kim Wah. *Political Development in Singapore, 1945–1955*. Singapore: Singapore University Press, 1973.

Yeoh, Brenda S. A. *Contesting Space: Power Relations and the Urban Built Environment in Colonial Singapore*. 2nd ed. Singapore: Singapore University Press, 2003.

Yeung, Yue-man. *Changing Cities of Pacific Asia: A Scholarly Interpretation*. Hong Kong: Chinese University Press, 1990.

——. "Periodic Markets: Comments on Spatio-Temporal Relationships." *Professional Geographer* 26, no. 2 (1974): 147–51.

Yong Sai Shing, and Chan Kwok Bon. "Leisure, Pleasure, and Consumption: Ways of Entertaining Oneself." In *Past Times: A Social History of Singapore*, edited by Chan Kwok Bon and Tong Chee Kiong, 153–81. Singapore: Times Editions, 2003.

Yung, Sai-shing. "Territorialization and the Entertainment Industry of the Shaw Brothers in Southeast Asia." In Fu, *China Forever*, 133–53.

Zhang Zhen. *An Amorous History of the Silver Screen: Shanghai Cinema, 1897–1936*. Chicago: University of Chicago Press, 2006.

Zukin, Sharon. *Points of Purchase: How Shopping Changed American Culture*. New York: Routledge, 2004.

environments, urban: bungalows as refuge
from, 66, *66*; dynamism of, 56–59,
71–72, 218; expatriates, residential segregation and, 57, 63, 64, 65; spectacles
and, 88–89
Epifanio de los Santos Avenue (EDSA),
Manila, 3, 23, 185, 195, 223
Esco Hour (radio show), 38
Escolta Block Festival, 223
Estrada, Joseph "Erap," 23, 154–55, 156,
166, 167–69, 195
La Estrella del Norte, 34, 35
exhibition booklets, 22, 78
expatriates. *See* white male expatriates

Facebook, 200, 223
Fahmy, Mohamed, 89
Fajar (underground magazine), 114
fake news, 216, 223
FAMAS (Filipino Academy of Movie Arts
and Sciences), 167
fantasy, postcolonial: cinematic landscapes,
155–57; gossip in coffee shops, 174–77;
movie stardom and paradoxical duality,
166–70; public figures of youthful dynamism, 170–74, *173*; sanitary modernity
and urban informality, 161–66; self-
determination and metamorphosis, 23,
157–61; waiting as modernity, 177–81
femininity, 20, 40–43, 48, 51, 80
Fernandez, Ignacio, 90
Filipino Academy of Movie Arts and Sciences (FAMAS), 167
Filipino Struggles through History (*History of
Manila*), 172–73, *173*
films. *See* cinema
First Quarter Storm movement, 131
First United Building, 223
Florida, Richard, 191
"Footprints in the Jungle" (Maugham),
63–64
Foreign Policy, 188
Foreman, Harrison, 129, 130, *130*
The Forsaken House (Guerrero), 41
Foucault, Michel, 16, 90–91, 121

FPJ Productions, 156
France, 5, 8, 10, 12, 28, 35, 89
Francisco, Carlos "Botong," 172–73
Fraser, Arthur, 46
free speech, 119
Freire, Paulo, 177
Fried, Michael, 92
Frisco, Young, 90
full play, 85, 86, 88, 95

Galt, Rosalind, 164
gambling, 34, 72, 84, 86, 96, 147, 210,
211
gangs, 131, 147, 167
Gardner, Young, 89
Geertz, Clifford, 111, 127
Gellner, Ernest, 125
gender, 8, 9, 11, 98, 101, 115, 199
genealogy: archeology and, 16–17; of
capitalist modernity, 3, 6, 17
George, Cherian, 121
Germany, 28, 35, 45
Geron Busabos, Ang Batang Quiapo (film),
167, 168
Gibson, William, 192
Gladwell, Malcolm, 193
glass: displays, 2, 16, 22, 34, 43–48, *45*,
52, 58, 210, 219, 220, 222; with magical
self-renewal, 30; stained, 45, 47; win-
dows, 12, 21, 30, 44, 47, 48, 217
Glissant, Édouard, 20–21
Global Cities Index, 188
Global Investor Programme, 209
Goh Chok Tong, 187, 189
Goh Keng Swee, 106, 122, 164–65, 171
Gonzales, Luis, 156
gossip: in coffee shops, 23, 141, 154, 155,
157, 174–77; about Marcos, Ferdinand
Edralin, 172
Gothic cathedrals, 47
Great World Amusement Park, Singapore,
75–76, 82, 86–87, 93, 96, 186, 224
Great World Entertainment Center,
Shanghai, 82, 84
Great World Mall, 186, 224

sanctuary, *66*, 74, 217; temporality of, 67–70
Vera-Perez, Azucena "Mama Nene," 155
Victorian Eclectic style, 61
Villegas, Antonio J., 22, 120–21, 155, 157, 169, 172–74, *173*
Violator (film), 194–95
violence, 121–22, 129, 132, 144, 145, 166
virtual infinitude: buzz and, 194; of commercial streets, 192; of consumerism, 152; of neon lights, 23, 139–43, *140*, 155, 173, 218; of popularity, 143; in *Sa Mga Kuko ng Liwanag*, 135–36
visual infinitude, neon lights and, 131, 139
von Simson, Otto, 47

waiting, as modernity, 177–81
Walker, Gavin, 216
Watson, Jini Kim, 17, 161
wayang troupes, Chinese, 111–12
wayang wong performances, Javanese, 84
wealth inequality, 4, 214, 218
Western Europe, 3, 5, 8, 15, 18, 177, 186, 204
Westerns, cinema, 165
white beauty, 14, 49

white male expatriates: in "The Door of Opportunity," 70; dynamism of urban environment and, 57–59; languor of, 54–55, 71; moral degeneration of, 54, 62, 63; with postcards, 22, 54, 71, 73; residential segregation and, 57, 63, 64, 65; verandahs and bungalows as sanctuary for, *66*, 74, 217
whiteness, 80, 150, 151
"Why I Believe in Socialism" speech, 122
Williams, Raymond, 19
Wilson, Ara, 9, 10
Winsemus, Albert, 117
women, 30, 40–44, 48, 50, 52, 101
wooden sandals (*bakya*), 137
working class, 94, 160, 161. *See also* labor

youth, 118, 132, 200; activism, 114–15, 117, 130–31, 166; delinquent modernity and restless, 143–49; public figures of dynamism, 170–74, *173*
YouTube, 222

Zhang Zhen, 11–12, 13
zoning, 64, 190–91, 207–14
Zukin, Sharon, 8

Elmo Gonzaga is an Associate Professor in the Division of Cultural Studies and Director of the Master of Arts in Intercultural Studies Programme at the Chinese University of Hong Kong (CUHK). His work has appeared in the *Journal of Cinema and Media Studies, Cultural Studies, South East Asia Research*, and the *Journal of Asian Studies*. He is a Member of the Advisory Board of *Verge: Studies in Global Asias*.

Printed in the USA
CPSIA information can be obtained
at www.ICGtesting.com
LVHW091032031123
762979LV00005B/135